" You
Can't
Enlarge
the Pie "

" You Can't Enlarge the Pie "

Six Barriers to Effective Government

MAX H. BAZERMAN

JONATHAN BARON

KATHERINE SHONK

BASIC
BOOKS

A Member of the Perseus Books Group

Published by Basic Books,
A Member of the Perseus Books Group

Designed by Jeffrey P. Williams

Bazerman, Max H.
    You can't enlarge the pie : the psychology of ineffective government / Max H.
    Bazerman, Jonathan Baron, Katherine Shonk.
        p. cm.
    Includes bibliographical references and index.
    ISBN 0–465-00631-0
        1. Political planning–United States, 2. United States–Politics and
    government–Decision making.   I. Baron, Jonathan, 1944-   II. Shonk, Katherine.
    III Title.

01 02 03 04 / 10 9 8 7 6 5 4 3 2 1

Contents

Preface

Every day, citizens of democratic governments must cope with problems caused or perpetuated by the well-intentioned decisions of the officials they elected with good intentions. A child in the United States waiting in vain for a life-saving heart donation is the victim of the American government's failure to confront the desperate shortage of available organs. Some European nations have largely eliminated this problem by encouraging citizens to adopt a surprisingly simple change of mindset. When citizens are assumed to be potential organ donors unless they explicitly opt out, the great majority cooperate; thus many more organs are made available for those who would otherwise die. Despite the success of such reforms, politicians in the United States have been reluctant to take on this cause.

Few government policies are as inefficient as the organ donation system in the United States, and yet many of them are troubling. Why do we tolerate a court system that discourages pharmaceutical companies from marketing drugs that would alleviate suffering and save lives? Why does Congress force taxpayers to subsidize tobacco farmers to grow a crop directly responsible for the death of more than 430,000 American citizens each year? Why have countries across the world allowed entire species of fish to disappear from the oceans? Why do some governments continue to rely on inefficient and environmentally harmful energy sources such as coal?

These big questions have been debated for years by scientists, lawyers, politicians, doctors and other professionals. Each group has contributed new approaches toward solving these problems. Yet we believe that most policy debates have neglected a fundamental issue: the underlying psychological components of decisions made by citizens and government officials. Since the early 1980s, researchers have come to understand the errors that people commonly make when forming judgments and decisions. Much of this work has concerned the difficulty of discovering and understanding tradeoffs. In this book, we take a first step toward adding this perspective to the discussion of how to create wiser government policies.

We argue that difficult and pervasive social problems can be effectively addressed through wise trades. Our core argument is that large gains can often only be achieved when citizens learn to accept small losses in return. Time and again, the human tendency to ignore mutually beneficial tradeoffs and resist changes to the status quo has been reflected in flawed government decisions. This book explores these mistakes in detail, offers readers a better way of approaching stubborn social problems and explores the practical implications of this new mindset.

Collectively, we offer a perspective that has been overlooked by writing on government policy. Bazerman is a business school professor who has contributed to the study of judgment and decisions, particularly concerning negotiation in managerial contexts. Baron is a psychology professor who has also studied judgment and decisions, with a focus on those with moral implications. Shonk is a writer who has editorial experience with these topics. Although none of the authors is trained in policy analysis, we believe we can offer unique insights into the search for wiser decisions in government.

The ideas in this book derive from an approach that now dominates the curriculum of business schools. MBA students are trained to identify and correct the hidden biases that inform their decisions. Once they have been taught to analyze the likelihood of various consequences, these students learn that the best decisions are those that minimize expected costs and maximize expected benefits. When more than one decision maker is involved, negotiation strategies become relevant.

There is no reason why this approach cannot be expanded to society at large to bring about improved decisions regarding the environment, poverty and international relations. Governments and the citizens who elect them often fail to make decisions according to a rational-analytic model. Business school professors and other experts can contribute to this knowledge gap by offering decision-making and negotiation training to elected bodies—from city councils to Congress—and community groups.

Some of our concrete proposals might be criticized from both ends of the political spectrum on matters of detail. We will illustrate our ideas with recommendations that may not even be on the table for discussion, yet which we believe to be eminently defensible. Some of our proposals might seem radical, such as the argument that consent for organ transplantation should be presumed unless it is explicitly removed. Some may not be feasible in the context of a specific political era.

We are much more interested in introducing a new way of thinking than in advocating specific government policies. Our broad interest is to identify the flawed decisions that underlie failed policies and generate new ideas about how to expand the pie of social resources—goals relevant to all political eras.

The book is not positioned ideologically; rather, it is a call for pragmatic reform. We have written it for those who are disgusted on a daily basis by the latest partisan debate, in which a political victory appears to be more important than creating wise policy. Our readers want government to work better, yet they are frustrated by decisions that consistently seem to lead to failed policies.

We wish to thank Dov Brachfeld for his research and editorial assistance during the book's early stages. We are also grateful to several people for their helpful comments on each draft of the book: Linda Babcock, Nick Phillipson, Phil Tetlock, Barbara Rifkind and

Marjorie Williams. We especially thank William Frucht, our editor at Basic Books, for his thorough and thoughtful comments. Vanessa Mobley and Lori Hobkirk were invaluable in guiding the manuscript toward publication; we also appreciate the excellent copyediting of Jennifer Blakebrough-Raeburn. While these readers improved the quality of the book, the authors alone are responsible for any short-comings in the finished product.

Writing this book has given us a deeper understanding of the many failures that occur in the very best democracies in the world. These failures offer a challenge for the future. We offer this book as one step toward responding to this challenge.

Introduction

An Argument for Wiser Government

Imagine that you are listening to a series of campaign announcements, each made by a different politician running for national office. Consider how you would react to each politician's promises:

> If elected, I will do everything possible to ensure that all Americans will be treated by the doctor of their choice and receive as much medical attention as they require.
> If elected, I will do everything possible to enable every American to attend any university in this country.
> If elected, I will do everything possible to ensure that America has the strongest defense forces in the world and that we are prepared to fight two major wars at a time.
> If elected, I will do everything possible to protect the right of all Americans to carry the weapon of their choice without government interference.
> If elected, I will do everything possible to guarantee that there will be no real reduction in Social Security or Medicare spending.

If elected, I will do everything possible to protect our natural
    environment and ensure that no additional species of ani-
    mals or fish become extinct.
If elected, I will do everything possible to enact an across-the-
    board fifteen percent tax reduction.

Undoubtedly, some of these positions appeal to you more than
others. Some you simply do not like. Now consider the ones you
like best. What is your opinion of the candidates who hold these positions? Do they strike you as wise?

We will argue that all these politicians are lacking in wisdom. Each
expresses a view on a single position and promises to do "everything
possible" to enact it. None of them mentions the possible tradeoffs
or costs related to each new policy. Nor do they discuss how their
proposed policy would interact with other policies and issues. The
fact is, increased spending on medical care, defense, education and
so on guarantees that fewer taxpayer dollars and government resources will be available for other initiatives. It may also mean that
the national debt will increase, imposing a heavy burden on future
generations. Similarly, politicians who vow to protect the freedom
to own all types of firearms are implicitly condoning the death of innocent people through lax gun laws. Candidates who promise to do
"everything possible" to enact a specific policy are neglecting the
tradeoffs inherent in all political decisions.

When people engage in political discussions, they typically focus
on specific issues, such as those mentioned in the campaign promises
presented above. They then evaluate politicians based on how well
the politicians' positions match their preferences on these key issues.
In other words, they focus more on goals than on results. Yet when
evaluating business leaders, most people judge them primarily by results: profitability, return to shareholders, innovation and so on. This
is the more rational measure of effectiveness. An organization's overall health will generally have a greater effect on an individual employee or citizen than its stance on specific issues. Why do we judge
government by one standard and the private sector by another?

In this book, we argue that the way citizens and government currently think about real-world problems is dangerously narrow. We believe that a core objective of any government should be enlarging the pie of resources that society has available to distribute. Yet few citizens judge their leaders according to this key attribute. By focusing on vivid issues covered widely in the media, they ignore one of the most important issues: Valuable resources are often misused, squandered and ignored.

These resources are vast and diverse, ranging from tax dollars and the time of government bureaucrats and officials to national resources such as forests and mineral deposits. All these commodities are finite, and all have been squandered in nations across the globe as a result of inefficient government decisions. This book documents the many realms in which we miss the opportunities to increase the resources available to society. Here are a few examples:

People who die in automobile accidents are often buried with their healthy organs intact. Meanwhile, thousands die because of the lack of organ donors. Most of us would be willing to trade our organs upon our deaths in exchange for access to organs if we needed them. This mutually beneficial trade occurs far too rarely.

Environmentalists want to strengthen legislation to better protect biodiversity. Land developers do not want "Washington" telling them what they can and cannot do with their property. Both sides battle for increased or decreased legislation while ignoring possibilities for wiser regulation through joint problem solving.

When a sports team threatens to move to a new location, a bidding war ensues among different American cities. The winner typically pays more than the team is worth, and the losers often end up with empty stadiums. By focusing on keeping their teams with little or no regard for the long-term costs, taxpayers have spent vast sums of money making wealthy sports team owners even wealthier.

The American government currently subsidizes timber and paper companies for chopping down national forests. A business that operated as the government does would quickly go out of business. The government provides welfare to the timber industry because the public consistently ignores the degree to which special-interest groups have corrupted the legislative process.

The world's great fishing basins are in decline. New England's proportion of the world fishing harvest is down by ninety percent. Although the warning signs were clear fifteen years ago, fishers have successfully fought the regulation of their industry. Their rash behavior will deprive future generations of entire species of nutritious fish. Long-term thinking about intergenerational issues is lacking in this and many other public decision-making arenas.

Free trade prevents war, cuts inflation through price competition, increases efficiency and makes better goods and services available to citizens across the world. Why then do so many people fight free trade? A primary reason is loyalty to the short-sighted interest of a group. Groups that benefit from import restrictions organize to maintain their prerogatives at the expense of others. Another reason is the human tendency to resist any policy change that leads to harm as well as benefit.

These are complex issues. Politicians and activists have been trying to solve some of them for decades; but these same politicians and activists have consistently ignored others. We believe that partial solutions to these problems are surprisingly clear.

The Psychology of Flawed Decisions

We write from the perspective of psychologists who study imperfections in the way people make decisions. Since the early 1980s, it's become clear that many of the errors people make have to do with the difficulties they have in making and understanding tradeoffs. This book will illustrate how this new understanding of tradeoffs can clarify the flaws in existing government policies and lead to better policies.

By identifying wise tradeoffs, we can expand the resources available to society as a whole. This may mean, for example, increasing the average income per citizen; meeting the demand for donated organs; or improving the natural environment. We will present real-world examples in which we can increase two or more social goods at the same time—for example, improving both the economy and the environment through creative trades.

Although other scholars have written about flawed government decisions and the failure of policymakers to discover wise trades,[1] these writers have typically viewed such problems through the common lenses of political science and economics. We seek to expand the discussion by focusing on the limitations of the human mind. Most people recognize tradeoffs as exchanges that result in both a gain and a loss, but the human mind consistently overlooks *wise* tradeoffs—trades in which gains significantly exceed losses for all parties involved. This tendency is pervasive: It affects the educated and the uneducated, those inflamed by passion for an issue as well as those who pride themselves on their cool-headed rationality. Virtually everyone can benefit from incorporating a search for wise tradeoffs into their decision making.

Wise tradeoffs involve a type of policy change that economists call "Pareto improvements." A Pareto improvement is a change in policy that makes some people better off and no one worse off. Unfortunately, true Pareto improvements are very rare in government policy making; most changes will require sacrifices from some members of society. Thus, in many cases, we will be advocating what economist Joseph Stiglitz calls "near-Pareto improvements."[2] Near-Pareto improvements include policy changes that create vast benefits for some and comparatively trivial losses for others, as well as changes that would hurt only a small, narrowly defined special-interest group—in many cases, a group that has already manipulated the political process to its advantage. We agree with Stiglitz's argument that "if everyone except a narrowly defined special interest group could be shown to benefit, surely the change should be made."[3]

Social change must occur at two levels: How citizens think, and how the government creates policy. It will not suffice if only those who work in government learn to incorporate these principles.

Citizens, too, need to become more familiar with the reasoning decision scientists use when they think about government. As citizens broaden their mindsets, they will influence other voters and special-interest groups, and pressure the government to create wiser legislation.

Ideological, moral or religious debates such as struggles over abortion and capital punishment may seem to resist the type of tradeoffs we advocate. Parties who view the opposite side as morally wrong will often refuse to yield the slightest bit from their positions. Although we recognize that our recommendations will sometimes be impossible to apply, these cases are far rarer than most people realize. In certain instances, claims of intractability may be bargaining ploys that will yield to reasonable compromises. Negotiations promoting tradeoffs and compromise have proved effective in some of the most long-standing and bitter feuds—as recent peace accords in Northern Ireland suggest.

Strategies for Increasing Social Gains

This book presents six ways in which current government decision making is flawed. We propose explicit and practical strategies for increasing social gains and decreasing losses through wise tradeoffs. These are the subjects of Chapters 1–6. The chapter titles describe cognitive barriers to efficient government decisions. Each chapter highlights a set of specific existing government policies, explains the problems that exist under the current system, links these problems to flawed decision making and documents a specific strategy for improvement based on identifying wise tradeoffs.

Do No Harm

Chapter 1 explores how we can improve social decisions by reconsidering our approach to risk. When citizens resist changes to government policy, it is often because they irrationally expect to suffer from a small increase in a known risk. Many people, for instance, resist beneficial vaccinations for fear of vivid side effects, even though the diseases prevented are much more common and far more serious than the side effects. When people believe that a vaccination has made them ill they are outraged, and typically file a lawsuit against the vaccine's manufacturer. Juries often side with these plaintiffs, even when the scientific evidence linking the vaccine to the illness is questionable. Fearing such lawsuits, pharmaceutical firms often fail to develop new, potentially life-saving vaccinations to market—the business has simply become too risky. The same psychological forces that cause people to resist risky changes, even when the risk is small, also make them resist many government policies that might improve their lives.

In Chapter 1 we present three public-health dilemmas that illustrate the harm caused by our biased risk preferences. The dilemmas are: A rise in spurious lawsuits that inhibit the development of beneficial medical products and devices, an organ donation system that needlessly deprives people of life-saving transplants and a drug approval system that overlooks the harms caused by lengthy delays. In all three cases, society could achieve large benefits, but only by allowing a smaller risk to increase. We will document the suboptimal way that current systems handle risk and consider practical solutions based on reassessing risk.

Their Gain Is Our Loss

Chapter 2 offers citizens and government officials a strategy for negotiating strategically. Most people, including legislators, enter negotiations with the mistaken belief that resources are a pie of a fixed size: "Anything good for them must be bad for us." This mindset is the most common barrier to the wise resolution of political negotiations. Negotiators typically fail to find optimal outcomes because their fixed-pie mindset hinders them from looking for tradeoffs that might enlarge the pool of resources to be distributed. In the realm of government, the myth of the fixed pie causes legislators to fight political battles rather than pursue tradeoffs that would benefit the collective society.

In Chapter 2, we focus primarily on environmental disputes. Environmentalists and corporations have traditionally taken extreme, opposing positions on conservation issues. In the United States, the Endangered Species Act illuminates the strong and often detrimental role that self-interested pressure groups play in creating, revising and enforcing new laws. We will examine this law in-depth as a means of showing how cooperative attitudes can lead to better results for all parties involved.

Competition Is Always Good

Chapter 3 promotes a strategy for reducing dysfunctional competition in domains where cooperation should rule. Competition is good for business, but competition between government units (such as municipal and state governments) often leads to unnecessary expenses for taxpayers and wasted resources. Typically, in these situations, the primary goal of politicians is the satisfaction and notoriety of winning a public battle. Examples of dysfunctional competition include charitable organizations that fight with each other for donations, cities that compete with each other for sports teams and states that bid against each other for employment-producing plants. When governments and charities take part in these dubious activities, taxpayers and contributors become the unwitting sponsors of wasteful competition. We will consider psychological explanations for citizens' acceptance of irrational competition and suggest ways to avoid destructive political battles.

Support Our Group

Chapter 4 shows how controlling special-interest groups will improve government decisions. Regardless of whether you support welfare, most people assume that government welfare funds are given directly to poor people. In truth, the majority of welfare in the United States subsidizes corporations—often to engage in activities that have negative effects on society.[4] For example, the American government subsidizes tobacco farmers while suing cigarette companies for suppressing information about the dangers of nicotine addiction. The government also subsidizes the cutting of national forests, at the same time earning mere pennies from timber for every dollar it invests in building roads in national forests.

In Chapter 4 we document the negative effects of special-interest groups. American industries, ranging from cigarette manufacturers to telecommunications firms, spend millions of dollars in lobbying fees and campaign contributions each year in their attempt to sway the decisions of Congress and the president in their favor. The cost often exceeds the benefit gained by the smaller group. Why do we, as citizens, tolerate these destructive decisions? We will explore the basis for this irrational acceptance.

Live for the Moment

In Chapter 5 we present a strategy for confronting intergenerational dilemmas, particularly the worldwide fishing crisis. When harvested in a sustainable manner, fisheries can provide enormous quantities of protein-enriched food forever. Why then are fish harvests on the decline? Each fisher, and each fishing nation, becomes profitable by fishing as much as possible. When they all engage in this self-serving behavior they all suffer over the long term. With so much at stake, restraint does not occur spontaneously but must come from some coordinated action. Why aren't people willing to seek solutions to this problem?

The reason for this shortsighted behavior is that people tend to focus on the present, thus neglecting the future. They also engage in wishful thinking to convince themselves that indulging their immediate interests does no long-term harm. Because many wise tradeoffs occur across time, decision makers must be willing to accept small losses in return for long-term rewards, even when these benefits will accrue only to future generations. Policies promoting balanced budgets and wise land management also fall under this category. Government leaders and voters need to keep in mind that their short-term sacrifices can improve the lives of their children and grandchildren.

No Pain for Us, No Gain for Them

Chapter 6 examines tough situations in which we can improve society as a whole by redistributing resources. Government, like wise philanthropic organizations, must learn to assess where its dollars will do the most good. Some tradeoffs benefit all interested parties, but others help some and harm others. When making decisions, government should not rule out opportunities to improve the lives of a great many people by requiring minor costs from a smaller, less needy group. Some of the losers will object to these decisions, and even those who view the problem from the outside are often reluctant to impose losses on some for the benefit of others. We can try to compensate the few who are hurt by the tradeoff, but this is not always possible. Like generals who send troops into battle, we must be willing to require sacrifices from some for the great benefit of numerous others.

We explore two worldwide resource redistribution initiatives in Chapter 6: removing barriers to free trade and reducing global poverty. Enacted wisely, the loss that these policies will require from some is much smaller than the potential gain to the others. They will bring about long-term benefits such as lower prices, a better supply of goods and improved health and welfare for many people, thereby enlarging the pie of resources. If societies were organized to take full advantage of wise tradeoffs, most people would be better off in the long run.

Decision-Making Skills and Public Policy

The field of behavioral decision research has had a profound influence on management schools, negotiation training, and the financial markets. Many people have learned to audit the cognitive biases in their own intuitive decision-making repertoires, and have used these new skills to improve the rationality of their business decisions. This book applies the same ideas to the public-policy arena. Using principles of cognitive psychology and management practice, we will show how normal deficiencies in our intuition limit government effectiveness, and we will suggest solutions aimed at overcoming these human flaws.

The connection between decision making and public policy is not new. Two decades ago, Richard Nisbett and Lee Ross wrote:

> One of philosophy's oldest paradoxes is the apparent contradiction between the greatest triumphs and the dramatic failures of the human mind. The same organism that routinely solves inferential problems too subtle and complex for the mightiest computers often makes errors in the simplest of judgments about everyday events. The errors, moreover, often seem traceable to violations of the same inferential rules that underlie people's most impressive successes. . . . How can any creature skilled enough to build and maintain complex organizations, or sophisticated enough to appreciate the nuances of social intercourse, be foolish enough to mouth racist cliches or spill its lifeblood in pointless wars?[5]

A small set of judgment biases commonly underlie failed government decisions. What we present below is not a comprehensive list of known biases—such lists can be found elsewhere[6]—but a selection of those that best account for current practices in social decision making. They all arise from one common human limitation: the failure to make wise tradeoffs by accepting small losses in exchange for larger gains. These cognitive mistakes make up the tool kit we will use to analyze social problems in the chapters that follow. Although our analysis will not be limited to these biases, they form the core of our argument.

Omission Bias

Both this bias and the next (the status-quo bias) stem from a general rule that most people follow in their daily lives: "Do no harm." This is often a useful guideline, but not always. For example, many potential trades exist that require society to cause harm as a means to a greater benefit. In a study of hypothetical decisions about vaccination, many people expressed an unwillingness to vaccinate children against a disease that was expected to kill 10 out of 10,000 children when the vaccine itself would kill 5 out of 10,000 through side effects.[7] These people would not tolerate any deaths from the "commission" of vaccinating–even when their decision would cause five additional deaths. Similarly, many people avoid committing themselves to programs that would improve society, such as organ donation. Failure to act in these areas can be regarded as a harm–but many people prefer not to see it that way. The omission bias helps people believe that they are completely moral if they obey a list of prohibitions while otherwise pursuing their narrow self-interest.

Status Quo Bias

A closely related bias is the human tendency to maintain the status quo. The most direct effect of this bias is that people are often unwilling to give up what they already have–their "endowment"–for a better set of options. In such instances, the loss looms larger than the gain. A person who receives an offer for a new job that on some dimensions is much better than his or her old job, but marginally worse on others, will probably turn down the offer after paying more attention to the losses than to the gains. Similarly, most changes to government policy will require certain losses in exchange for greater gain. For many decision makers, these losses will be more salient than any gain, even when the losses are much smaller. As we will see, the status quo bias is an irrational barrier to legislative change.

The Fixed-Pie Approach to Negotiations

Issues under negotiation often have multiple dimensions. For example, it is rare for a bill being debated by Congress to affect only one facet of citizens' lives. Negotiations in which parties have differing assessments about the importance of these various dimensions are called "integrative." The trouble is that people tend to over-simplify negotiations, viewing them as "fixed pies."[8] In other words, parties tend to believe they are fighting over a limited amount of resources whose size cannot be increased–even though most negotiations allow for tradeoffs that will improve the overall quality of the agreement. Once again, when these opportunities are realized, each party makes a small sacrifice in return for a larger gain. Unfortunately, we intuitively ignore creative opportunities for mutual gain.

Unwillingness to Help Solve Social Dilemmas

A central role of good government is to resolve conflicts in which individuals must decide whether to pursue their self-interest or the broader interest of the group. When individuals pursue their self-interest in these situations, society suffers. But, again, the benefit of cooperation for all is larger than the loss of self-interest. Air pollution in urban areas is a social problem that is the result of people's self-interest; each time we choose to drive rather than walk or take public transportation, we dismiss the long-term harm we are inflicting on others. Solutions to social dilemmas exist, but coordinated action is required. Government can contribute to solutions such as better public transport systems. At this point, a new social dilemma arises: It is in each citizen's narrow self-interest to let others do the work of persuading public officials to take action. But the sacrifices required are small, and they can bring about great benefits. We will explore why citizens, industries and government so often fail to respond to the need for social cooperation.

Ignoring Secondary Effects

Some politicians emphasize the need for campaign finance reform. They argue, and we agree, that the current system gives too much power to wealthy special-interest groups and decreases the amount of resources available to society as a whole. Nonetheless, the public and the media consistently allow Congress to quietly defeat or weaken reform measures year after year. Why does the notion of campaign finance reform bore the public? We argue that most people do not think about the secondary effects of boring issues on vivid issues, even when these secondary effects have enormous collective importance. This bias works against the cooperative solution of social dilemmas. We would all benefit if we could cooperate on campaign finance reform, and the losses would be small, but most people do not see this as an issue worthy of their attention.

Discounting the Future

Most people apply an inappropriately high "discount rate" when they purchase a household appliance. In other words, they fail to pay extra for a more energy-efficient refrigerator, even when they will be paid back the extra cost in utility bills within a year. Why? Generally, human beings underweigh the future, a tendency that gets worse when the future includes future generations. Most people agree that "we should leave the earth in as good a condition as we received it." But in far too many cases—including fishing, timber, global warming, urban planning and the national debt—we discount the future pain we are causing by our current actions. In the long run, the gains of attending to the future are often greater than the immediate loss.

Egocentric Perceptions of Fairness

Although many people strive to be fair to others, most of us have very self-serving assessments of fairness.[9] Ample evidence suggests that negotiators tend to believe that neutral parties will side with them in a conflict. For instance, when fishers meet to discuss the pending crisis, they express very different ideas about who should be responsible for finding solutions—even if they agree that a problem exists. Although developed nations often consider the world's leading environmental issue to be overpopulation in developing nations, the developing nations more typically see the leading problem as over-consumption by those in developed nations. When it is time to negotiate a solution, all parties want what is "fair"—yet they have differing notions of fairness. Egocentric perceptions discourage cooperation of the sort required to solve social dilemmas.

Collectively, these cognitive errors are the central barriers to finding the wise tradeoffs necessary to resolve the complex decisions facing government. We will use this cognitive understanding to identify and propose remedies to specific social mistakes.

One of the main goals of this book is to reduce public cynicism toward government. This is a necessary first step toward motivating citizens to believe that they can play a valuable role in improving government decisions. Many organizations rate members of Congress based on how well the politician advances the goals of the specific organization. But we know of no organization that rates members of Congress on the overall degree to which they improve the quality of life for the Earth's inhabitants. Yet it is precisely this ability–to know when to compromise on specific goals in pursuit of the larger good–that constitutes wise government.

1

Do No Harm

SINCE THE EARLY 1960S, MILLIONS OF AMERICAN WOMEN HAVE
undergone surgery for silicone breast implants, either as reconstruc-
tion after a mastectomy or for the cosmetic enlargement of normal
breasts.[1] These silicone pouches, usually filled with saline solution,
are intended to improve the quality of life rather than its duration.
The popularity of the procedure suggests that many women expect
implants to enhance their confidence, well-being and enjoyment of
life.

When the U.S. Food and Drug Administration (FDA) began regulating breast implants in 1976, it acted on the assumption that
these devices were safe. Meanwhile, in Japan, reports in medical
journals were beginning to document illnesses—particularly connective-tissue disease—among prostitutes who had received direct injec-
tions of silicone or wax. In 1982, connective-tissue disease was reported in three Australian women with implants. Soon after,
American women with breast implants who developed connective-
tissue disease or another disorder began to initiate lawsuits against
the manufacturers. In 1990, after the television show *Face to Face with
Connie Chung* interviewed victims of these diseases and implicitly

blamed the manufacturers and the FDA, Congressman Ted Weiss began public hearings to explore a possible link between breast implants and these ailments.

Just a year later, in 1991, a jury awarded $7.34 million to a woman who claimed that her Dow-Corning implants had caused her connective-tissue disease. In 1992, after failing to receive evidence of their safety, FDA Commissioner David Kessler placed a ban on most implants; at the same time, he assured women who already had them that there was no evidence of danger. The ban galvanized tens of thousands of women to launch lawsuits against implant manufacturer Dow-Corning; these were eventually consolidated into one class-action suit. Some of the women involved in the suit blamed their implants for poor health. Others had no sign of disease but joined the suit for fear of future illness. In 1994, Dow-Corning agreed to an initial settlement of $4.25 billion, at the time the largest class-action settlement in history. One billion of the settlement went directly to the plaintiffs' lawyers. Under the terms of the settlement, a woman had only to present a doctor's diagnosis of some illness to receive a share of the money. Other women were allowed to file for their shares retroactively, making the per-person amount very small. Dow-Corning filed for bankruptcy in 1995.

Many of the facts of this case may already be familiar to you. But you may not have heard about the surprising scientific results that emerged—without much attention from the press—when implant manufacturers began to put their products to the test. This research began at the time of the lawsuit and continues today. Consider that about 1 percent of adult American women have implants, and about 1 percent of adult American women have connective tissue disease. If the implants had no relation to the disease, we would expect about 10,000 American women (1 percent of 1 percent of the 100 million women in the United States) to have both. Several studies showed that this rate was approximately correct. The only study that showed a small association between implants and disease was conducted after the negative publicity; the criterion for "disease" was a self-report questionnaire, raising the possibility that some women might have been more likely to report signs of disease after hearing that it could be caused by implants.

By 1999, a panel appointed by the Institute of Medicine had reviewed the existing evidence and concluded that, to date, there was no connection between implants and the diseases blamed on them.[2] Meanwhile, as more and more women have filed claims, the amount paid out by Dow-Corning in the class-action settlement has surpassed $7 billion.[3] The fear of unfounded lawsuits led DuPont to refuse to supply Dacron polyester for vascular grafts. In 1994, foreign suppliers refused to supply American manufacturers with Dacron for the first time.[4] Because silicone is used in catheters, pacemakers and artificial-heart valves, it is possible that these products could some day be in short supply. After all, in the aftermath of a lawsuit based on no scientific evidence whatsoever, why would any company supply a product that could bring about its financial ruin? It would not be surprising if firms chose to steer clear of this risky business altogether.

Dow-Corning is not the only company that has paid huge settlements to victims of diseases its products did not cause. Drug companies have cut back on research on contraceptives and vaccines because these products, given to healthy people, inspire lawsuits. Obstetricians are switching to the less risky field of gynecology, and the specialists who remain sometimes refuse to deliver lawyers' babies. In addition, companies guilty of outrageous crimes spend millions on attorneys' fees to protect themselves from litigation.

An obscure backwater of the law since the Middle Ages, the law of torts has today become almighty. Every day, plaintiffs win millions of dollars in damages for harms that cannot be considered crimes, and our existing tort system funnels as much money to lawyers as it does to victims. These fees could be avoided if parties were able to settle disputes through efficient negotiation.

Why don't we change the American legal system? The underlying psychological reason is that we pay too much attention to the losses that might result from action or change, but we ignore potential gains. As a consequence, we refuse to take small risks in order to reduce a large risk. People often resist changing jobs, homes or relationships because, biased toward the status quo, they focus on what they will lose rather than what they might gain.

The same psychological forces that cause people to adhere to the status quo also make them resist government policies that might improve matters for them as individuals. Citizens and government officials oppose tort reform proposals because of the vivid but small risk that recouping losses in court will become more difficult. This fear of risk overshadows the greater benefits they will gain in the form of lower health care costs, tax reductions and product availability. Through wise tradeoffs, citizens will discover where their true self-interest lies, and they will be more accepting of government policies that advance this interest.

The Way We Look at Risk

On December 21, 1988, 270 people died when a bomb planted by a terrorist on Pan American Airways Flight 103 exploded over Lockerbie, Scotland. In response to the tragedy, the U.S. Federal Aeronautics Administration (FAA) tightened regulations on air travel, including more thorough baggage checks and mandatory early arrival for travelers on international flights.

In 1989, reporter Henry Farlie made a conservative estimate of the cost per life saved by the new regulations.[5] Taking into account that the main cost factor is extra time, Farlie figured lost time to passengers at what was then the minimum wage, $3.35 per hour, even though most international travelers earn quite a bit more. He generously assumed that the new regulations would prevent all deaths from terrorism, which had averaged sixty-one each year since 1976. Given the 221,471,000 people who take international flights each year, this comes to $6,081,375.81 per life saved.

Perhaps this is not an outrageous amount to spend to save a human life. In other realms, the cost per life saved by governmental regulation is much higher. Still, there are far less expensive ways of saving lives, such as reducing air and water pollution. In general, developed nations spend far too much money on reducing certain risks. For example, the complete removal of asbestos from American school buildings would save about 400 lives over 40 years—at an estimated cost of about $100 billion, or $250 million per life saved.[6] Of course, because of the danger to asbestos-removal workers, it's possible this $100 billion might save no lives at all. Estimates of the amount of money it costs to save a certain number of lives are full of inaccuracy; but even if each figure given in the examples above were off by a factor of ten, the allocation of resources to reduce risk would still be shockingly high.

Why fixate on excessive expenditures? Because resources such as money and time come in limited quantities. Just as companies generate a finite amount of profit, governments collect a limited amount of funds each year. Government officials and employees can devote only a fixed amount of hours to solving a problem. Once money and time run out, they're gone for good.

Most changes to government policy carry some degree of risk. Ideally, reforms reduce one risk more than they increase another, achieving an overall improvement for each individual. Yet citizens often resist reforms, believing that they will suffer from the increased risk. Why, for instance, do we have so few organs to allocate to those who need them? Because people focus on the contributions they will be making—and by association, the risks they will be taking—without thought for the benefits they may receive as potential organ recipients. The solution may be a system in which people accept or reject both roles at once. An even simpler solution would be to assume that all citizens are both potential donors and potential recipients unless they specifically opt out of the program. These measures would frame organ donation as a cooperative enterprise in which the benefits to the individual far outweigh the costs.

There are many areas in which government has failed to create optimal legislation for society, and there are numerous reasons for these failures, including partisanship, political processes, special-interest groups and incompetence. We will examine many of these in later chapters. For now, we will focus on the most central explanation: the failure of the human mind to make wise tradeoffs. Citizens and legislators make a variety of systematic cognitive mistakes that lead to suboptimal legislation.

Opportunities for beneficial trades abound: We could direct time and money spent on very expensive measures to control one risk and use them to reduce other risks. This would save money and lives. Instead, we tend to react to each catastrophe with new regulations, which pile up to massive size and become institutionalized. When someone suggests the repeal of an existing regulation, activists rush to its defense regardless of its cost inefficiency.

The poor distribution of government funds is not a case of the government's ignoring the wishes of the people. When elected officials vote to pay huge sums on regulations aimed at risk reduction, they are usually responding to the demands of their constituents. The problem is that citizens look at risk through the lens of a variety of irrational biases. By supporting the status quo, these biases become roadblocks on the path of beneficial change–the type of change that requires a small increase in one risk in return for a large decrease in another risk.

The Omission Bias

Suppose you have a 10 percent chance of catching a new strain of flu virus. The only available vaccine completely prevents this type of flu, but it has a 5 percent chance of causing symptoms identical to those it is supposed to prevent, and with the same severity. If all other factors (such as cost) were the same, would you get the vaccine? Many people would not. They would be more concerned about the risk of harm from action–the 5 percent risk of an adverse reaction to the vaccine–than about the risks of inaction, or the 10 percent risk of catching the flu without the vaccine. This is true even though the vaccine reduces the chance of flu symptoms by 5 percent. Although the flu example is hypothetical, the same bias affects people's decisions about vaccination in real life.[7]

This irrational preference for harms of omission over harms of action is known as the omission bias. More than any other cognitive error, the omission bias pervades our decisions regarding risk. When contemplating risky choices, many people follow the rule of thumb, "Do no harm." Implicit in this advice is the notion that "do" means "do through action," making harms of omission easy to ignore. Our susceptibility to the omission bias means that every year many more people catch the flu than need to. The bias is not limited to government officials who oppose the wishes of super-rational citizens; nor is it the case that citizens need to be set straight by all-knowing officials. While the strength of the bias varies from person to person, it is found in every group of people.

The Status Quo Bias

One feature of the omission bias is that it usually supports the status quo. When contemplating a change, people are more likely to attend to the risk of change than to the risk of failing to change. Taking losses more seriously than gains, they will be motivated to preserve the status quo.

A classic psychology experiment demonstrates the pitfalls of the status quo bias. Students were divided into three groups: "sellers," "buyers," and "choosers."[8] The sellers were each given a coffee mug from their university bookstore and were asked to indicate on a form whether they would sell the mug at each of a series of prices ranging from $0 to $9.25. On a similar form, buyers indicated whether they were willing to buy a mug at each price in the same range. The choosers were asked to choose between a mug (which they did not "own") and various amounts of money. Sellers valued the mug at a median price of $7.12, while the average buyer thought it was worth only $2.87 and choosers gave it a median value of $3.12. Motivated to avoid a "loss" and maintain the status quo, sellers irrationally overvalued the mug.

The status quo bias is a general principle of decision making that aggravates many of the problems discussed in this book. Any kind of reform requires some losses and some gains. If it is a good reform, gains outweigh losses. But because people worry more about losses, they will tend to oppose the reform.

The Preference for Natural Risk

A final cognitive bias that interferes with rational decision making regarding risk is the human preference for natural risk over artificial risk. In general, "don't mess with nature" is a good rule for human beings to follow. We have evolved by adapting to the natural world and learning that tampering with nature–by bleeding people as a medical treatment, for example, or destroying entire forests for firewood–can lead to trouble. But, as often happens with such cognitive shortcuts, we fail to recognize important exceptions to the rule. In particular, we follow it even when the consequences of letting nature take its course would be worse than the consequences of altering it by "artificial" means.

Our preference for natural risk has two effects. First, we react to the same consequences differently depending upon whether they are brought about by humans or by nature. Specifically, we are more tolerant of "natural" disasters than of artificial ones. "I don't mind natural extinctions, but I'm not too enthusiastic about extinctions that are directly caused by man," commented a subject in a study of environmental values.[9] This bias toward nature leads us to ignore opportunities for lessening the devastation of natural risks such as hurricanes, earthquakes, floods and epidemics. People tend to regard such disasters as the inevitable "will of God." Of course, we cannot prevent hurricanes and earthquakes, but we can do a great deal to protect ourselves against their worst consequences (such as not building homes on sandbars in hurricane-prone regions).

In general, people are more willing to pay to reduce risks when the source of harm is human error than when it is a nonhuman natural source.[10] Subjects were willing to contribute about $19 to an international fund to save Mediterranean dolphins when the dolphins were "threatened by pollution," but only $6 when they were "threatened by a new virus"–even though the same number of dolphins were expected to die in both cases. Similarly, subjects in one study (some of whom were judges) thought that workmen's compensation paid by a state panel should be greater when an injury is caused by a drug rather than by a natural disease.[11] These questionnaire studies suggest that economic allocations are based on the psychological properties of human judgment rather than on the amount of benefit from the allocation. This leads to a misallocation. We could spend the same money more fairly by dividing it equally among those with the same need.

The second effect of the preference for natural risk is our tendency to be suspicious of new technology, even when we have every reason to believe that the technology will improve on natural outcomes. Synthetic chemicals added to food are often banned because they cause cancer in laboratory animals. Yet when natural foods are broken into their constituent chemicals, they too have been found to cause cancer in lab animals.[12] Caffeic acid, for example, is a carcinogen found in coffee, lettuce, apples, pears, plums, celery, carrots and potatoes. One review found that 94 percent of synthetic carcinogens were subject to government regulation, compared to 41 percent of a sample of natural carcinogens;[13] the review also showed that the average risk to humans from synthetic chemicals was lower than from natural ones. Researchers have argued that animal tests require such high doses of the chemicals that cancer is an almost inevitable result of increased cell division brought on by an overdose of the chemical in the animal's body.[14] At lower doses, a given chemical typically does not cause cell poisoning; for this reason, animal tests may be highly inaccurate. If these tests provide inaccurate and alarming information about natural chemicals, they probably do the same for synthetic chemicals.

The irrationality of the preference for natural risk is illustrated by the human tendency to consider some technologies "natural" simply because they are old. For example, although most of our crops are the result of breeding–a technology–people resist further improvements from biotechnology on the grounds that they are "unnatural." It is inefficient to spend money reducing the risk of artificial chemicals when these risks are no more serious than those of nature itself. If expenditures are needed at all, we should treat all risks equally and simply strive to save the most lives per million dollars spent.

We will consider these three biases—omission, status quo and preference for natural risk—in the context of cases in which gaining a large social benefit requires acceptance of a small risk. The examples we will explore are:

1. The benefit is a product and the risk is some rare harm caused by that product—or, as in the case of breast implants, merely believed to have been caused by the product. These products are sometimes withdrawn or withheld because of fear of lawsuits.
2. The benefit is an organ transplant for a patient who would die without it. The risk is removing organs from a person's dead body without knowing the wishes of the deceased. Potential donors fail to recognize that their omission—refusal to consent to donation—may cause irreparable harm. From the perspective of those who will die waiting for an organ transplant, inaction causes at least as much harm as action.
3. The benefit is the development and approval of a beneficial drug, and the risk is harmful side effects from the drug. The introduction of new drugs has been slow in the United States because of the fear of harm resulting from action, while the harm caused by inaction has traditionally been ignored.

All three cases involve an imbalance in which citizens and policy-makers worry too much about one risk and not enough about another. To restore balance, we, as a society, will have to reduce one risk greatly and increase the other risk by a small amount. The human tendency to be more concerned about losses than gains often prevents us from taking such potentially beneficial action. We will explore these three dilemmas, consider practical solutions to each one and offer a better way to think about tradeoffs across a broad array of policy decisions.

Lawsuits and Corporate Inaction

In his book *Galileo's Revenge: Junk Science in the Courtroom*, Peter Huber presents several alarming signs that something is wrong with the American legal system.

- Cancer victims have sued successfully for damages after developing cancer at the site of an injury, even though the best evidence indicated that the association was coincidental.
- The Audi 5000 was one of the safest cars on the road, but the close proximity of the brake and the accelerator—a safety feature on the highway—may have led some drivers to step on the accelerator instead of the brake in parking lots or garages. Drivers argued successfully in court, despite strong scientific evidence against their claim, that the Audi accelerated suddenly on its own. Audi sales plummeted.
- Bendictin, an anti-nausea drug that has probably saved the lives of many mothers and infants in cases of severe morning sickness, was withdrawn from the market after courts decided that it caused birth defects despite good scientific evidence that it did not. Since then, research on drugs for pregnant women has declined drastically.[15]

Huber blames these events on judges' and juries' abandonment of scientific standards and tolerance for "junk science" in the courtroom. All sorts of shady characters are paid to pose as expert witnesses, regardless of their credentials. By leaving juries with the impression that "experts disagree," lawyers enable them to rationalize siding with the plaintiff purely out of sympathy. After all, who can truly judge which experts are credible?

One common point among lawsuits gone haywire, from the Dow-Corning breast implants case to these triumphs of junk science, is that companies are sued for their actions–but never for inaction. No company will ever be taken to court for refusing to manufacture a silicone product or an anti-nausea drug. Thus, the omission bias is practically built into the law. The result? Lawsuits tend to encourage the omission bias in the companies themselves. If lawsuits were predictable and preventable, companies could fend them off by establishing adequate safety measures. But when companies can be sued for misfortunes they have not caused, they may refuse to take the risk. Large corporations, whose deep pockets make them an easy target of spurious claims, will be afraid to act when action involves developing a beneficial product that carries some degree of risk, as most medical products do. They will choose to avoid the healthcare industry and turn to other markets in which lawsuits are less likely.

Of course, this reluctance decreases societal resources because the harms of new medical devices are often small compared to their benefits. Lawsuits are supposed to deter the production of goods that have few benefits and many harms, such as automobiles with faulty brakes or drugs that don't work as advertised. But when producers are sued for unforeseeable harms that are in any case minor when compared with the benefits, the lawsuits lead to the withdrawal of beneficial products, and the legal system has done a poor job of balancing harms and benefits. A prime example is the case of vaccines.

Vaccines

Lawsuits against pharmaceutical companies have led to the withdrawal of beneficial drugs, research cutbacks and price increases for drugs that remain available. Because manufacturers are always sued for actions rather than omissions, the easiest solution is to withdraw from the market any product that, despite its benefits, causes small harms that could lead to punitive lawsuits.

The vaccine for pertussis prevents a bacterial infection that causes whooping cough, a deadly disease in infants and toddlers. Pertussis is the "P" in "DPT," a commonly used combination vaccine that immunizes babies against diphtheria and tetanus as well as whooping cough. Before the DPT vaccine was introduced in the late 1940s, about 7,000 children died in the United States each year from whooping cough.[16] The death rate is now less than 100 per year.

Despite its success, until the late 1990s, the DPT vaccine was a source of controversy. Why? Because a tiny fraction of a percent of children vaccinated experienced serious side effects—brain damage and perhaps even death—from pertussis. When a few cases of brain damage attributed to the DPT vaccine were reported in England and Japan in the mid-1970s, vaccination requirements lapsed. In Great Britain, after vaccination rates fell from 79 percent in 1971 to 37 percent in 1974, a two-year epidemic of whooping cough killed 36 people. The epidemic ended when vaccination rates increased. Similar epidemics occurred in Japan, also involving 30 to 40 deaths per year.[17]

The reported instances of brain damage may not have been caused by the vaccine at all.[18] Infants are subject to brain damage from such diseases as naturally occurring encephalitis, which could occur immediately—and coincidentally—just after a child is vaccinated. Even if some of these cases were caused by the vaccine, they are rare, occurring in just eight children out of a million.[19]

In the United States, following a spate of lawsuits from people who contracted polio from the polio vaccine or who developed disabilities around the time of their DPT vaccinations, research on new vaccines declined. Meanwhile, millions of people throughout the world continue to suffer and die from preventable infectious diseases.[20] In addition, companies stopped making the vaccines targeted by the lawsuits. By 1986, only one company, Lederle, was left manufacturing the DPT vaccine; within a few years, its price had risen from less than a dollar per shot to more than ten dollars, with most of the increase used to pay liability claims.[21] The National Childhood Vaccine Injury Compensation Act, passed by the U.S. Congress in 1986, has stabilized the situation by providing a fund for limited compensation.

The distinction between harm caused by action and harm caused by inaction and the implicit bias toward the status quo are built into many laws that affect pharmaceuticals. In the special case of synthetic drugs, the human bias against artificial risk also strongly influences policy decisions. Consider Tamoxifen, a drug that seems to reduce the risk of breast cancer (research to test this preventive effect is underway). Unfortunately, it also appears to increase the risk of cancer of the endometrium of the uterus. The beneficial effect on breast cancer is apparently many times greater than the harmful effect of endometrial cancer, so we can think of Tamoxifen as a drug that decreases the risk of cancer overall. Because of a California law requiring warning labels on anything manmade that causes cancer, the scientific panel that labels carcinogens in California felt that it had to include Tamoxifen. As a result, a large experimental study intended to measure the overall effects of Tamoxifen took longer than expected, and the experiment's sponsors believe the warning discouraged women from participating.[22] Despite these setbacks, the study was a success, and Tamoxifen is now in widespread use. Nonetheless, many women may have died unnecessarily because Tamoxifen was unavailable for so long.

Warnings about drugs and vaccines should be based on overall risk relative to the risk of doing nothing (failing to approve the product), rather than on whether the risk is natural or artificial. If this change were made, people would not have to calculate a product's relative costs and benefits on their own. Most people lack the necessary data to conduct such an informed analysis. When they hear about a potential risk, they become afraid to act—even if the risk of inaction is much greater.

Contraceptives

Effective contraception was a major technological achievement of the twentieth century—and just in time. Overcrowding is a serious problem in many countries. Populations in African nations are growing faster than their food supplies, and as many as a quarter of African children are undernourished to the point of reduced physical and intellectual development.[23] Bangladesh and China appear unable to support many more people despite their fertile land. Both of these countries use contraception to help manage population growth. Even in wealthy nations such as the United States, where overpopulation is not a problem, contraception is indispensable for preventing unwanted pregnancies and disease.

Despite the enormous need, present contraceptive methods are less than ideal. Condoms sometimes fail; birth control pills often produce unpleasant side effects. Sterilization is risky and difficult to reverse. Every method has its drawbacks, and they all cost money, a serious problem for the poor. These disadvantages discourage people from using contraceptives and exacerbate the problems of population growth.

It would be nice to report that researchers are working diligently to develop new and better forms of contraception, but they aren't. Despite the huge potential market, contraceptive research is the neglected stepchild of the drug industry. Why? Because contraceptives, like vaccines, are developed for healthy people who do not expect to suffer in any way from a drug or a device. When infections occur, people sue, even when package inserts have warned them about side effects.

These problems began with the Dalkon Shield, an intrauterine device (IUD) that, when implanted in a woman's uterus, prevents the egg from being fertilized.[24] When the Dalkon Shield entered the market in 1968, it had a 1.1 percent pregnancy rate, which compared favorably to other IUDs. When the Dalkon Corporation was taken over by the A. H. Robins Co. in 1970, the Dalkon Shield did not need FDA approval. In 1971, a quality-control supervisor reported to management his finding that the string attached to the Shield could carry bacteria from the vagina into the uterus, thus causing infection. The report was ignored, as were reports the following year of several infections and miscarriages as well as the death of one woman using the Shield. In 1975, Robins recalled all unsold Shields, but it was not until 1980—after paying $4 million in one year for settlements and legal costs—that it advised physicians to remove the Shield from anyone still using it. In 1985, Robins filed for bankruptcy, and the judge ordered the company to set aside almost $2.5 billion to compensate women injured by the Shield. Beginning in 1983, as a result of the negative publicity the Shield had attracted, three other companies withdrew their IUDs from the market; leaving only two in the United States—even though few lawsuits had been filed against the three companies and even fewer had been argued successfully in court. Why did the companies abandon the IUD market? Because they no longer trusted the American legal system. They believed Robins was ruined not because it was more careless than other companies but because it made a medical device used by healthy people.

Once again, we see the imbalance between acts and omissions and the opportunity to increase societal benefits by treating these behaviors more equally. We are not arguing that lawsuits are inherently wrong; they provide a strong incentive for companies to design and test their products carefully. The problem is that healthy people are less forgiving of a product's side effects and malfunctions than sick people are. Sick people do not sue if a drug or device intended for the relief of pain or the prevention of death has severe side effects (as long as they have been warned). Most important, people do not sue drug companies for failing to develop new products. Given a choice of where to put its development funds, a company will choose to work on a new medicine for cancer rather than develop a new contraceptive.

Lawsuits are supposed to deter carelessness, but executive decision makers are more likely to regard them as random lightning bolts that strike certain products for no good reason. Experience has taught them that the result of a lawsuit may depend more on the skills of a lawyer or the sympathy of a jury than on whether the company was negligent. Negligence is difficult to avoid. Hindsight suggests that someone at Robins made a terrible decision when he or she chose to ignore the reports of danger. But if a company adopts a rigid policy requiring that all such reports be investigated, research costs might drive it out of business. Often, companies decide that it is easier to direct their energies elsewhere.

Our liability system encourages individuals to think of themselves as plaintiffs and big corporations as defendants. This mindset forgets that we all pay the costs incurred by losing defendants, whether through higher prices, the sudden disappearance of a product or the failure to research new products. People who have invested their pensions in mutual funds or other stock should think of themselves as potential defendants; when companies lose big lawsuits, the value of their stock and dividends often decline.

Changing the Way Lawsuits Work

Lawsuits, as we have seen, often do more harm than good. Because they are such a crude and unreliable instrument, businesses often pull out of useful enterprises, fearing an irrational and capricious legal system. Two reforms can help.

1. *Ensure that laws and court decisions are based on sound science.* The U.S. Supreme Court moved strongly in this direction with its 1993 *Frey v. the United States of America* ruling, which advised judges to ask for expert advice in matters of science rather than leaving the selection of expert witnesses to the opposing lawyers. If this ruling were mandated and universally followed, juries would less often be subjected to the presentations of unqualified "experts." It is important that the experts be paid by the court (or by assessments on both parties) so that they are not financially obligated to either side.
2. *Allow the FDA to be the arbiter of good science.* Establishing a central agency to certify scientific evidence used in trials would have the advantage of making the facts clear to all parties. While the FDA's conclusions would be open to challenge, they would be assumed correct until proved otherwise.

Negotiated settlements could also alleviate the problem, but the rules would have to be changed. Now, negotiated settlements in lawsuits are the usual outcome–but the problem is that in most states, the results are secret! Secrecy defeats the major function of lawsuits:

defining and deterring negligent behavior. Secret settlements leave everyone but the immediate parties in the dark about what is and what is not permissible. These settlements may be based on cost-benefit analysis, but others will not benefit if the analysis must be done over from scratch. If other companies in the same situation cannot accomplish the same settlement because they don't know what it is, then this standard is unfair. Settlements should generally be made public so that everyone can learn the rules, and so that the rules apply to everyone. When privileged information is involved, specific information should be guarded, not the entire case. Because secrecy is one of the benefits of negotiation, more cases might go to trial if settlements were made public; if so, other means of encouraging negotiated settlements would have to be found.

The American legal system has tended to punish harms arising from action, regardless of the benefits caused by these actions, while ignoring the harms that arise from inaction. In the next section, this same selective mindset will emerge as a barrier to solving the worldwide shortage of transplantable organs.

Organ Supply: Should Bioethics Have a Warning Label?

Which option do you prefer:

A. If you die in an accident, your heart will be used to save another person's life. In addition, if you ever need a heart transplant, you will have a 90 percent chance of getting the heart.
B. If you die in an accident, you will be buried with your heart in your body. In addition, if you ever need a heart transplant, you will have a 45 percent chance of getting the heart.

If you're like most people, you chose Option A. So why do the United States and most other countries maintain an organ donation policy that resembles Option B?

In the United States, the waiting list for organs grew from 13,000 in 1987 to 44,000 in 1996. Over a third of those on the list will die before an organ is found. A quarter of those waiting for liver transplants are less than ten years old. Meanwhile, the number of potential donors has decreased. Because the most eligible donors are young people who die in accidents that do not harm their transplantable organs, increased use of seatbelts and motorcycle helmets has reduced the number of these donors. Still, only 4,500 of the 11,000 eligible donors donate their organs. If we could double this figure, we could save an additional one-quarter of the approximately 15,000 people who die each year in the United States because of the lack of organs.[25]

In the grand scheme of things, the problem of organ donation is small. The 40,000 Americans waiting for organs at any given time pale beside the million children in Africa who die from malaria each year and the hundreds of thousands who die from AIDS because they lack medicine. But if you or someone in your family is one of those 40,000, the problem is not trivial at all. For some, it means growing weaker day by day as their hearts degenerate, yet always hoping along with their families that the phone will ring with good news. When seven-year-old Nicholas Green, an American boy, was killed by gunfire in Italy, his kidney was donated to Tino Motta, an eleven-year-old Italian boy. Tino's mother recalls: "I cried. I felt so sorry for the child who had died, but I was so happy for Tino. . . . I give thanks to the parents of Nicholas. For them to donate the organs was a beautiful decision. My child has come back to life."[26]

If an action is known to benefit one person immensely and harm almost no one, most people would agree that the action should be taken. The benefits of cadaveric transplants are perhaps the greatest gift a person can receive. So why aren't more people willing to donate organs?

Ways to Enlarge the Pie

The organ donation system that exists today in the United States favors donors over recipients, yet the pool of donors and recipients is nearly the same. Most of us have no idea which role we will assume, if either. Just as we must learn to think of ourselves as both plaintiffs and defendants in lawsuits, citizens must learn to view themselves as both potential donors and potential recipients. This change in mindset is the key to solving the organ donation problem. The system that naturally follows from this approach assumes that a potential donor consents to donation unless she explicitly removes her consent before death. This approach is known as "presumed consent."

The biases discussed in this chapter cause people to oppose presumed consent. When we take an organ from one person to help another person, we risk harming the donor by going against her wishes, or those of her family. If we do not take the organ, we risk harming the potential recipient, who may lose years of life or suffer a lower quality of life if he is unable to obtain an organ elsewhere. Of these two risks, the risk of harm to the donor is arguably less serious and less likely, but because it is a harm of commission, we worry about it more than we worry about the harm of depriving a sick person of an organ. In addition, because transplants may seem to go against the "wishes" of nature or God that the recipient's time on Earth is up, many people view them as "unnatural." We can assume that this is not the view of potential recipients who are eager to improve or prolong their lives; rather, it is a view imposed on them by the human preference for natural risk. Finally, many countries place the burden of positive consent upon the donor. The status quo bias makes us reluctant to change a system that presumes donor consent has not been given.

Discussion of organ donation in the United States has focused on how to divide the small pie rather than how to enlarge it. The debates concern priority for local versus distant recipients, and whether the sickest patients should have priority over those who have been waiting longest. Initiatives aimed at enlarging the pie have been limited primarily to publicity—convincing more people to sign donor cards, for example.

Three solutions have been proposed to the broader task of expanding the pie by securing more organs. Presumed consent, the most radical of these solutions, is the one we will recommend most strongly.

Required Request.   According to "required request" laws, which have been passed in most states, when a potential donor dies, a doctor or nurse must ask the next of kin to consider donating one or more of the deceased's organs. While hospitals in these states have adhered to these laws, donation rates have not increased. Families often refuse to donate, or at most, make relatively minor donations, such as corneas. Even without such laws, request rates are fairly high, but about half of the families of potential donors in the United States refuse, as do about a third in Britain.[27]

Why do so many families reject the opportunity to save a life? Consider the typical case. The most promising potential donor is a young, healthy person who has suffered a sudden, devastating head injury. Although the patient is still breathing, often with mechanical support, his brain is dead. Sometimes he can be kept in this state for a long time; other times, injuries will cause his heart to stop. The doctors and nurses caring for the patient must wrench their attention away from him to give the family the terrible news and then to ask permission for organ donation. Although the victim may have filled out an organ-donor card or a living will, or indicated his wishes on his driver's license, the hospital staff does not automatically look for such information. If the family is against donation or cannot be located, the organs will not be removed. Clearly, the confusion and grief of such moments work against organ donation. In addition, hospital staff are well aware of the bad publicity, lawsuits and anguish to the family that might follow if they were to remove organs without consent.

"Required request" laws could force citizens to decide for themselves whether they want to donate organs. Although several states now require people to make this decision when they apply for a driver's license, these reforms have not improved organ donation rates. One study found that more than half of potential donors refuse when asked about donation in advance.[28] In Texas and Virginia, the vast majority decline to donate, and the wishes of those who say "yes" are rarely followed.[29]

Given the nature of the decision and its consequences, the explanations people give for refusal often sound like rationalizations. Potential donors often say they want their family's input in these decisions. Family members of dead or dying potential donors question whether the allocation system is fair. We suggest that the omission bias, the status quo bias and the preference for natural risk lie at the root of the problem. The last, in particular, produces a kind of disgust reaction to the thought of transplantation.

Preferential Access/Donor Compensation.   Another possible solution, donor compensation, has been hotly debated by physicians and ethicists but never tried. Several forms of compensation are possible for those who promise to donate their organs upon death, including a reduction in insurance rates, preferential access to transplants if needed or simply money. Payments ranging from $1,000 to $3,000 for funeral expenses have been proposed.[30] Those who sign a donor card could be immediately compensated, or the money could be set aside for their estates. Compensation to the estate might make it easier for family members to honor the donor's wishes. Given the influential role that families have played in these decisions, though, it is still not certain that signing a donor card would have much effect.

There are two related objections to the idea of donor compensation. First, some have argued that the trade of organs for dollars is inherently immoral. According to this argument, things such as sex, votes, freedom and human organs should never enter the marketplace. Although the rationale for these moral principles varies considerably, the general term applied to them is "commodification," or the process of making something into a commodity that should not be one. There are good reasons why many of these things should never be given a dollar value.[31] But why add organs to the list?

Before entering this fray, we should consider another main objection: Moral quibbles aside, compensation may not work. Payments for blood donations have had little effect on the number of donations. An irrational psychological principle of motivation may be at issue here: Many people are happy to donate out of altruism, but when money enters the equation, their goodwill dries up. Compensation may attract new donors, but almost as many people who would have contributed out of altruism will decide not to do so. We seem to require exactly one reason for doing something; if that reason is financial reward, then it can't also be altruism.

Giving donors preferential access to organs could, in principle, solve both of these problems. We imagine a system where all citizens are given the opportunity to opt in or opt out of organ donation. Those who opt in would enter into a legally binding agreement to donate their organs at death. In return, they would have preferential access to available organs over all people who opted out. This structure would avoid the egocentric tendencies of the many people who believe it is religiously or morally inappropriate to harvest organs from themselves or from loved ones, but who would willingly receive an organ if they needed one. This type of system would require all citizens to decide whether they wish to cooperate in a system that offers minor costs and great benefits. We believe it would create a great increase in donation.

While technically a form of donor compensation, this solution involves no financial incentive. Thus we would expect people to regard preferential access as a form of cooperation rather than bribery. Donors' families would still be the biggest stumbling block to a preferential access system because they would presumably continue to control donation decisions, in many cases ignoring the wishes of their loved ones. Thus, such a system would need to state clearly the binding nature of each person's decision.

Presumed Consent.   Our final option reframes the issue of organ donation. Under "presumed consent," instead of requiring consent for donation, people are asked whether they object to donating. Instead of handing out donor cards to those who consent, the government gives objector cards to those who refuse. Citizens who do not object are automatically assumed to be donors. In our current system, non-donation is an omission, not an act. Although this omission is potentially harmful to someone else, nondonors do not regard their omission as immoral, and find ways to justify it. When consent is presumed, potential donors are forced to view refusal as a harmful act that is less easily rationalized away.

Many countries have adopted presumed consent laws, including several European nations, Singapore and, most recently, Brazil. The laws vary in the degree to which hospital staff must work with the donor's family from simply informing them to giving them a chance to opt out. Presumed consent laws have dramatically increased rates of donation. In Belgium, donations rose by 140 percent after the law was introduced. In Austria, after a presumed-consent law was passed in 1983, the waiting list for organs fell to a small fraction of its previous size by 1990.[32] Presumed consent may be particularly effective because it applies not only to donors but to their families, who also must act to deny a donation.

Objections to Organ-Donation Reform

Why haven't we enacted reforms that would save tens of thousands of lives each year? Objections to presumed consent and other reforms are much the same as objections to the very notion of organ donation. In Brazil—where opposition to the new law is intense and a majority of citizens in some cities opt out of the system—support for organ donation in general is declining, and the subject is hotly debated in the news media.[33] Some of the opposition in Brazil has occurred because that country's system for distributing and transplanting organs was unprepared for the increase in available organs. Horror stories abound, such as the tale of a worker who got drunk, fell asleep in a field and woke up without his eyes.

Aside from such urban legends, one argument against presumed consent prevalent in Brazil is similar to those made throughout the world: We should not concern ourselves with survival—let nature take its course. One person wondered whether donation "may change destiny . . . like Frankenstein."[34] "I don't believe in this idea that you have to live as long as possible," said one Brazilian. "I think our lives are what we do with them. I can live to ninety and not have as good a life as somebody who dies younger."[35] This fatalistic attitude is off the point. One person's ninety years may indeed be less fulfilling than another's fifty, but as Damon Runyan said, "The race is not always to the swift, nor the battle to the strong, but that's the way to bet." Every transplantation patient makes the optimistic bet that years regained will be worth the risk, high costs and challenges of recovery. For most people, this gamble pays off.

Many religious and spiritual traditions, such as Catholicism, have based their moral systems on the idea of natural law. Most of these faiths do not object to the beneficial interference of medicine and technology in the natural course of events. The Catholic Church, for example, seeks a deeper moral law through the observation of the natural and social order, and advocates intervention, when needed, to satisfy the demands of that law. Catholicism actively supports organ donation as an act of charity, as do most other major religions, including Islam.[36] Some people interpret their religion's laws to dictate life support at all costs. Throughout history, time of death has been determined by the cessation of breath and heartbeat. But given that most people now consider the brain to be the locus of earthly experience, those who think of breathing as the primary indication of life are failing to question the reasons that anyone would want to live. This failure to search for ultimate purposes is a common cause of fallacious thinking about organ donation.

Perhaps out of wishful thinking, many nondonors fall victim to "belief overkill": the tendency to accept any argument, no matter how spurious, that reinforces the stand they have taken. For example, some people insist that organ transplants almost always fail— even when they are confronted with cases in which someone has benefited immensely. Even college students, who might be expected to be more open-minded than most, often oppose organ donation.[36] Their objections take various forms: They do not want to think about death; they do not want their organs given to an undeserving or undesirable recipient; they worry that their organs will not be transplantable; they feel they will need their organs in the afterlife;

they do not want their bodies disfigured; they worry that a doctor will declare death prematurely. We might generalize this group of objections—most can be easily disputed—as the "ycch factor" resulting from the idea of one's dead body being cut open. Granted, it is not a pleasant image to contemplate; but thoughtful citizens must separate their immediate emotions from serious consideration of the issue. Interestingly, such concerns come up much more frequently for organ donors than for recipients—which is one of the reasons we endorse preferential access. It forces a healthy person to separate selfishness from legitimate objections.

Bioethicists, members of an emerging field that draws its knowledge base from philosophy, medicine and the law, have recently weighed in with their own expert opinions on presumed consent. Before presenting their arguments, we will first define a few terms: informed consent, patient autonomy and the do-no-harm principle. The first two, informed consent and patient autonomy, are the guiding principles of bioethics. We have discussed the do-no-harm principle as a cognitive rule of thumb that is biased toward omissions. This rule is also built into many doctrines espoused by bioethicists.

Informed consent reinforces the property right that people have to their own bodies. Proponents of informed consent insist that a person's body cannot be trespassed without permission; a person is able to give such permission only when fully advised of the nature of the proposed procedures, its implications and its risks. Informed consent obliges medical personnel to help their patients make an informed decision. In the absence of such information, consent to any drug or medical procedure does not exist.

Autonomy, the right to do as one likes with one's body—including the right to refuse medical treatment—extends beyond death. Just as people can control their property through wills, they can control their bodies through "living wills." And if they fail to do so, the current default prevails: Their bodies will be buried intact.

The do-no-harm principle states that it is wrong to harm one person to benefit another, even if the benefit outweighs the harm. As we have discussed, harm refers only to actions, not to omissions.

Thus failing to save the life of a dying patient is not considered a harm. But taking an organ from a dead body without previous consent, or without the consent of a family member, does count as a harm.

The objections that bioethicists have raised to presumed consent are founded on these three principles. A report from the Council on Ethical and Judicial Affairs of the American Medical Association argues that presumed consent laws are harmful to those who would not consent if their wishes were known.[38]

> To be ethically acceptable, presumed consent would require intensive, sustained educational efforts to inform individuals and families of their right to opt out of the system by registering an objection to donation. The absence of known objections does not mean that consent may be presumed; rather, when a decedent has not indicated his or her preference regarding donation, families must be asked if they have knowledge of the decedent's true wishes.[39]

What the report fails to mention is the harm done now to those who would want to donate but whose wishes are not known. Neither harm causes pain to the dead person, and both harms involve going against someone's wishes. Why do we count one as "harm" but not the other? Perhaps because the harm of failing to donate results from inaction and follows the course of nature. Surely education about options is an essential component of any organ donation system, yet education offers no increased benefit under presumed consent than under the present system of expressed consent.

The families of the deceased are the major concern of another opponent:

> Presumed consent laws . . . ignore those interests from the donor side of the equation which deserve the most protection. The current system of organ procurement shows a great deal of respect for the wishes of the donor. But once the donor dies, she is not the one who

is going to be affected by what we do to her body. The people who are going to be affected are the family members she leaves behind. They are the ones who must live with the decisions that are made.[40]

Because the potential donor will presumably have made her own decision, this focus on her family is odd. When a family is allowed to override the donor's wishes and refuse organ removal, that family is the party causing the harm—to the transplant recipient as well as to the deceased. Surely the choices made by adults should be respected after death. Just as we would not, and legally cannot, disobey the decisions a person makes for the disbursement of her possessions in a will, we should not be permitted to act against the stipulations she makes about her body.

Others argue that presumed consent violates the autonomy of the deceased because of the possibility of error.[41] Through ignorance, carelessness or bureaucratic mishap, a citizen's objection to donation could fail to be registered. Surely such errors will occur under presumed consent—just as they do now under expressed consent when, for example, medical personnel neglect to examine a patient's donor card or driver's license for evidence of consent. Why should the principle of autonomy be brought to bear on one kind of error and not another? If a person seeks to help others when she can and views organ donation as a way to help others at no cost to herself, and if she forgets to sign a donor card or her family fails to communicate her desire, hasn't her autonomy been violated? Given that a majority of the population say they favor donation when asked, we might expect that, in the absence of information, a person is more likely to want to donate than not. Autonomy is selectively interpreted to favor inaction and "nature."

The principles of autonomy and do-no-harm clearly *do* harm, especially when combined. Why do we support them? The bioethicists haven't come up with good answers, but legislators listen to them nonetheless. "Presumed consent has been tried in Europe with unimpressive results," argues bioethicist Arthur Caplan. But the doubling of the donation rate in Belgium is in no way unimpressive.

Caplan's claim is sheer belief overkill. Bioethicists resist the undeniable fact that their moral principles work to the detriment of people awaiting organs.

A Final Argument for Organ Donation

When a society assumes that people do not want to donate their organs upon death, it has shown a preference for one of two options. This default option allows organs to be buried in the ground or burnt, and allows a person who could have used that organ to die or to continue with dialysis for the rest of her life (in the case of patients in need of kidney transplants). The other option, transplantation, is of little consequence to the dead person save for that person's beliefs about what is morally right; in addition, it allows another person to live longer or better. Ordinarily, actions that shorten or substantially reduce the quality of someone's life, and that have no compensating gain, are considered crimes. This can even be true when these actions are motivated by religious or moral beliefs, as in the case of religious terrorists or of Christian Scientists who withhold medical treatment from their children.

Under current law, we define donation as an act and the withholding of donation as an omission. Ordinary intuition leads us to believe that harms caused by omissions are less blameworthy than those caused by acts. This is sometimes true for reasons having nothing to do with the distinction itself—for example, acts require more effort than omission, and we are reluctant to require people to expend effort on each others' behalf. But in the case of organ donation, the distinction in citizens' minds between acts and omissions is created entirely by the law. Presumed consent reverses this situation: By requiring an act to refuse donation, rather than making refusal the default, the do-no-harm rule works against refusal. In return for a small risk that someone's wishes not to donate will be ignored—because that person feels pressured to consent, for example—many lives are saved.

Perhaps the story of the Venutti family illustrates better than any ethical, practical or spiritual argument why the existing organ donation system in the United States should be changed. Tina Venutti's three-year-old daughter, Lauren, was left brain dead in the aftermath of a severe seizure. "You're just numb when you're told your child is dying, is brain dead," Mrs. Venutti recalled. Despite her shock and grief, when Mrs. Venutti was asked about organ donation, she faced the situation. "It was a very immediate decision," she says. "Just knowing that through your child's death you're giving hope and dreams to someone else helps tremendously. They already knew that there was a little girl down at Loma Linda [Hospital] who needed a heart and was a perfect match. It's the greatest gift you can give." The transplant was undertaken and the little girl survived. A year later, Mrs. Venutti gave birth to a son with a heart defect. The boy did not survive more than a few days, but if he had, he would have been a prime candidate for a heart transplant. "Would there have been an organ waiting for him?" Mrs. Venutti wondered. "Probably not. It was hard to accept this. We've been at both ends."[42] Like the Venuttis, any one of us could someday find ourselves at either end of this debate.

The Drug Lag

Throughout history people have taken drugs, potions and lotions to treat illness. While the rise of capitalism has made it worthwhile for companies to invest billions of dollars in new drugs, it has also made room for snake oil, magic elixirs and other frauds. This possibility of deception provides a justification for government involvement in the drug trade; capitalistic markets work only when buyers are well informed about what they are purchasing. A second reason for government intervention is the need to protect people from themselves. Even when people are warned of the dangers of smoking, drinking and drug addiction, they tend to minimize the risks. Protection can come in the form of taxes, regulated sales or outright bans.

In this section, we focus specifically on the problem of regulating new drugs to treat diseases. Under the current system, thousands of people have died while waiting for new drugs to be approved. Government officials who regulate drugs often seem to worry more about the harm they could cause by approving a potentially harmful drug than about the harm caused by approval delays. Recent reforms in the United States have overcome this problem to some extent, but greater benefits can be accomplished in this country and elsewhere.

U.S. Drug Regulation: A Brief History

By the end of the nineteenth century, quack medicine had become a near epidemic in the United States. Patent medicine salesmen crisscrossed the country peddling their concoctions at touring shows and pharmacies. These mixtures were not only ineffective but often dangerous. "Poor mothers doped their babies into insensibility at night with soothing syrups containing opium or morphine. . . . Cancer 'cures' flooded the market," recalled Harvey W. Wiley, the Department of Agriculture's chief chemist at the time.[43]

The Food and Drug Act, signed by President Theodore Roosevelt in 1906, attempted to stanch the flow of bogus medicine by prohibiting interstate commerce of misbranded and adulterated food, drinks and drugs, and by requiring such products to be properly labeled and not poisonous. The law was later tightened to prohibit false therapeutic claims. The Food and Drug Administration was formally established in 1930; by 1938, Congress had passed the Federal Food, Drug and Cosmetic Act, which provided the framework for drug regulation in the United States. Manufacturers of new drugs, cosmetics and therapeutic devices were now required to prove the safety of their products before they were put on the market.

The powers of the FDA were increased substantially in 1962, when European doctors discovered that the tranquilizer Thalidomide caused severe birth defects—such as absent or incomplete limbs—when taken during pregnancy. After the disturbing image of "Thalidomide babies" increased public support for the FDA, Congress established the process for drug approval that still exists today.

The FDA's Approval Process

Obtaining FDA approval for a new drug is a lengthy and expensive process. First, the drug company submits an "Investigational New Drug" (IND) notice to the FDA, which contains information about animal tests, other relevant safety data, and a plan for testing the drug on humans. Unless the FDA objects within thirty days, Phase I studies on humans can begin. Typically involving fewer than a hundred subjects and lasting about a year, Phase I is designed to determine dosage levels and to answer questions about how the body absorbs the drug. Phase II, which also lasts about a year, tests for side effects and effectiveness in a few hundred patients. Phase III typically involves thousands of patients and can last two years or more. This is the main test of the drug's effectiveness and the most difficult part of the process, both financially and ethically. The anticancer drug Taxol, for example, had to pass nine years of human testing before it was deemed effective, despite having undergone six years of lab tests. At the end of Phase III, the company submits a "New Drug Application" (NDA) to the FDA, which can take up to a year to respond. Finally, after approval of the drug for clinical use, Phase IV studies continue to monitor its effects.

Not surprisingly, such an arduous process discourages the development of new drugs in the United States; and when new drugs do make it to market, high research costs drive up their prices. The American public has generally supported these rigorous policies, in part because, as we have seen, we tend to regard harmful acts as worse than harmful omissions, especially when the harm in omissions can be blamed on "nature" or the occurrence of natural disease. In 1974, FDA Commissioner Alexander Schmidt expressed his frustration with this contradiction: "In all of FDA's history, I am unable to find a single instance where a congressional committee investigated the failure of FDA to approve a new drug. But the times when hearings have been held to criticize our approval of new drugs have been so frequent that we aren't able to count them."[44]

The 1962 legislative changes created a "drug lag"—a slowing down in the approval of new drugs. Thousands of Americans have died in recent decades because they were unable to obtain life-saving drugs already approved in other countries. This deadly lag is a direct result of the human tendency to worry more about the harms that come from action than those that come from inaction. As one critic pointed out, "[The] introduction of a new drug that produced fatalities anywhere approaching this magnitude would be regarded as a major disaster, but the undoubted occurrence of deaths through failure to introduce a drug has so far gone unremarked."[45]

A Call for Reform

The FDA began seriously to consider the negative effects of the drug lag in 1987, when its decisions regarding a drug called tissue plasminogen activator, or TPA, caught the attention of the public. A naturally occurring substance developed by Genentech, a genetic engineering company, TPA promised to be more effective at breaking up blood clots caused by heart attacks than other remedies—including a drug called Streptokinase, which had been in use since 1982. As the makers of Streptokinase applied for the FDA's approval of an improved administration of the drug, Genentech pushed for TPA to be considered at the same meeting. At first, the FDA refused.

A *Wall Street Journal* editorial responded: "Last Friday an advisory panel of the Food and Drug Administration decided to sacrifice thousands of American lives on an altar of pedantry. . . . Patients will die who would otherwise live longer. Medical research has allowed statistics to become the supreme judge of its inventions. . . . We'll put it bluntly. Are American doctors going to let people die to satisfy the bureau of drug's chi-square studies?"[46]

While the story was more complicated than this editorial implies,[47] it appears that public criticism may have led the FDA to speed the TPA approval process. Reversing its early decision, the FDA allowed discussion of TPA at the Streptokinase meeting. In the end, the two drugs were approved in the same week. The incident was one of many that caused the FDA to rethink its procedures.

The major impetus for overhaul arose from the spread of AIDS. The political efforts of AIDS patients represent the first time the victims of the drug lag have organized themselves effectively. The main mobilizing organization was ACT UP, the AIDS Coalition to Unleash Power. In the United States in the 1980s, AIDS primarily afflicted male homosexuals, many of whom were politically active and well educated. Many ACT UP members met for the first time at funerals, where their shared frustration over the horrendous killer of young people eventually gave way to action. Under the leadership of Larry Kramer, ACT UP demanded more research on AIDS from the government, as well as faster access to potentially beneficial drugs, even if their safety and benefits were not proved to the FDA's satisfaction. AIDS patients showed—quite reasonably—little concern with the small safety risks of a drug that might prolong their lives.

The slow approval of a drug called Dextran Sulfate was one case that called ACT UP to action. A preliminary test of the drug, which had been used in Japan for many years to lower cholesterol, showed promising results in treating AIDS, according to a report issued in June 1987. As the FDA worked on a year-long study to approve a study of the drug in the United States,[48] thousands of AIDS patients began importing the drug illegally from Japan. As it turned out, the drug didn't live up to its promise and was never approved. But the uproar over the slow testing helped create changes in the law.

Another FDA policy under fire by activists was the research use of placebos—inactive sugar pills given to subjects instead of the active drug. "It's proven that without treatment, AIDS is fatal, so it's inhumane to have protocols with placebos," argued one demonstrator at an AIDS rally in October 1988. "They're jeopardizing people's health and lives for research that may not even be useful."[49] Partly in reaction to these protests, the FDA introduced Parallel Track, a new policy that allows patients who are not a part of clinical trials to take drugs being tested in Phases II and III. The new program enables researchers to study patients who take drugs on their own rather than as subjects in a controlled experiment. Participants in these "natural" experiments are compared to people who do not take the drug. These studies are poorly controlled and thus difficult to generalize.

As Parallel Track studies increase, it will become much more difficult to recruit subjects for controlled placebo studies.

While most potential AIDS-fighting drugs were disappointments, one was not: AZT (azidothymidine) was shown to reduce the symptoms of AIDS and to delay death. In 1987, the FDA allowed 4,000 patients to use AZT after the drug was found to be so successful in a Phase II trial that withholding it from the control group would have been unethical. In 1991, DDI (dideoxyinosine), a drug similar in its effects to AZT, was approved after testing under the Parallel Track plan; the benefits of DDI were later borne out. When some expressed concern over the fast approval of DDI, FDA Commissioner David Kessler addressed the implicit tradeoff involved in speeding drugs to market: "There is no question that one day we are going to be wrong. Everyone needs to keep their eyes wide open."[50] Kessler was willing to admit that a large reduction in errors of omission were worth the small increase in errors of commission. His statement reflects wise preparation for the future, when an error of commission could trigger a backlash against the new policy.

The Parallel Track program was a response not only to the AIDS protests but also to the FDA's own internal problems. The agency had reached a standoff with pharmaceutical companies in the 1980s. Anticipating several years of review for each new drug, the companies sent undigested data to the FDA by the truckload to get applications in the pipeline. FDA workers were overwhelmed; a vicious circle ensued, resulting in greater delays and demoralization. More money would have helped the situation, but Congress refused to provide it.

Negotiations started between the FDA (then headed by David Kessler), Congress and the drug companies. The result was a win-win solution: The pharmaceutical companies agreed to pay fees for drug approval in return for guarantees that drugs would be reviewed in six or twelve months (depending on priority) or else be automatically approved. The Prescription Drug User Fee Act of 1992 went a long way toward eliminating the drug lag caused by the FDA approval process.[51] Other new regulations permitted unsafe drugs to be marketed if the diseases they cured were much worse than the harm they caused. The Food and Drug Administration Modernization Act of 1997 added provisions designed to speed approval; these included faster reviews of drugs for life-threatening illness and permits for outside reviews (e.g., by academic centers).

Faster review implies that more bad drugs will reach the market than before, but the FDA was satisfied that this had not occurred through 1999.[52] In 2000, the FDA withdrew several newly approved drugs (Propulsid, Rezulin and Lotronex) that caused three deaths and adverse reactions in a small number of patients. The doctors of those who were harmed may have been partially to blame for inappropriately prescribing these drugs. Nonetheless, the agency now believes its six-month approval of Rezulin was premature, and speculates that two members of the drug's advisory board were too closely tied to Rezulin manufacturer Warner Lambert (since acquired by Pfizer).

These incidents appear to have given the FDA second thoughts about its fast-track process. As the pendulum swings back again, new drugs will doubtless face long review periods—and patients will have to suffer through long waits for beneficial drugs.[53] But if these mistakes remain rare, the benefits of faster approval would greatly exceed the costs, as hundreds of thousands of patients in the United States receive new drugs sooner. Beneficial change is possible only when people are willing to accept small losses for greater gains. Accepting small losses means accepting the risk that some drugs will be approved only to be found flawed later. The monitoring of industry consultants is also a problem of risk management: If the FDA is too cautious, it will lose the advice of some of its best consultants. We do not advocate neglecting the problems conflict of interest cause; but there is a cost to being careful enough to catch every case.

FDA approval may no longer be the major impediment to the marketing of new drugs. As the FDA has added more drugs to its fast-track approval process, managed-care companies have become wary about paying for the drugs before they have passed Phase IV trials. The same fear of causing harm through action that used to bedevil the FDA now frightens these companies.[54] As a result, approval is playing a smaller role in determining which drugs patients actually get. Since 1988, Americans have been allowed to import drugs not approved by the FDA; thus, those who can afford to buy medicine from overseas have not been constrained. Most Americans, however, are limited by their insurance—and insurers are increasingly demanding evidence of the cost-effectiveness of a drug before agreeing to pay for it.

Expanding Opportunities Through Wise Tradeoffs

Despite the FDA's recently improved efficiency, the process of approving a drug still takes years and is based on the do-no-harm principle. According to law, a drug is illegal until it is declared safe and effective. Most people regard the harm that comes from making a drug legal more serious than the harm that comes from failing to do so. We believe the best solution is to educate citizens about the irrational distinction they make between acts and omissions and train them to weigh the harms and benefits of both. While this change in mindset is unlikely to happen quickly, there are several practical ways of managing the tradeoff between acts and omissions.

More Information, Less Command and Control. The new structure for approving drugs in the European Community (EC) makes automatic approval the default under certain circumstances. The EC now has one drug approval agency, the European Medicines Evaluation Agency (EMEA). When the EMEA approves a drug, it is automatically approved in all EC countries. Drugs can also be approved by individual countries, but only for sale within that country. According to one proposal, the FDA and EMEA should automatically accept each other's approvals as evidence of safety and effectiveness, but with the ability to override.[55] This would at least make approval the default when a drug is approved by one of the two agencies. Presumably, the Europeans have learned their lesson from Thalidomide and will be more cautious. In any case, the option to override an agency's decision ensures that each group will be able to maintain its own standards.

Some writers have taken this strategy a step further: They propose that all potentially beneficial drugs should be considered legal until tests lead them to be banned. In this case, the action would ban a drug rather than approve it. A reversal of the default would force the FDA to pay more attention to the harm that arises from withholding a drug from those who might need it. Of course, the government would have to continue to monitor the manufacturer's claims about the drug's benefits so that potential users could make their decision based on the best available research rather than on wishful thinking.

One notable drawback of this idea is that the prohibition of drugs can be useful in the early stages of research. Once a drug is in wide use, it becomes difficult to find subjects willing to participate in a study in which they know they may get a placebo rather than the drug itself; on the other hand, if there is serious doubt about the drug's safety and effectiveness, subjects may be willing to do without it temporarily for the sake of science. A more serious drawback is that there might be long delays in banning harmful drugs, although the FDA has shown that it is capable of reversing its own decisions when drugs have later been found to be harmful.

We need not go to this extreme to improve the availability of beneficial drugs in the United States. Various in-between strategies can easily be devised, such as new forms of provisional approval for life-saving drugs. Drug regulation has two functions: keeping harmful drugs off the market and making sure that consumers are well informed. Despite the FDA's success at meeting the first goal, the second function remains important. Drugs are approved for specific uses, but once they are approved, doctors can use them for anything, and often do. Their decisions are based on information provided by drug companies and medical journals.

If we were to alter the burden of proof, the certification and dissemination of information on drugs would become increasingly important. Once the government shifted its emphasis from protecting consumers from themselves and their doctors to providing good information about drugs and medical devices, beneficial products could come to market more quickly. Other agencies besides the FDA—such as professional societies—could help disseminate information. Organizations such as the American Council of Obstetricians and Gynecologists, the American Cancer Society and the American Medical Association, which are accustomed to making treatment recommendations to their members, could become official advisers to the FDA. This would reduce the possibility of conflict between the FDA and professional societies.

It is important, however, that the government continue to fund drug research rather than abandon it to drug companies. Critics of automatic approval want to know where society will draw the line if the government allows people to buy untested, unregulated medical drugs. The distinction between medical and recreational drugs has always been hazy. Alcohol, in moderation, can reduce the risk of heart disease; heroin is used as a painkiller in some countries; and cancer patients on chemotherapy have found marijuana an effective anti-nausea drug. If the government's regulation of medical drugs becomes less paternalistic, the line between medical and recreational drugs will become more arbitrary—an important consideration if the United States were to switch to an approval default.

Improving Research Studies.   Another way to reduce the drug lag is to consider the research process itself. New techniques are permitting pharmaceutical companies to produce many more candidate drugs for testing. The bottleneck is no longer within the FDA but rather within the companies as the time required to test these candidates increases. Much of this time is spent looking for subjects. For example, only 3 percent of cancer patients take part in studies, although three times as many are needed. It often takes four years or more to enroll enough subjects in a Phase III (efficacy) cancer trial. Most of these drugs will be duds—but some will be lifesavers.[56]

To speed up the testing process, companies turn to specialized firms or individual practitioners who recruit subjects and test them. Because some of this testing is conducted outside of universities or medical centers that receive federal funds, it is not subject to review by Institutional Review Boards (IRBs). *New York Times* reporters Kurt Eichenwald and Gina Kolata exposed some of the abuses that result from doctors' being paid—sometimes huge amounts—to enroll subjects in trials and test them.[57] The temptations to ignore exclusion criteria, deceive potential subjects, or fabricate data are apparently difficult to resist.

In response to these abuses and others, the Human Research Ethics Group had several recommendations: extending a regulation (known as the "common rule") concerning the treatment of human subjects in federally funded research to institutions that do not receive federal funds; finding new ways for researchers and IRBs to interact with potential subjects; monitoring financial conflicts of interest, such as "finders fees," more closely; and creating more readable consent forms that help subjects understand when benefits to them may be unlikely.[57] We would expand this last recommendation to include informing subjects about the potential benefits their participation will bring to others. Consent forms are currently almost devoid of information about the science behind the study; but we see no reason to withhold it, especially since this knowledge could be expected to increase participation.

We have an additional suggestion: Instead of paying finders fees to doctors, why not pay the subjects? Yes, this idea has drawbacks. Payment could induce some subjects to engage in wishful thinking; they might pretend the study's risks are minimal, when in fact the risks are the reason they are being paid. But a lot of wishful thinking goes on under the existing system. If the steps recommended by the Ethics Group were put into practice, paying subjects would have little (but some) risk and would yield the important benefit of speeding up drug testing. Here is another case where the fear of risk from action is preventing the reduction of a greater risk from omission.

As we have seen, opportunities for valuable tradeoffs abound. The present system neglects the long-run benefits of making drugs available sooner and focuses unduly on the more immediate costs to research subjects or to those who suffer side effects. To strike an appropriate balance, we must be willing to tolerate some losses in return for greater gains, even when these losses, like the gains, are measured in human lives.

A Rational Approach to Risk

Money spent by the American government on expensive regulations could be better distributed. Some increases in regulation could save lives at little or no cost because they would pay for themselves, either through savings in efficiency or through reduced medical costs. Examples include safety improvements in automobile design and the reduction of pollution from coal-burning power plants.[58] Funds could be better spent on testing and remediation of water pollution, medical screening tests (PAP smears and colon cancer screening) and the regulation of guns. In poor countries, even greater benefits could be accomplished (see Chapter 6). Through vaccination and vitamin supplements for children, lives could be saved for just hundreds of dollars each rather than millions. The prevention of AIDS transmission to fetuses and the distribution of condoms to prevent the spread of AIDS are two other programs that would save lives at low cost.

When we sue people for actions but not for omissions, or worry more about the harmful effects of approving drugs too soon than about the harm of excessive delay, we lose opportunities to enlarge the pie of resources available to all citizens. In the arena of public health and safety, our intuitive, irrational assessments of risk cause unnecessary deaths every day. By transferring resources to the areas that will yield the most benefit, we can expand the pie of value.

One way to improve our risk assessments is to look at situations quantitatively. This does not mean that we must reduce every problem to a mathematical formula; rather, we must learn to accept that a well-made decision requires comparisons of quantities. If we develop a good sense of the quantities, we will be able to make a well-reasoned decision without having to know the exact numbers. We make these kinds of effective cognitive guesses all the time in our daily lives. When we pay more for a brand-name computer, for example, we are trading off such factors as price and expected reliability. We do not know the probability of failure or of the company's going out of business and being unable to provide technical support; but even without these numbers, we consider the factors in a quantitative manner.

When we think this way, we will be able to judge when public decisions, such as whether to build more nuclear power plants, require a more detailed quantitative analysis by experts. We will also understand that it does not matter whether risks arise through action or omission or whether the cause of a risk is human or natural. And we will understand why we should not pay more to reduce a risk to zero if we can achieve better results by reducing another risk imperfectly.

These principles can be applied to such government regulation decisions as the mandating of clean air standards. When we ask individuals how much money they are willing to pay in taxes to prevent one person from getting asthma or emphysema, the answer is a reasonable amount, as is the amount of time they feel should be expended. Yet when Congress passed the recent revisions of the Clean Air Act, and when the Environmental Protection Agency (EPA) proposed new regulations requiring extra inspections for motor vehicles, people angrily protested the idea of intrusive government regulation. Exasperated EPA officials accused the public of inconsistency: Their representatives, after all, had voted overwhelmingly for this act. But *none* of these officials' public statements and none of the news articles discussing these issues mentioned how many cases of which diseases were expected to be prevented by an unspecified number of extra car inspections. With such a lack of information, it becomes easy to understand why public opinion swings wildly. Better information is available, but it is left out of the process because journalists, government officials and private citizens do not understand the importance of balancing one risk against another.

Finally, quantitative thinking may show us when a risk is too slim to be worth considering. We face too many real risks to waste time worrying about those that don't exist, or about freak accidents that have happened once or twice. Should we stop going to the dentist after reading that a few patients contracted AIDS from their dentist? Or stop eating grapes because one grape containing cyanide was found in a shipment? Or never take aspirin because there is a remote chance it will cause internal bleeding? At a minimum, we must establish evidence of a statistical association between a cause and an effect before deciding to treat it as a legitimate risk. Citizens should expect government officials at all levels to make decisions with a view to saving lives and preventing illness, not to satisfying their faulty intuition. This type of change will be difficult in a democracy because the citizens themselves share this intuition. Once citizens confront their own intuitions, they will be better equipped to detect them in the decisions of their leaders and press for change.

2

Their Gain Is Our Loss

WHEN BENJAMIN CONE BOUGHT 7,200 ACRES IN NORTH CAROLINA'S Pender County in the 1930s, the deforested land seemed so unpromising that his friends labeled it "Cone's Folly." By the time Ben Cone, Jr., inherited the land from his father in 1982, the once-barren tract had become a profitable forest where songbirds, wild turkey, quail and deer thrived. For decades, the Cones managed their land for wildlife by planting fodder, conducting controlled burns and keeping their timber sales low.

This all changed in 1991, when a wildlife biologist hired by Cone informed him that approximately twenty-nine red-cockaded woodpeckers, members of an endangered species, were living on his property. Acting on the authority of the 1973 Endangered Species Act (ESA), the U.S. Fish and Wildlife Service took control of the woodpeckers' habitat—1,560 acres, or about 15 percent of Cone's property.[1]

After the Fish and Wildlife Service had moved in, Cone drastically altered the way he forested the remaining 85 percent of his property. He abandoned the moderate, sustainable practices he learned from his father—in which 50 acres of land were clear-cut (cleared of all trees and vegetation) every five to ten years—and began clear-cutting up to 500 acres of forest *every year.*[2] Why did Cone resort to these destructive practices? He explained his actions this way: "I cannot afford to let those woodpeckers take over the rest of the property."[3] By harvesting the oldest trees on the land that remained within his control, Cone prevented the woodpeckers from expanding their habitat. In the process, he also destroyed vast quantities of his forest, perhaps permanently. The clear-cut land had once again become "Cone's Folly."

The ESA, which was designed to protect endangered or threatened species and restore them to a secure status in the wild, forbids the killing, harassing, possessing or removing of protected species from the wild. Cone's response was not what the authors of the ESA had in mind. Yet Cone would not have resorted to clear-cutting if he hadn't felt cornered. Why did this dispute between economic and environmental concerns turn out so badly for both sides? Senators and members of the forestry industry have argued that the Cone story illustrates the failure of the Fish and Wildlife Service to consider economic factors when carrying out its species regeneration plans; however, the argument that the Fish and Wildlife Service is intractable in its dealings with landowners is overly simplistic. Only after the Cone story became a touchstone for ESA critics did it become clear that endangered species considerations had affected only a fraction of Cone's property. He was free to do as he wished with the remaining land.

Cone had many alternatives to clear-cutting huge stretches of forest. The ESA had offered its own solution in the form of a Habitat Conservation Plan (HCP). In simple terms, HCPs give private landowners permission to violate the specifics of the ESA by allowing the "incidental take" of listed species during lawful development—provided the landowner also takes certain steps to preserve the species. HCPs can break the win-lose mentality by creatively developing plans that serve the interests of the endangered species and the economic interests of landowners. The Fish and Wildlife Service repeatedly approached Cone with proposals for HCPs that would insulate him from future ESA responsibilities. He rejected the offers and stuck to his slash-and-burn strategy.

Cone rejected the government's compromise because he assumed that if the plan was desirable to environmentalists, it must be bad for his business. He was so fearful of seeing his assets completely devalued that he embraced a radical protective strategy. Antagonists on both sides of environmental disputes hold similar beliefs, leading to similarly dysfunctional results.

The "myth of the fixed pie" is pervasive in many political negotiations. It is evident in these remarks from Floyd Spence, a South Carolina congressman: "I have had a philosophy for some time in regard to SALT, and it goes like this: the Russians will not accept a SALT treaty that is not in their best interest, and it seems to me that if it is in their best interests, it can't be in our best interest." The assumption that "anything good for them must be bad for us" eliminates the search for solutions that bring benefits to both sides of a negotiation.

Spence's confused reasoning is unfortunate yet surprisingly common. In the environmental domain, a recent article advocating tighter regulation of hazardous waste dumps declared, "We must pass an effective Superfund law. If the polluters win, then we lose— our tax money, our environment, and our health."[4] (Unfortunately, the government has spent far more money trying to force polluters to pay than it has spent on cleaning up Superfund sites.)[5]

Negotiators typically fail to reach optimal outcomes because they do not look for tradeoffs that can enlarge the pool of resources to be distributed. They approach the negotiation with a mythical fixed-pie assumption, even when the situation allows for tradeoffs that will improve the overall quality of the agreement. Mr. Cone acted rashly because he misinterpreted the Fish and Wildlife Service's intentions, not because the Service carried out its policy.

In this chapter, as we explore the conflicts between environmental and economic interests, we will show that the myth of the fixed pie dominates these disputes. We will discuss two groups of applications, specifically habitat conservation and pollution, and consider the broader consequences of the mythical fixed pie in political decision making. We will conclude by proposing negotiation strategies that will benefit citizens and politicians alike.

Environmental Versus Economic Disputes

"Cone's Folly" shows us that differing opinions about the relationship between economic competitiveness and species protection may lead to a contentious stand-off—in which politicians choose sides—between industry officials and environmentalists. Members of each camp typically view the situation as "win-lose," a polarization that reinforces combative rather than cooperative approaches to solving real-world conflicts. Parties with a win-lose perspective believe that the environment can be saved only through economic sacrifices.[6] Economic and environmental interests thus try to claim as great an advantage as they can, often by demonizing and even destroying the other side.

Overall, the ESA has been a tremendously successful piece of legislation. Fifty-nine percent of the 128 species that were on the endangered species list when the ESA was passed in 1973 have since recovered, have improved or are in stable condition.[7] But because the ESA appears to pit the interests of economic development against those of environmental protection, it has led parties to adopt a win-lose attitude toward negotiation. Because protecting the human economy is paramount to ESA critics, the idea of giving up jobs or perhaps even crippling a regional economy to save a few animals strikes them as an absurd proposition. Many American industry leaders and their stakeholders view environmentalists as tree-huggers who are willing to sacrifice entire communities for one owl or kangaroo rat. To proponents of the ESA, economic sacrifices are unfortunate but necessary; to them, protection of the natural ecosystem is priceless. Environmentalists tend to view loggers and fishers as villains eager to harvest every last tree and fish for their personal profit.

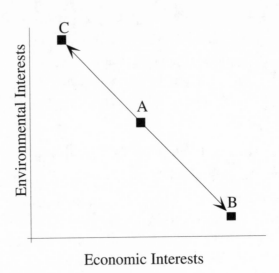

FIGURE 2.1   The Win-Lose Negotiation

This is how ESA debates most often play out: Both sides establish intractable positions and fight a distributive battle over concessionary agreements. For example, the Sierra Club voted to oppose *all* logging on *all* federal land, allowing no room for mutually beneficial negotiations. By viewing their opponents from this mythical fixed-pie perspective, these groups are forfeiting the creation of mutually beneficial solutions through cooperative decision making. Although almost all negotiations involve a distributive element, these parties err by ignoring integrative elements inherent in their dispute. According to this framework, gains achieved by one party always come at the expense of the other, as Figure 2.1 shows. If species protection is weakly enforced, economic interests will triumph over environmental interests (Point B). If species protection is strengthened, environmental interests gain at the expense of economic interests (Point C).[8] Because both sides consider the pool of resources fixed, allocation is virtually the only issue discussed.

An integrative element can be found in most negotiations. The pool of resources is rarely fixed, and parties can work together to increase its size. Win-win proponents believe the American economy

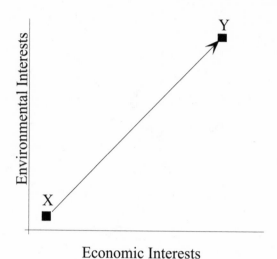

Economic Interests

FIGURE 2.2   The Win-Win Negotiation

can be improved by methods that protect and restore the natural environment.[9] Former Vice President Gore, for example, argued that "some companies have found that in the process of addressing their environmental problems they have been able to improve productivity and profitability at the same time . . . an emphasis on environmental responsibility makes good business sense."[10] A win-win advocate might point out that a given piece of land is valuable to environmental interests and suggest that it be traded for a piece of land a corporation would value more highly. Issues such as the type and timing of harvesting and specific habitat protection efforts increase the opportunity for mutually beneficial trades.

When these issues are identified, parties can weigh their value to each side, thereby establishing opportunities for integrative trade-offs. Figure 2.2 shows how two opposing parties can reach a mutually satisfying agreement by integrating each other's interests.

Still, the win-win perspective is no more complete than the win-lose perspective.[11] It is simplistic to describe the relationship between environmental and economic interests as either purely cooperative or purely competitive; the balance between economics and

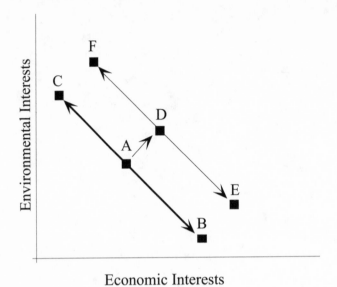

FIGURE 2.3   The Mixed-Motive Negotiation

the environment involves mixed motives. Expanding the pie through wise tradeoffs will not eliminate the need to divide the pie because actors would simply be arguing over a larger pool of resources. Figure 2.3 demonstrates how the win-win and win-lose perspectives can blend to expand the possible outcomes (moving from Point A to Point D) and lead to a position from which each party can argue over whether to move toward Point E or Point F.[12] The mixed-motive model shows that all parties can be made better off without ignoring the realistic need to divide the larger pie.[13]

Parties frequently fail to notice easy gains because they are preoccupied with negotiating distributive aspects. Ben Cone had the law on his side. With the endangered species of woodpecker not yet populating most of his land, he could have chosen to maintain his forest as he liked. Rather than resorting to rapid clear-cutting, he could have negotiated with the government for an HCP that would strengthen his rights, increase the profitability of his forest and contribute to the goal of removing the red-cockaded woodpecker from the ESA's list. Note that although an HCP might have led to a more integrative agreement, one party was still likely to gain at the expense of the other. For example, even had Cone agreed to reduce his overall cutting in exchange for less governmental regulation, the woodpecker could still have suffered great damage, depending on the details of the negotiated agreement. The combination of distributive and integrative aspects makes this a complex, mixed-motive negotiation with many possible outcomes.

Can a better solution for both parties be reached in most negotiations? Yes! Flexibility and creativity are the key ingredients to efficient and satisfying economic and environmental agreements. These solutions are not limited to such polarized issues as the protection of endangered species. Consider the large amount of money that oil companies are required to spend on environmental protection. The Unocal Corporation developed an innovative way to reduce its costs for complying with the hydrocarbon and nitrogen oxide standards in the Los Angeles basin. By collaborating rather than competing with the state of California and the public, Unocal met its mandated emissions reductions at a reduced cost. Rather than undertaking costly and inefficient refinery renovations, Unocal initiated a creative program in 1990 for removing old, high-polluting vehicles from the Los Angeles area. The company began buying pre-1971 cars for $600 apiece and scrapping them. By estimating how many miles the vehicle would have been driven had it not been scrapped, Unocal determined that it had removed nearly 13 million pounds of tailpipe pollution per year from the air of the L.A. basin. The company (in conjunction with the State of California) managed to reduce noxious emissions to a degree that would have cost ten times as much and taken ten times as long had they been made at the company's L.A. refinery.[14] This outcome might initially appear to be win-win, but it also possessed a distributive element. The final solution was not a fixed target but a negotiated endpoint that allowed both parties to create and claim value.[15]

In another example of a mixed-motive negotiation, Amoco joined with the Environmental Protection Agency (EPA) to examine pollution reduction possibilities at its refinery in Yorktown,

Virginia. The team determined that if Amoco was allowed greater flexibility in choosing where it spent its regulatory dollars, it could meet the emission reductions required by the Clean Air Act Amendments of 1990 (CAAA) at one quarter of previous costs ($10 million versus $40 million).[16] This end result combined the claiming of value (the EPA's insistence on CAAA compliance) and the creating of value (greater economic efficiency gained through flexible rulemaking). Blending the distributive and integrative elements created an outcome that allowed gains for environmental and for economic interests.

Results like these could only have become apparent through a mixed-motive perspective on the debate between economics and the environment. In each case, the pursuit of more efficient solutions led interested parties away from a distinctly win-lose or win-win scenario. Ultimately, this mixed-motive perspective can lead to rational searches for optimal outcomes that maximize both environmental and economic gains.

Endangered Species Protection: The Role of Habitat Conservation Plans

The win-lose perspective appears to predominate most often in debates regarding endangered species. Yet contrary to popular belief, mixed-motive solutions that enhance environmental and economic interests are possible under the ESA.

One way to increase the likelihood of efficient agreement is to provide landowners with a voice in negotiating their ESA compliance options. But as long as the mythical fixed-pie mindset persists, these solutions will be difficult to imagine. The HCPs discussed earlier are a means toward this end. Many private landowners have used these plans to work with other stakeholders, from government agencies to citizens' groups, to identify optimal means of ESA compliance. At the end of 1997, 243 HCPs in sixteen states covered 6.2

million acres of land.[17] Because they can help break an impasse, HCPs are a useful negotiation tool.

The San Bruno Mountain HCP is one of the most successful. Comprising 3,600 acres of unique habitat close to San Francisco, the San Bruno Mountain is the largest urban open space in the United States. It is home to two endangered and one threatened species of butterflies and ten species of rare plants. When Visatacion Associates, a major land-holding company, announced plans to build 8,500 residential units and 2 million square feet of office space on the mountain, environmentalists were outraged—especially when the government appeared powerless to stop the development. In 1982, a HCP negotiation led to results that all the major parties could live with. The county bought 1,100 acres of the disputed land from Visatacion; Visatacion donated 546 acres to a county park and 256 acres to the state of California; and 368 acres were allocated for the planned development. Although this HCP resulted in the loss of about 14 percent of the habitat for the Mission Blue butterfly, the majority of the habitat was preserved, and a permanent funding source to manage the habitat was created. Seventeen years later, the San Bruno Mountain HCP remains an excellent example of the constructive trades HCPs can create.

Although HCPs increase the chances that the resulting outcome will bypass the traditional win-lose perspective, they have not created as much value as they could. The problems are numerous. The government agencies authorized to create HCPs often have insufficient and undertrained staff. Companies affected by the ESA are often uninformed about the HCP process. Thus, both sides lack the knowledge and training essential to this kind of intricate negotiation. In addition, political changes continue to both weaken and strengthen the ESA, so that neither side can depend on the consistent enforcement of the law. Environmentalists and landowners, as a result, spend more time and effort lobbying to change the law than they spend trying to act wisely within it. Finally, by producing analyses that focus only on the success or failure of species preservation efforts, the scientific community has also failed to understand and assess the HCP process.

We are less concerned about these setbacks than about the broader implications that tradeoffs being made in HCP negotiations have for society. We believe the most important question to ask is whether the HCP process is improving the environment and the economy more than they would have improved in its absence. Overall, the results are positive but fall far short of ideal. The biggest barrier to optimal agreements is the pervasiveness of the fixed-pie myth among opposing parties.

Pollution Prevention: Project XL

One of the regulatory reforms undertaken by the Clinton administration was a 25-point agenda for "Reinventing Environmental Regulation." Project XL, which stands for "eXcellence and Leadership," was one of the initiative's four pilot programs. It aimed to improve the adversarial relationship between government regulators and manufacturing companies by encouraging the development of alternative methods for establishing environmental policy and enforcing regulations. Launched by the EPA in May 1995, Project XL is designed to test innovative ways of accomplishing environmental protection that is more effective *and* more cost-effective than conventional "command and control" regulatory and policy approaches. The program allows the regulated community—private and federal facilities, industry sectors, states and local communities—to gain greater regulatory flexibility in exchange for a commitment to a higher level of environmental results; for instance, reductions in air and water pollution. The program is based on the idea that regulators should set environmental standards for businesses, but should then let the businesses figure out the best methods for meeting these levels. In essence, Project XL prompts both government and industry to search for solutions that are better for the environment and the economy than those that mere compliance would accomplish. The EPA committed to fifty pilot projects at XL's inception in 1995.

Although the concept of Project XL has received widespread support from the business community, reaching agreement on the specifics is typically a thorny process. By the end of 1996, of the forty-five project proposals received by the EPA, only two had reached the stage of realization.[18] Following negotiations with the agency, at least fifteen industry participants withdrew their proposals; another twenty-four projects remained stuck in development. Companies that dropped out complained the EPA was unable to abandon its traditional enforcement-oriented ways; they accused the agency of imposing conditions on agreements that—contrary to Project XL's mission—were decidedly inflexible, such as requiring guaranteed and quantified "superior environmental performance" in advance. In addition, Project XL negotiations often move too slowly for companies striving to remain competitive. Government bureaucracy is largely responsible for the tortured pace. EPA officials might convene an exploratory meeting purely to discuss the pros and cons of various issues, but corporate executives expect a business meeting to produce swift decisions and concrete results.

Meanwhile, environmental and citizens' groups, contending that "XL" stands for "Extra Leniency," fear that the program allows corporations to trample environmental regulations.[19] Environmental and citizens' groups want assurances that stakeholders will not be reduced to mere observers during the process of making agreements with companies. These groups complain that the EPA is ill equipped to assess what it can extract from a company in return for flexible regulation. "Regulatory flexibility is hard to define," says Deputy Administrator Fred Hansen in the EPA's defense. "What one party sees as a regulatory obstacle that should be removed, another perceives as a fundamental protection."[20]

One disgruntled Project XL participant was 3M. The company proposed a project for its Hutchinson, Minnesota, facility, which was planning to replace its manufacture of audiovisual tape with several new products. The Minnesota Pollution Control Agency allowed the company one permit for plant modifications in exchange for the promise of exemplary environmental performance. But the

EPA objected to certain conditions in the permit and the company's definition of "superior environmental performance." Following eleven months of talks, Project XL negotiations collapsed. "We simply ran out of time," says 3M spokesperson Rick Renner. "We decided to go with traditional permits to be sure we could get our products out on time."[21]

One of the first finalized projects was a November 1996 agreement between the EPA and the Intel Corporation regarding the company's Chandler, Arizona, computer-chip manufacturing facility. Among other promises, Intel agreed to keep its emissions at the Arizona facility below an EPA cap and to reduce chemical and water use and vehicle-miles traveled by commuting employees. In return, the EPA expanded its preapproval of air-emission sources, thus allowing the plant to sidestep operating-permit revisions.[22]

The Intel project has drawn mixed reviews. Public participants complain that their voice was lost during Intel's extended negotiations with the EPA.[23] The seventeen-month process of hammering out the agreement was also frustrating from Intel's point of view. "There is a certain mindset that can't understand that things might be better without following every jot and tittle of the regulation,"[24] said Timothy Mohin, Intel's government affairs manager. Government bureaucracy caused the project to stall during the second tier of review: "There were too many EPA offices and too many levels of regulators involved," Mohin said. "We were negotiating with people who weren't making the decisions."[25]

In January 1997, the EPA held a meeting to address the public's criticisms of Project XL and make mid-course corrections. Regulators promised more roundtable meetings to air concerns and announced that it would provide $25,000 per project for independent technical assessments. Not surprisingly, this decision was objectionable to industry leaders. "Citizens are going to make decisions . . . that are binding on Fortune 500 companies?" Mohin asked skeptically.[26]

Perhaps the biggest obstacles to Project XL have been cultural, both within the agency and in its relationship with industry. After twenty-five years of command-and-control, this project has offered opportunities to experiment with new ways of thinking—yet neither the EPA nor corporations appear to follow a road map. According to Fred Hansen, "When [we were] announcing Project XL, a number of companies said, 'We're interested in this, but tell us what you really want.'"[27] Like the EPA, companies tended to fall back on a fixed-pie mentality despite the possibility of cooperation. "It's almost like a religious war," commented Jay Benforado, the "reinvention" coordinator for the EPA. "People are just fighting because their forefathers fought."[28]

Another drawback for industry participants in the early days of Project XL was the uneasiness they felt about making agreements that might not have the force of law behind them if challenged in court. "If the EPA had clearer statutory authority to approve more dramatic experiments, firms would be more likely to propose them," a spokesperson for the National Academy of Public Administration commented. "Certainly it is important to firms, if they are to put their reputations on the line while investing in an essentially open-ended process."[29]

Project XL has been touted by some as a "regulatory blueprint" for a site-specific, performance-based pollution control system. But the XL experience so far suggests that perhaps the financial burden of developing regulation site-by-site is too high. Researchers Blackman and Mazurek estimated that the average cost of forging the first seven Project XL agreements—not to mention carrying them out—was about $686,000. The companies picked up most of the tab, about $516,000, and EPA's expenses averaged $170,000.[30] A Resources for the Future report estimated the average cost of XL agreement slightly lower, at $450,000 per firm.[31] The report also argued that the interaction between project participants and the EPA was the biggest expense and that EPA management was the main culprit in generating unnecessary costs. Finally, the critical factor that affected whether a project's development was particularly expensive was the scope and content of its proposal. Costs were particularly high for firms that submitted relatively complex proposals, which suggests that Project XL favors large firms that can afford to pay project development costs. Unfortunately, project complexity and innovation are correlated; they create a significant economic bias against the type of proposals that Project XL was designed to inspire.

In defense of these many critiques, the EPA points out that, aside from contending with the slow but steep end of the learning curve, many of industry's early proposals were "'duds'—too focused on regulatory flexibility, with insufficient attention given to environmental benefits."[32] Learning from its failures as well as its successes, the EPA subjected Project XL to a reengineering operation. In an interview with *Industry Week*, EPA Associate Administrator Charles J. Fox said that he believed one of the lessons learned was that "the time may have come for the agency to exert a little more leadership—to identify good projects out there and actually recruit candidates for Project XL, rather than have companies come to us."[33] In March 1999, the agency announced changes, developed in conjunction with Union Carbide and Dow Chemical, to streamline the XL process and "make it more user-friendly." Although only twelve projects were being carried out in April 1999, dozens more were in the planning and preliminary stages, according to EPA coordinator Jay Benforado, with more projects to be announced in the near future.[34]

Both the HCP and Project XL programs have been created with a shockingly large amount of bureaucracy. The bureaucratic demands of the EPA can be overwhelming for industry employees charged with negotiating their company's plan. On the other side, these programs are often added to the existing tasks of overworked government officials, who also lack experience and expertise with the programs. As a result, inexperienced negotiators find themselves trying to cope in an environment that is far more complex than necessary. This structure creates significant barriers to accomplishing the visions these programs were meant to create. The main reasons the HCPs and Project XL have failed to live up to their potential are the fixed-pie perceptions of the protagonists and the institutionalized systems that encourage them to maintain their narrow mentality.

Barriers to Expanding the Pie

We believe that wise environmental negotiations have the potential to improve outcomes for both economic and environmental interests. Unfortunately, our minds intuitively work against methods that would help us create mutual gain. Negotiators fail to find optimal outcomes because they do not look for tradeoffs that can enlarge the pool of resources to be distributed. Increasing the value of an agreement by finding effective trades increases the expected value of each individual's outcome. By hiding the opportunities that exist in a complex negotiation, the fixed-pie assumption leads to competitive behavior that ignores cooperative possibilities. Psychologists Lee Ross and Connie Stillinger have shown in several studies that negotiators typically degrade the value of opponents' offers. When parties assume that the other's gain is their loss, "reactive devaluation," or the tendency of negotiators to interpret any proposal offered by the opponent as negative, is likely to follow.[35] Essentially, they assume that anything an opponent wants must be bad for them. These biases are exacerbated when the other side is viewed as the enemy. The process is antithetical to the cooperative processes necessary to make the types of wise tradeoffs that can improve the overall quality of negotiated outcomes.

Executives from corporate and environmental organizations attending negotiation seminars taught by one of the authors are often asked why they fail to make mutually beneficial tradeoffs in simulated negotiations. They commonly respond that they did not know tradeoffs were possible—either in the simulation or in their real-world negotiations. Negotiators may not oppose tradeoffs but may overlook them because they assume that parties' interests are perfectly opposed. Creating trades across issues is not part of our repertoire of negotiation strategies.

A win-lose orientation makes sense in athletic competition, admission to academic programs, corporate promotion systems and many other contexts. The problem is that citizens and government decision makers tend to generalize their experiences in these situations to those that are not win-lose. When confronted with a situation requiring both cooperation and competition, most negotiators focus too narrowly on the competitive aspect; the result is a distributive approach to bargaining. They choose strategies aimed at obtaining the largest possible share of a fixed pie. This approach inhibits the creative problem solving necessary for developing integrative solutions that could enlarge the pie for everyone.

Some social institutions have encouraged the fixed-pie myth. For example, lawyers, who are often at the core of legislative and regulatory disputes, have historically been trained in adversarial litigation. Only recently have leading scholars argued for reforms in legal education that would place less emphasis on lawyers as adversaries and ask them to become creative negotiators instead.[36]

Lawyers are not the only group known for circumventing wise negotiations. Two-party democracy may inhibit creative problem solving with "the other side." To a party's ideological leaders, creative solutions often look like inappropriate compromises. Yet in independent work,[37] Deb Gruenfeld of Stanford University and Phil Tetlock of Ohio State University have argued that the wisest policies often result from "integratively complex" thinking rather than from the intransigent positions typical of political ideologues. Gruenfeld and her colleagues have found that the integrative complexity of thought processes—the degree to which one considers a problem from multiple perspectives—predicts whether a negotiator will move beyond the fixed-pie mentality.[38]

At the lowest levels of integrative complexity, people look at negotiations in black and white: They see all the advantages of the option they favor and none of its drawbacks. At higher levels, people become aware of the pluses and minuses of various options and think of the decision as a matter of finding the best overall balance. Negotiators who have adopted integratively complex thinking are more likely to consider the advantages of the other side's proposals. When these advantages are great, and when the disadvantages to themselves are small, they are likely to accept the proposal. This shift in mindset is needed to realize the opportunities to expand the pie.

After he left President Clinton's Council of Economic Advisors, economist Joseph Stiglitz observed that White House staffers discouraged economists from proposing well-reasoned, integrative solutions to complex economic issues. According to these strategists, only policy arguments that could be articulated in tidy sound bites would find public support.[39] Like Stiglitz, we consider it unacceptable that integratively complex thinking is a political liability. How can we persuade citizens to be more tolerant of the type of thinking that brings about wiser government policies? The logic of tradeoffs is not as complex as it seems—it just isn't intuitive. When corporate decision makers are taught the logic of negotiation analytics,[40] they discover that incorporating these ideas into their business negotiations is relatively simple. We hold the same hope for government officials and voters.

Stiglitz argues that one inherent problem of government negotiations is that presidential administrations are unable to commit to long-term agreements.[41] Yet in its HCPs, the government did agree to "no surprises" provisions that explicitly promised landowners that the deal would not change. The problem of government commitment is not a terminal barrier but another challenge to be solved.

Broader Consequences

This chapter has focused on environmental negotiations because of their extreme adversarial nature. As we see every day from discouraging news reports about gridlocked federal debates on education funding, health care, social freedoms and other issues, government is rife with disputes that need to be handled more effectively. The political left and the political right behave as if they were fighting over a fixed pie—which they are, if their only goal is to remain in office. We hold the less cynical view that politicians are primarily interested in creating wise policies. But when beating the other side becomes their primary focus, they thwart this goal. Unfortunately, the fixed-pie myth is deeply ingrained in political systems.

A recent battle over taxation in Vermont shows the limitations of this mindset. The dispute began in 1997 when the state passed a new law that called for the more equitable distribution of education dollars across the state. Whereas school funding had previously been based on property taxes and therefore varied widely across municipalities, Act 60 mandated a new statewide tax that would be distributed evenly at a rate of $5,000 per student per year. Money from "gold towns" (wealthy communities with a large pool of funds coming from real estate taxation) was thus transferred to poorer towns to level the educational opportunities of Vermont schoolchildren.

Never mind whether you agree with this policy. We will focus instead on the misguided fulfillment of Act 60. Realizing that the gold towns were accustomed to spending much more than $5,000 per student annually (the statewide average was $6,300), the state legislature encouraged these communities to raise additional education funds through local property taxes. But it then stipulated that the extra dollars must be shared with other communities to maintain the goal of school funding equity. The richer the town contributing extra taxes, the lower the percentage of dollars that would stay local.

For the town of Stowe, which spends nearly $9,000 per student each year, this meant that up to 70 percent of the extra money it raised from property taxes would go elsewhere. Not surprisingly, many Stowe residents rebelled against this "Robin Hood" policy. A local lawyer, Hal Stevens, sued the state on behalf of his 11-year-old daughter and her classmates, arguing that Act 60 discriminated against wealthy towns. According to Stevens, lifting the per-student expenditure significantly above the statewide $5,000 minimum would be disproportionately difficult for a town like Stowe, which would be required to give away a much higher percentage of additional property taxes raised than a poor town would be.[42] He lost, but other lawsuits followed, and a citizens' group known as the "Gang of Ten" sponsored seven bills that sought everything from the minor tweaking of Act 60 to its repeal.[43]

The town of Stowe eventually found a way to avoid sharing its wealth: With the help of matching funds from the Freeman

Foundation, it has raised almost $2 million in private contributions for local schools. By May 1999, nearly forty of Vermont's communities had formed their own private education funds based on Stowe's model. Because these donations are held by nonprofit corporations, the money is off-limits to the state of Vermont—and therefore off-limits to poor children, whose education was supposed to have benefited from a "spread the wealth" policy.

Some readers may find these contrivances stingy and uncharitable. We argue that Vermont is to blame for not anticipating that its citizens might balk at an enormous redistribution of their tax dollars. A wiser restructuring could have encouraged the prosperous communities to contribute more funds to their own schools and, in turn, a smaller portion of the extra money could have gone to other towns. If Stowe taxpayers had been told that 20 percent of extra voluntary taxes would be funneled to other communities, it is likely they would have accepted the loss of this small percentage and raised tax revenues, leading to improvements in their own schools and in those across the state. Instead, Act 60 created tremendous conflict, forced Stowe and other towns to adopt an extra level of administration for educational purposes (the new foundations), and cut the gain to poorer communities.

Because a state government is considered to be free from the distorting effects of self-interest, it is uniquely positioned to assist impartially in a negotiation between rich and poor communities. When we view the government of Vermont as a third-party arbitrator, it becomes clear that the state would have done well to search for mutual gains. Instead, politicians acted as if they believed that whatever benefited poor communities would harm rich communities. They applied this fixed-pie mindset to the state as a whole, and all parties ended up worse off.

Sometimes solutions emerge that break the mythical fixed pie. One example comes from the realm of prescription drugs, explored in Chapter 1. Although by the 1990s the Food and Drug Administration (FDA) had become a large, powerful agency with over 8,000 employees and a budget exceeding $900 million, the demands for drug review continued to outgrow it; a paralyzing backlog in drug applications resulted.[44] The solution, the Prescription Drug User Fee Act of 1992, was good for the FDA, the drug industry and those who needed the new drugs. It was also simple: A drug company that sent in an application would pay a fee to compensate the FDA for the time and costs of the review. In return, the FDA would hire more help and guarantee a faster review. The trade has been a great success. The FDA has more resources to do its job, the drug companies generate products and revenue much faster, and the new drugs have improved the health of many people. The fixed-pie mindset that whatever is good for industry is bad for citizens had blocked discussion. By overcoming this obstacle, the parties were able to find a mutually beneficial solution.

Overcoming the Myth of the Fixed Pie

Environmental debates do not have to degenerate into squabbles over a fixed pie of resources to be divided. They can be settled instead by finding creative resolutions and trades. The objective of all environmental protection measures should be the discovery of efficient, innovative tradeoffs between environmental and economic concerns. We disagree with the right wing's unwillingness to trade jobs for nature, and we oppose the left wing's assertion that no price can be put on nature. Efficient solutions to environmental problems require a balanced perspective that recognizes the mixed motives inherent in all these negotiations.

A primary vehicle to change the way we make decisions is to better educate our leaders and our citizens. Since 1980, mutual-gains negotiation has become central to management schools. Executive centers at management schools often include negotiations training as a central topic. Business leaders want to learn how to negotiate more effectively and they are willing to pay for this knowledge. But we need to expand this training to a broader context. Jared Curhan has created an organization called the Program for Young Negotiators, based in Cambridge, Massachusetts, to teach children in middle school to resolve their differences by negotiating and engaging in mutual-gains bargaining rather than in fighting. Similar programs have been introduced to increasingly younger children, and they have been tried out in high schools as well. We think this is a great way of teaching future voters to make wise decisions. Readers of this book can become part of the movement by encouraging their local school districts to add these programs to their curricula.

Meanwhile, our government officials need even more training, and evidence suggests they are not getting it. We advocate that federal, state and local governments and not-for-profit organizations place the same value on executive/professional education that we currently see in corporations as a means of eliminating the fixed-pie mindset and creating lasting change. In return, citizens must become more supportive of politicians who take creative, cooperative approaches to resolving long-standing problems.

3

Competition Is Always Good

WITHIN FIVE YEARS, TWO OF SEATTLE'S PROFESSIONAL SPORTS franchises went up for sale, threatened to leave town and, as a result, received huge public assistance deals for new stadiums. The deals saddled King County taxpayers with one of the biggest sports debts in recent history: New homes for the baseball Mariners and football Seahawks cost almost $1 billion.

Competition between cities for sports teams has become so commonplace in recent years that politicians and citizens often throw themselves into these battles as a matter of course. Winning teams are a great source of civic pride, and even mediocre ball clubs carry long traditions and the hope of future glory. The more practical minded argue that professional sports teams are an economic boon to the community because they generate jobs and revenues that ultimately repay the cost of keeping them in town. At least, that's the argument you'll hear on radio call-in shows whenever a pro team threatens to leave for greener pastures. But is this logic sound? Will the people of Seattle, for example, recoup their investment in the

Mariners and the Seahawks in their lifetimes, or even in their children's lifetimes? We will argue that the saga of pro sports in Seattle is a prime example of dysfunctional competition.

In the early 1990s, insurmountable debts and a dwindling fan base prompted Mariners team owner Jeff Smulyan to put the team up for sale. Early fears that the team would leave Seattle were assuaged when a consortium of local businessmen calling themselves the Baseball Club of Seattle bought the Mariners for more than $100 million in 1992. Less than a year later, the new owners began pressuring the state of Washington for a new baseball-only stadium—even though the team's current home, the Seattle Kingdome, was not yet twenty years old.[1] A September 1995 referendum for a sales-tax increase to fund a new Mariners stadium was narrowly defeated, but the team's owners were undeterred. They declared that if the state didn't commit to building a new stadium by October 30, they would put the team up for sale. Ignoring the protests of irate citizens, the state legislature held an emergency session and approved a plan to fund a $320 million stadium by imposing new taxes on restaurants and car rentals.

In mid-1996, the Public Facilities District declared that the new facility would cost $45 million more than initial projections, and that its retractable roof would not be ready for the planned 1999 opening. Meanwhile, the Mariners put off signing the new facility's lease. Wary of forking over extra funds, city council members wrote a letter urging the Public Facilities District to delay the stadium's opening until these issues could be better addressed.

Within two days, the Mariners' owners announced that they were selling the team and pulling out of the stadium project. In a statement read live on local radio, they declared:

> Reluctantly, after more than five years of work, The Baseball Club of Seattle has concluded that there is insufficient political leadership in King County to complete the new stadium by 1999. [The] owners of the Mariners take great pride in having fulfilled all commitments and

obligations to those who looked to us to preserve Major League Baseball for Seattle. To them, and to everyone, we cannot explain why those who represent the people have chosen to let baseball go.[2]

Although the team's owners asserted that they weren't interested in negotiating further with King County officials, Republican Senator Slade Gorton managed to broker yet another deal with the owners—one that handed them greater profits and fewer expenses. Under the terms of the new deal, the city of Seattle would pay for police traffic control, cleanup and extra transit to the stadium and also compensate the surrounding neighborhood for the stadium's impact.[3]

When the Mariners' new home was completed in the summer of 1999, it had become the most expensive single-sport stadium in North America, the epitome of high-tech opulence. And yet the very group that had commissioned the stadium's Internet kiosks, retractable roof and heated grass field continued to behave like paupers. The Baseball Club of Seattle, which had previously agreed to cover all cost overruns, demanded an additional $60 million in funding from the citizens of King County and threatened to sue the Public Facilities District for that amount if it did not comply. The owners hinted that contractual fine print would make them the sure winners in a legal battle. "I think all the unmitigated gall on the face of the earth right now resides at Mariner headquarters," commented Cynthia Sullivan, a member of the King County Council.[4] The stadium's grand opening was marred when incensed taxpayers, who carried signs reading "No More Corporate Welfare" and "Keep Your Word," marched in protest.[5]

At about the same time, a parallel set of negotiations and intrigue were going on. In early 1996, Microsoft cofounder Paul Allen, one of the ten richest people in the world, purchased an "option" giving him the right to buy the Seattle Seahawks at a specified price from the team's California-based owner. Allen indicated that he would not exercise his option unless a new football stadium replaced the Kingdome. Many in the northwest community were enthusiastic about the possibility of a local team owner—despite the warning signs that hundreds of millions in public money were about to be requested once again.

The Seahawks launched a massive public relations campaign to win the hearts and votes of the public. The unconvinced nonetheless spoke out against public assistance for a new stadium. "A bigger concern is that 40,000 legal residents of Washington State are going to lose their food stamps this summer," noted one citizen. "About 8,000 are going to lose social security benefits. Legal residents. That's an emergency, not building a new stadium for a billionaire."[6]

In February 1997, after months of wrangling in the media and the state legislature, Washington's governor, Gary Locke, called for a statewide referendum on the question of the public's share of the bill. Allen paid for the election, which cost $4.2 million. A narrow 51 percent of voters approved construction of the new $430 million stadium.

Here is the deal the voters of Washington won for themselves: Allen promised to contribute $130 million for construction of the stadium and to pay for cost overruns. The public portion of the construction budget, which was capped at $300 million, came from four revenue streams: (1) a $101 million diversion of sales tax revenues from the state's general fund; (2) lottery revenue worth $127 million from a new sports-related scratch game, plus additional funds from other lotteries if the new game proved unsuccessful; (3) an extension of King County's share of the existing hotel/motel tax, worth $15 million; and (4) $56 million in parking and facility admissions taxes from game attendees. As "owners" of the complex, taxpayers were promised a mere 20 percent of the profits from an adjoining exhibition center.

And this is the deal that Paul Allen—who plans to name the arena "Microsoft Stadium"—will receive: television rights and advertising, personal seat licenses, luxury seat sales and 100 percent of the profits from the stadium.

Politicians and other interested parties naturally tried to portray these deals as win-win situations that benefited the public as well as the teams' wealthy owners. But the local residents were the ones who, time and again, were asked to make sacrifices to prevent the other party from walking away from the bargaining table. The case of the two Seattle sports franchises illustrates what happens when governments get caught in an escalating spiral of competition.

Sports teams are not the only prize that draws local government into competition. Every day, states, counties and cities compete to lure new manufacturing plants into their areas, often in the name of jobs. The "winner" in these high-stakes negotiations often ends up paying many hundreds of thousands of dollars per job. Why? Because the competition between states (as well as regions, counties and cities) is inherently dysfunctional.

Whether companies are striving to build better mousetraps, computers, or airline reservation systems, private sector competition generally improves the local or national economy. But competition becomes dysfunctional when an organization invests resources simply for the satisfaction of winning, or even worse, to hurt a competitor rather than improve its own product.

When governments participate in these contests, citizens become the sponsors of wasteful spending. Government competition can be far more destructive than competition between private-sector organizations; unlike corporations, governments must provide a variety of public services, from highways to libraries. When competitive practices backfire, citizens suffer the consequences in the form of service cutbacks or tax increases. The valuable, finite resources of tax dollars and government land are squandered in destructive competition between states and regions. In private industry, competition fuels creativity and innovation; between states, competition channels taxpayer funds to selected private interests.

Competing for Sports Teams

The current system has led to the expenditure of billions of taxpayer dollars by state and local governments competing with one another to retain and attract sports franchises. These local governments struggle to provide schools, libraries, police and fire protection and other essential community services while millions of dollars are diverted to retain or attract sports teams. It is in the best interest of all our citizens that we seek a rational solution to this national problem.

—Representative Louis Stokes (D-Ohio)[7]

A national poll conducted by Media Research and Communications showed that 80 percent of Americans oppose using their tax dollars for sports stadiums and arenas. Yet city and state politicians continue to build them. At least thirteen communities now provide or have proposed providing at least $250 million each in subsidies for professional sports: Baltimore (and Maryland), Cincinnati, Cleveland, Denver, Detroit (and Michigan), Hartford, Milwaukee, Nashville, Pittsburgh, San Diego, Seattle, Scottsdale and St. Louis. Raleigh, North Carolina, will spend $120 million on an arena to house the National Hockey League's (NHL) former Hartford Whalers. The Minnesota Twins have threatened to leave Minneapolis unless the city builds a $400 million, retractable-roof stadium, even though the Metrodome is only about fifteen years old.[8]

On occasion, local officials have blocked or ignored referendum elections held to resolve these matters. When voters in Milwaukee overwhelmingly rejected a sports lottery to fund a new stadium, the Wisconsin state legislature went ahead and granted $160 million in subsidies for the facility.

State and local officials across the nation are frantically spending billions of tax dollars on new sports facilities in the hope of attracting or retaining a professional sports franchise. Costs have skyrocketed as team owners pit city against city in the scramble for new sports venues with profit-generating restaurants, luxury suites and seat licenses. This catering to the demands of team owners is one of the most extravagant corporate welfare systems in the United States today.

Like most entrepreneurs, owners of professional sports teams aspire to invest in ventures that yield the highest return, increase the value of their holdings, and maximize their profits. Experience shows that new or renovated stadiums generally increase the profits of team owners, at least temporarily.[9] It is no surprise, then, that owners faced with losses or low profits have demanded public assistance to build or improve their stadiums. Most of the profits from a new stadium come from sky boxes, special seating and other revenue-enhancing elements. In addition, the resale value of the team soars when it moves into a new home. In *Major League Losers: The Real Cost of Sports and Who's Paying for It*, Mark S. Rosentraub points to the example of the Texas Rangers. Before The Ballpark in Arlington was constructed, the estimated value of the Rangers franchise was $101 million, sixteenth among Major League Baseball teams. After the new stadium opened in 1994, the team's value jumped to $157 million, making it even more valuable than the Los Angeles Dodgers.[10]

Seeking a public subsidy is an attractive business strategy for the owners of professional sports teams. Because team owners join together in leagues to limit the teams available, more cities and states desire major league franchises than there are franchises to go around. Although teams move infrequently, the excess demand provides team owners with plenty of alternatives to staying put. Their threats of relocation drive cities into expensive bidding wars and give team owners great leverage with local politicians.

Franchise owners and their political allies often justify the resulting subsidies by crying poverty and proclaiming that their teams benefit the local economy. In truth, teams are doing quite well—thanks in part to the sweetheart deals owners have won from local officials, along with media revenue. In the 1994 and 1995 seasons combined, for instance, the Dallas Cowboys earned more than $75 million from ticket sales and luxury seating revenue at Texas Stadium alone. President George W. Bush earned $15 million on his $600,000 investment after taxpayers funded a new baseball stadium for his Rangers.[11] In the 1994 season, the Indianapolis Colts reported the *lowest* media income of NFL franchises—$37.2 million.[12] It's little wonder the potential owners of professional expansion teams must fork over upwards of $100 million in franchise fees to put an untested product on the field—hardly the sign of a dying industry.

The question public officials undoubtedly ask themselves when negotiating with a team owner, usually over the building of a new stadium, is whether the public benefits of attracting and retaining the team justify the associated public costs. Although stadiums are alleged to produce three types of benefits to a community—increased tax revenue, increased economic activity (i.e., increased income or jobs) and nonmonetary or intangible benefits such as civic pride and community vitality—most do not generate sufficient public revenue to pay back the public assistance provided. One study found that of fifteen new or renovated stadiums, only the Dodger stadium in Los Angeles generated enough tax revenue to pay for the original public assistance and interest cost.[13] One main reason is that sports are merely one form of entertainment among many. A large proportion of the spending on sports is transferred from one form of entertainment to another. States using public assistance as an investment strategy would likely do better elsewhere.

The claim that a stadium contributes to a region's economic prosperity is also unfounded. Most employees connected with sports facilities receive low wages as janitors, concession workers and parking lot attendants. The high salaries paid to players and managers tend to flow out of the local economy.[14] Public financing for stadiums is essentially a transfer of income from those in lower and middle income brackets, who pay sales taxes, to owners and players, who take their huge salaries out of the state.[15] And it's not just locals who must foot the bill: A change made under the Tax Reform Act of 1986 fueled the stadium-building trend by permitting the use of federally tax-exempt bonds in arena construction. The costs of building a stadium are now diffused throughout the country.

Some suggest that conventional economic analysis does not account for important nonmonetary "public goods" such as increased civic pride and community vitality. But if public officials use these benefits to justify stadium subsidies, they must weigh the value of the team to the community against the cost of the subsidies by considering the nonmonetary public costs of increased traffic congestion and air pollution.[16]

At the very least, taxpayer financing for the construction or reno-
vation of a sports stadium must be considered in relation to other
potential civic investments. Because public resources are limited,
spending money on sports stadiums may reduce funding for goods
that are far more important than stadium deals. Citizens who support stadiums may be less willing to pay for them when presented
with alternative uses for the money, such as increased spending on
schools, parks, or community policing. Or, instead of investing in a
civic project, the state might consider the benefits of reducing the
taxes imposed on its citizens.

The merry-go-round of professional teams has made cities without teams eager to attract them. These cities will be tempted to try
to steal away another city's team by offering the owner more money,
more luxury suites and a better stadium. Many team owners have
close relationships with legislators, and sports fans will always
staunchly fight to keep their team in their hometown. When a team
leaves a city, residents often accuse their city or state government of
failing to meet its civic responsibility. Thus, instead of trying to fix a
flawed system, local officials adopt such short-term remedies as stadium building to prevent their teams from migrating. Until changes
are made, the teams will likely remain in the driver's seat.

Why Does Dysfunctional Competition Occur?

The unhealthy competition between states for professional sports
teams can be explained by a variety of psychological mechanisms.
At a basic level, one might argue that people are by nature greedy
and competitive; they are motivated to win a resource away from
another party at any cost. But this explanation does not account for
dysfunctional competition among people in public and not-for-
profit spheres who are entrusted to safeguard and enhance the lives
of their constituents. Why do public servants sometimes make decisions that shrink the pie of resources for all, including themselves?
Why do politicians make bad stadium deals?

We offer three explanations that help us understand why our judgment leads us to dysfunctional competition when cooperation would be a far wiser long-term strategy. First, we examine *social dilemmas,* payoff structures that create an environment in which, when each party in a negotiation acts out of self-interest, the overall quality of outcomes is reduced for all parties. Second, we explore how *internal conflicts* create a tension between what people want to do for themselves, their organization, or their local community versus what they think they should do for society as a whole. Finally, we discuss a pervasive phenomenon known as the *winner's curse,* in which the highest bidder in an auction ends up the biggest loser.

Defection in a Social Dilemma Game

In many situations where individuals or organizations act out of self-interest, all parties end up with the same suboptimal result. In his famous "tragedy of the commons" paper, Garrett Hardin introduced a dilemma confronting a group of herdsmen who graze their cattle in a common pasture. Each herdsman knows that it is to his advantage to "defect" on the other herdsmen by increasing the size of his herd, because each additional animal represents personal profit. But all the herdsmen share the damage done to the pasture. If too many animals graze, the pasture will eventually be destroyed. The herdsmen have a combined interest in limiting the population of cattle to a size that allows the pasture to replenish itself. Hardin predicts that most of the herdsmen will defect from the group goal and expand their cattle beyond their allotment out of selfish best interest; thus, they will all be worse off in the long run. Economists have cited "cooperation failure" as an explanation for the unrestrained and irresponsible behavior exhibited by participants in a social dilemma. When a group lacks cooperation, individual members have no incentive to act according to the greater good of society; any member who did so would probably be squeezed out of the marketplace.

Since the publication of Hardin's work, many social scientists have drawn an analogy between the commons dilemma and the broader resource scarcity and pollution issues that we face as a society. For example, this analysis has been used to explain the increasing frequency of crises in the world's fisheries (see Chapter 5). Currently, four of the world's seventeen major fisheries are commercially depleted, and nine more are in serious decline. The populations of many fish species will drop far enough below levels necessary to assure sustainable yields that many fish-dependent populations will have to search for other sources of food and economic livelihood. How did this situation come about? Each fisher or group of fishers harvested as many fish as they could, leaving too few fish to reproduce. As a result, many of the fishers have lost their jobs, numerous species of fish have been harvested out of existence, and the ecological balance of the ocean has been irrevocably disrupted.

Social dilemmas are also apparent in the dysfunctional competition that exists within governments and not-for-profit organizations. Competition among communities for sports teams, a scarce resource, is one example. As local governments compete for the resource by offering team owners better and better deals, the overall costs of competition increase over time. Eventually, communities defect on each other by trying to steal each other's teams. These competitive moves typically lead to unsatisfactory results for all parties except the team owners as some towns lose their teams and others pay too much to acquire them. The community that acquires the team gains the momentary satisfaction of savoring victory, and the politicians who inked the deal may secure their re-elections; but in the long term, parties caught in this trap generally lose far more than they gain.

Internal Conflict Within Governments and Not-for-Profits

In *The Odyssey* of Homer, the hero Ulysses faces a classic dilemma. During his long sea voyage, Ulysses realizes that his ship will soon pass by the Sirens, a clan of female "enchanters" who lure sailors to their deaths with beguiling songs. Ulysses is aware that no man has ever escaped the Sirens, and that their beach is "piled with boneheaps of men now rotted away."[17] To save his men from this fate, Ulysses orders them to put wax in their ears to block out the Sirens' beautiful voices. So that he will be able to hear the Sirens' songs without succumbing to them, Ulysses has his men bind him to the ship's mast, and forbids them to release him until they are out of danger. Ulysses' plan works, and he and his men survive this adventure.

Homer's hero was able to escape the Sirens because he recognized the power of the fleeting desires that threatened to conquer his sense of reason. In a sense, he acknowledged two conflicting sides of his personality. Contemporary scholars have also identified a dual nature within each of us. "Everybody behaves like two people," argues economist Thomas Schelling, "one who wants clear lungs and long life and the other who adores tobacco, or one who wants a lean body and the other who wants dessert . . . the 'straight' one often in command . . . but the wayward one needing only to get occasional control to spoil the other's best-laid plans."[18] Recent research argues that the most common competing selves can be distinguished as the "want self" and the "should self."[19] The instant gratification of the "want self" is evident in a wide range of illogical behaviors, such as running up credit-card debt, smoking, drinking and gambling. The rational behavior of the "should self" includes activities focused on one's long-term well-being, such as exercising, maintaining a healthy diet and saving for retirement.

Internal conflicts prevail within organizations as well. For example, in a typical corporation, the sales department tries to attract as many customers as possible while the credit department rejects potential risks. Similarly, some state representatives spare no expense to keep a football team in town, yet others weigh the costs and benefits. The want self desires a hero's glory; the should self recognizes the potential tax burden. Unfortunately, the selfish, short-term perspective of the want self often dominates these situations, and a pattern of destructive competition results.

The Winner's Curse

When a bidder wins an item at an auction in which the various parties have different ideas about what the prize is worth, the highest bidder is likely to overestimate the value of the prize.[20] This phenomenon is known as the winner's curse. Bidders often fail to draw a key inference: The winning bid is often made by the party who most overestimates the value of the prize.

The winner's curse is an important factor in dysfunctional competitions. When city leaders estimate the value of a baseball team, they often guess either too high or too low. The city that submits the winning bid is most likely to make the most overoptimistic estimate of the team's value. If a bidder assumes that her organization, city, or state will win an auction, this information should tell her that she may have overestimated the value of the commodity in comparison to other bidders. The other bidders obviously do not value the prize as highly, for reasons that the winning bidder may not have considered.

Corporate takeovers provide ample evidence that acquiring companies compete destructively against each other and pay too much for what they acquire. Often, in these situations, the winning bidder is cursed: One-third of all acquisitions prove failures (the winning bidder ends up losing money in the acquisition), and an additional one-third fail to live up to expectations.[21] In addition, any financial benefit from the merger usually goes exclusively to the shareholders of the acquired company.

Collectively, defection in a social dilemma, internal conflicts and the winner's curse account for much of the dysfunctional competition that occurs when governments compete for sports teams. As we will see, the same flaws appear when governments compete for manufacturing contracts and charities manage fund-raising.

Competition for Manufacturing

One of the fastest growing cities in the United States, Rio Rancho, New Mexico, boomed from a population of 10,000 in 1980 to 50,000 in 1998. As part of its aggressive development policies, in 1993, Rio Rancho beat cities in California, Oregon, Texas, Arizona and Utah to become the home for a $1 billion Intel semiconductor plant. Intel had sent its many suitors a 104-point "ideal incentive matrix"—a wish list of tax, utility and workforce subsidies—as well as regulatory relief demands. Rio Rancho won the bidding war with a $114 million package.[22]

Soon after the deal went through, the city began to feel the weight of its heavy promises. Microchip plants consume millions of gallons of water a day, mainly to wash microscopic dirt from the surface of chips. Although Intel had been assured that New Mexico's water supply could provide the amount of water Intel demanded, activists led authorities to the belated discovery that Intel was a great drain on the regional water table. After weeks of public hearings, the state of New Mexico granted Intel 60 percent of the water it had initially requested. The company's environmental regulatory relief created political conflict when noxious fumes emanating from the plant caused skin problems among the local population.

Rio Rancho soon had to tighten its municipal belt. It was unable to pay for essential public services, particularly schooling for the many families it had lured to the desert. In 1994, the town raised only $27 million in taxes to support its new school district, far less than it needed. Officials publicly admitted that they could have obtained ten times more funding had Intel's tax abatement not been in effect. When the school board went begging for funds from an unsympathetic state legislature, it used local children wearing ribbons proclaiming, "We're desperate."[23] In September 1995, Rio Rancho announced that it had found a way to construct a high school. After the community agreed to float an $8 billion industrial revenue bond on behalf of Intel—for an amount four times the annual state budget—Intel offered to pay $28.5 million toward the new high school building.

Rio Rancho paid a high price for its bold development plans. The town's story is extreme but far from unique. Alabama, for example, granted Mercedes-Benz an incentive package worth over $250 million—an estimated $170,000 per job—to secure a new factory for the state. Blue Water Fibre received approximately $80 million worth of convincing from the state of Michigan for a paper-recycling mill and its thirty-four employees—a subsidy of $2.4 million per job.[24] Amarillo, Texas, offered one of the most creative relocation schemes yet. City officials mailed checks for $8 million apiece to 1,300 companies around the country. A company could cash its check if it agreed to create seven hundred new jobs in Amarillo.

The development policies of many states now incorporate generous incentive packages to attract businesses and jobs; these incentive programs have more than doubled to an average of twenty-four over the past twenty years. Proponents say the incentives are an investment that builds a state's economic base by creating local job opportunities and enhancing private-sector productivity and competitiveness.

Critics contend that government largesse often costs more than the derived benefits warrant and diverts funds from the traditional public goods of education, libraries and infrastructure. Perhaps worst of all, businesses play states against one another in costly bidding wars to obtain the most favorable deals. In each case, a city or state is spending taxpayers' money to win a battle against other cities or states—a battle in which American citizens enjoy little net gain.

Instead of the healthy competition that most economists favor— in which states try to create an *overall* business-friendly environment to attract industry and jobs—states engage in economic warfare. The inducements applied in this war include selective tax abatements and credits, outright grants to specific high-profile businesses, job-training subsidies, low-interest loans, tax-exempt municipal bonds issued for private benefit and infrastructure spending that often goes well beyond what the governments would normally undertake.

The victors suffer from the winner's curse. The "winning" government in this type of auction frequently ends up with fewer jobs and tax revenues than expected.[25] In 1978, for example, Pennsylvania spent approximately $70 million to bring a Volkswagen factory to the state. The factory, which was expected to deliver 20,000 jobs, employed only 6,000 workers and closed within ten years when Volkswagen began consolidating its operations.

Despite these disappointing results, incentive packages are growing increasingly expensive. "A comprehensive review of past studies reveals *no* statistical evidence that business incentives actually create jobs," acknowledged the Council of State Governments. "They are not the primary or sole influence on business decision-making and . . . they do not have a primary effect on state employment growth."[26] There is no indication that government incentive programs bring a net benefit to the community; too often, the misallocation of resources leaves everyone worse off than they were before.

There appears to be only a minimal risk that incentive programs will induce managers to make poor business decisions regarding location. Firms are not as interested in states' limited-term incentive offers as they are in the overall tax burden, the price of a skilled labor pool, the relative cost of compliance with regulations, transportation facility (airports and roads), crime rates, quality of schools and the general quality of life in the area. According to a study by KPMG Peat Marwick, state and local taxes usually total between 1 and 2 percent of the cost of doing business—by no means enough to influence corporate decisions on location.[27] In a 1993 survey conducted by the International Association of Corporate Real Estate Executives and the American Economic Development Council, eight hundred corporate real estate executives and economic developers rated incentive packages low (fourteenth of seventeen factors) in their site selection process.

Although companies base site selection decisions primarily on their long-term needs, they have nonetheless found a way to use competition between states to their advantage: After sending a prospectus to each state, they use the responses to put pressure on the state where they most want to locate. The ensuing bidding war creates a lose-lose situation for the general public as the states drive down each other's revenue bases and as wealth is transferred from state taxpayers to corporations and their shareholders. As a result, these deals make several people richer but leave states fewer funds for schools, road construction, health care and tax relief.

Local communities in states that offer these overzealous development programs suffer a double burden: the increased strain that new businesses place on their infrastructure and social services, and the reduction of their share of tax revenues. In addition, companies that cannot or do not wish to relocate to another state can find themselves at a disadvantage: Perks go to companies willing to relocate, yet loyal, locally based businesses subsidize these competitors through their taxes.

This End Up, a furniture manufacturer, accepted $230,000 and other incentives from the state of Arkansas for a new plant near Fayetteville that would employ 200. The company subsequently closed a Raleigh, North Carolina, plant that employed 150. It is difficult to imagine that the stress faced by the 150 laid-off workers in Raleigh was balanced by the creation of fifty additional jobs elsewhere. Companies have even been known to cannibalize an operation in their eagerness to secure an incentive deal in the same state. Quaker Oats received $98,000 for a new 98-worker plant near Asheville, then closed another North Carolina operation that employed 70 workers. Overall, these tax incentives create few new jobs but simply shift jobs from one location to another. The dysfunctional competition created by the North Carolina politicians who signed these deals backfired when the high cost of incentives failed to pay off.

According to Lawrence W. Reed of The Mackinac Center for Public Policy, "The war is becoming an exercise in mutually assured destruction, or at least one in which all victories are Pyrrhic ones at best, with the victors losing almost as much as the vanquished."[28] The economic war between the states requires the victor to defect on other communities—and on society as a whole. If each community competed according to its natural assets, plants would go to the most appropriate locations with far fewer taxpayer dollars spent and more substantial employment and economic gains for local residents. Under the current system, politicians reap the biggest gains.

"Each battle in this war brings with it the pageantry of ribbon-cuttings and photo opportunities for the politicians, who claim new, mystical powers of distinguishing the winners from the losers in the marketplace," notes Reed.[29] We will discuss ways to eliminate this irrational behavior later in the chapter.

The Shrinking Charitable Pie

Dysfunctional competition is as common in the charitable world as it is in government, particularly in the way charities solicit donations. Just as there are many sources of donations, there are numerous ways of running a fund-raising campaign. The Nature Conservancy and similar large groups buy land with donated dollars to conserve it for future generations. Hospitals solicit research dollars from wealthy individuals and corporations, and colleges and universities often target alumni. The solicitation methods of churches, mental health organizations and other small groups tend towards more localized and informal methods—bake sales and raffles, for example. Many of these groups rely exclusively on their own volunteers. Others engage professional solicitors, principally telemarketing firms, to conduct their fund-raising operations. This last technique leads to dysfunctional competition.

According to the Institute of Charity Fundraising, approximately 63 percent of charities use external telemarketing agencies for fund-raising. Given that we are all sick of telephone solicitors' asking for donations to charities, why is this still such a prevalent fund-raising tool? Because for-profit companies have discovered a cash cow in charities, which are often only too happy to pass off the difficult chore of fund-raising. By offering charities a small portion of the money that is raised, and by paying callers minimum wage, these companies increase their incentives to call. For-profit telemarketing firms commonly take a cut of as much as 75 percent of the money they raise. In the state of Washington, a third of the for-profit fund-raisers managed to send only 20 percent of receipts to the charities that hired them in 1996; 8 percent of these companies gave 10 percent or less to the charities. Several charities wound up losing money after "expenses" were totaled.[30] All too often, professional telemarketers become a parasitic operating unit of the organization that hires them.

In California, the attorney general's office found in 1997 that only 37 cents of every dollar raised by commercial fund-raisers in the state was spent on charity. "Of the $175 million raised by commercial fund-raisers in 1996," noted Attorney General Dan Lungren, "only $64 million went to charities. This is consistent with other years where only 30–40 percent of all money raised by commercial fund-raisers went to charitable purposes."[31] Of the 525 commercial fund-raising campaigns run in California in 1996, 28 percent gave more than half the funds raised to the charity the money was raised for; 11 percent gave from 31 to 50 percent; 20 percent gave from 21 to 30 percent; 11 percent gave from 16 to 20 percent; and 29 percent gave less than 15 percent.[32]

The results of the New York attorney general's report, Pennies for Charities 1998 (reporting on campaigns conducted during 1997), were virtually identical: Of the $145.2 million raised in the state by professional telemarketers in 608 campaigns, only $35.9 million– 24.7 percent–made its way to the charitable organizations.[33] The rest of the donations went to the fund-raiser for fees and overhead costs. According to the report, only about a quarter of the telemarketers managed to funnel over 40 percent to the charities. The report further noted that the funds received by the charities dropped from 38 cents of every dollar donated in 1995 to 36.7 cents in 1996. The funds that went to charity for the 608 telemarketing campaigns conducted during 1996 are shown in Table 3.1.

Although most states make an effort to regulate this business, the courts have struck down attempts by some states to set caps on how much solicitors can make.[34] In 1994, for example, California enacted a new law requiring that at least 50 percent of all donations raised by commercial fund-raisers go to the charity. The National Federation of Nonprofits won a lawsuit barring application of the law on the basis of recent U.S. Supreme Court rulings, which have consistently

TABLE 3.1   Percentage of Funds Raised by Professional Telemarketers
Received by Charities Registered in New York State, 1997

Percent Received by Charity	Number of Campaigns	Percent of Campaigns
90-100+%	3	0.5%
80-89%	5	0.8%
70-79%	8	1.3%
60-69%	24	4.0%
50-59%	44	7.2%
40-49%	61	10.0%
30-39%	123	20.2%
20-29%	188	30.9%
10-19%	90	14.8%
Below 0-9%	62	10.2%

held that percentage limitations on charities or on professional fund-raisers are an unconstitutional burden on the First Amendment right of free speech. In a 1988 decision, *Riley v. National Federation of the Blind of North Carolina, Inc.*, the Supreme Court ruled that "the act of fund-raising is so closely intertwined with the dissemination and advocacy of ideas that the entire process is cloaked by First Amendment protection."[35] Furthermore, full disclosure of fund-raising costs at the point of solicitation might have a "chilling effect" on the solicitors' free speech and so interfere with their right to solicit for charity.

With so many telemarketing agencies getting rich off citizens' charitable donations, it is difficult not to view the free speech defense with cynicism. Consider the California fund-raising outfit that solicited $10.9 million for Toys for Tots—and delivered not one penny to the charity. The contract apparently allowed the fund-raiser to take the first $11 million it raised; additional proceeds would go to the charity. Perhaps not surprisingly, when donations hit $10.9 million, the firm simply stopped soliciting. In a 1995 interview, Attorney General Dennis Vacco of New York stated that there was no evidence that charities relying on professional fund-raisers were being deliberately ripped off; many of them were simply negotiating poor deals. "For many telemarketers, the margins they are taking are exorbitant. I don't believe it's fraudulent, just that some of these charities are unsuspecting and don't have the lay of the land."[36] We have a different view. When generous people are led to believe that their money is going to a worthwhile charity and it falls into the hands of a for-profit company instead, there is a systemic problem.

Why do charities and nonprofits continue to rely on inefficient donation methods? Driven by an increasingly competitive market for donor dollars, these groups say they are simply following the axiom profit-driven companies adhere to: You've got to spend money to make money. Meanwhile, professional solicitors manage to convince these groups that they are burdened with legitimate labor costs and expenses. "It's labor intensive," said one telemarketer, "People just don't give right away. Sometimes it takes several calls."[37] The president of a telemarketing firm that solicits charitable contributions observed that "If you talk to a major company, if they had 10 or 12 percent clear profit they'd be delighted."[38] Another said, "The bottom line is, it costs a lot of money to raise money. The small piece that goes to help is better than nothing."[39] Lee Cassidy, director of the National Federation of Non-Profits, noted: "Nobody forms a charity to be efficient. They form a charity to be effective. Are they effective: that's the only way to measure a charity."[40]

To give an indication of how the charity dollar pie is divided, consider that as of 1997 there were 626,226 charities in the United States vying for contributions and another 30,000 joining their ranks every year.[41] Because the competition for donors is becoming so fierce, charities are making greater investments in fund-raising. As a result, a greater percentage of charitable dollars is being paid out to professional fund-raisers rather than being spent on the projects themselves. On this point, Linda Mollenauer, president of the Canadian Center for Philanthropy, noted, "It costs money to raise money and what's scary is that individual donations are not increasing; the pie ain't getting bigger."[42]

Charities have allowed for-profit organizations to create a wasteful enterprise that shrinks the overall charitable pie and manipulates uninformed contributors. As fund-raising activities become more transparent, these practices will reduce the pool of contributors by reducing the attractiveness of being a charitable person. When people learn that 80 percent of the $250 that they thought they had donated to a charity actually went to a moneymaking corporation, they will grow less interested in being charitable in the future.

In a recent article, Janet Greenlee and Teresa Gordon addressed the broader issues that are exacerbated by this method of fund-raising: "If every charity reduced its fund-raising expenditures, all would benefit from higher net proceeds; if only one charity reduced its expenditures, the remaining charities would reap the benefits."[43] At the same time, if *all* charities reduced their fund-raising expenditures, one that didn't would reap huge benefits. As charities hire for-profit organizations to obtain new funds for their work, they are defecting in a social dilemma and reducing the productive charitable dollars available to all groups. Charities are confronted with the internal conflict of knowing that the collective good requires their shunning intermediaries that funnel profits for themselves; but their private interests are served by generating maximum cash flow whether their competitors act responsibly or not.

Thus the current system reduces the overall good that can be done for the amount of money available. A far more efficient system is within our reach.

What Can Be Done?

Identifying the problem and its underlying causes is simple. The more difficult and important step is to develop strategies to reduce dysfunctional competition. To conclude this chapter, we present a variety of success stories that demonstrate how individuals, corporations and government officials can develop and sustain innovative and effective alternatives.

Creating New Wealth

When Billy Shore decided to form a hunger-relief organization in 1984, he hadn't yet worked out a strategy for feeding the poor; but he did have strong convictions about the type of organization he *didn't* want to run. Shore articulated this early vision in his book *Revolution of the Heart:*

> The last thing I wanted to do was to start yet another organization that spent a lot of money just to beg for more money through shrill direct-mail solicitations or guilt-inducing photos of starving babies. . . . We couldn't have the necessary impact on hunger by competing with other organizations for our slice of the charitable pie and then redistributing those dollars along the lines of our own vision. New and previously untapped dollars and resources needed to be brought into the effort. New wealth needed to be created.[44]

Shore's charity, Share Our Strength (SOS), based in Washington, D.C., has slowly but surely accomplished great success in its goal of feeding the poor. Since its inception, SOS has raised and distributed more than $50 million to nearly five hundred antihunger organizations in the United States and around the world. Shore has nurtured the organization according to his ideas for expanding the charitable pie, primarily through entrepreneurial fund-raising.

To create "new wealth," SOS convinces corporations to sponsor events, products and services whose proceeds go to charity in exchange for positive public relations. This previously untapped resource of creative talent is a major key to SOS's success. The charity convinced Random House to publish *Louder Than Words*, a profitable book of new short stories by well-known authors, including Joyce Carol Oates and Charles Baxter, who contributed their work gratis to help this worthy cause. Renowned chefs clamor to donate their time and skills to SOS celebrity dinners, and vineyards eagerly offer crates of wine. American Express, Northwest Airlines, Starbucks Coffee and other large corporations chip in with sponsorships and goods in exchange for publicity.

By donating their talents instead of their cash, contributors feel connections to SOS they could never gain through the solitary act of writing a check. As a result, the ranks of SOS contributors have swelled to more than 100,000. Shore criticizes the traditional dependence of charities on cold solicitations, which he calls the "Blanche Dubois syndrome" because it relies upon the kindness of strangers.[45] Share our Strength is now showing other not-for-profits how to break out of a limiting mindset and expand the pie through more innovative and active fund-raising.

Some organizations are educating charities about wasteful fund-raising practices. Watchdog groups advise charities on how much of the funds they raise should be spent on fund-raising and administration. The National Charities Information Bureau and the American Institute of Philanthropy recommend that overhead costs be no greater than 40 percent, and the Better Business Bureau advocates a 50 percent maximum. They contend that although fund-raising certainly has cost implications, non-profits need to base their budgets on sound business principles. Because the courts have struck down again and again attempts to regulate the profit margins of professional fund-raisers, a more successful course may be to continue to increase the transparency of charities' spending habits. Full disclosure of costly fund-raising activities should eventually generate enough alarm among contributors to shut off the flow of dollars to for-profit agencies.

What about the sports team owners and corporations that prey on towns and regions across the United States by squeezing outrageous stadium packages and tax abatement deals in exchange for promises of jobs and prosperity that often don't materialize? A small minority of politicians and communities that have resisted the temptation to compete dysfunctionally with their neighbors have accomplished surprisingly effective results.

Disarming the Bullies

Immediately after buying the New England Patriots in 1994, Robert Kraft began angling for a new stadium. Led by Speaker Thomas Finneran, the Massachusetts House of Representatives made what it felt to be a fair deal in the fall of 1997 when it passed a bill offering $52 million in state money for improvements to roads, lights and other infrastructure surrounding Foxboro Stadium. In return, Kraft would pay $100 million to renovate the existing facility, and the team would pay $2 million per year to the state (generated through parking and ticket surcharges) to cover much of the debt service on the public funding. In February 1998, Kraft struck a sweeter deal with the leader of the Massachusetts senate, Thomas F. Birmingham; he promised Kraft an additional $20 million worth of land and $5 million for infrastructure improvements if the team promised to build a brand new $200 million stadium and pay $2.4 million per year in state debt service.

Finneran objected to the Patriots' argument that the senate's plan would ensure the commonwealth of Massachusetts a continued flow of $10 million per year in team-generated tax revenue. Addressing the house, he called on lawmakers to guard taxpayers against the endless demands of National Football League owners. "If, in fact, we were to open the public purse and the public treasury," Finneran declared, "the owners would never really tell us they had reached the end of their needs or the end of their wish list. . . . It's up to us in the first and the last instance to draw what are appropriate and responsible lines in regard to accountability and protection of the public purse."[46]

The situation soon became even more complicated: In mid-November, Connecticut Governor John G. Rowland thrilled many Hartford residents by offering the Patriots the most lucrative stadium package in NFL history. Connecticut promised a $374 million publicly financed stadium and other perks topping more than $1 billion over the thirty-year lease terms. Connecticut politicians, salivating at the prospect of luring an NFL team to their state, seemed not to care that the estimated 2,600 low-wage jobs generated by the Hartford stadium would cost taxpayers nearly $144,000 per position. And apparently they did not consider that $374 million might be better spent on Hartford's notoriously distressed school system, widely considered one of the worst in the United States.

Not surprisingly, Kraft agreed to bargain exclusively with the state of Connecticut for the time being. Meanwhile, back in Massachusetts, Finneran refused to become entangled in a bidding war. "Apparently, there's a more generous suitor that's waiting in the wings. There's nothing I can do about that unless literally I was to say, 'Well, we'll open the door of the treasury all weekend, let us know when you've helped yourself to enough money.' That's not public service."[47] Finneran suggested that to accommodate Kraft would be to succumb to blackmail: "Once you begin to do that quite clearly you have sent a signal—that the Massachusetts House at least can be hijacked and can be bullied and will flinch in the face of economic bullying and economic pressure."[48]

Nevertheless, in an eleventh-hour meeting, Finneran, Birmingham, Massachusetts Governor Celluci and several NFL executives drafted an agreement to keep the Patriots in Massachusetts. Under the offer, Kraft would build a new stadium in Foxboro ($225 million), partially assisted by low-rate financing from other NFL teams, and the state would raise its offer from $57 million to $70 million in infrastructure improvements. Instead of selling the land under the new facility to the state as had been originally proposed, Kraft would grant an easement on his land that would allow the state to upgrade access ramps and sewer lines on his private property. As payback for the infrastructure improvements, the team and satellite parking lots would pay the state $1.4 million per year.

Meanwhile, talks with Connecticut stalled. On April 30, 1999, Massachusetts Governor Paul Cellucci attended a taping of *The Tonight Show*. When Jay Leno asked the governor during his opening monologue about the fate of the Patriots, the camera spun toward the audience where Cellucci sat smiling with his thumb in the air. "They're staying," the governor shouted, "in Massachusetts!"[49]

"In the end, we got an agreement everyone could live with, including, I hope, the team," Finneran said, looking back on the deal.

"But we did not pay tribute or ransom, and I think that might be a lesson for other states."[50] Although they reluctantly agreed to pay certain infrastructure costs, Boston and the commonwealth of Massachusetts resisted the national trend of using the public purse to pay huge sums for football stadiums. In the process, they saved hundreds of millions of dollars and showed citizens across the country that these negotiations can be resolved satisfactorily. They may have contributed to breaking a nationwide pattern of dysfunctional behavior toward sports teams.

Perhaps the ultimate solution to the problem of greedy team owners is to eliminate them from the equation completely. In Seattle, the team owner paid $100 million for the Mariners and the government chipped in well over $350 million. If a baseball team was indispensable to the community (an argument we question), it would have made more sense for the government to bid for team ownership, pay $450 million to buy the team, build the stadium and collect the profit rather than pay $350 million to make the team owners rich.

This idea isn't new. Since 1950, the Green Bay Packers football team has been a publicly traded nonprofit corporation. More than 111,000 Packers fans nationwide currently own a stake in the franchise. Stockholders elect a board of directors, which in turn elects seven officers; only the president receives a salary. Shareholders' dividends are funneled back into the franchise rather than disbursed as profit. To further ensure that the organization remains democratically run and locally based, individuals are prohibited from owning more than 200,000 shares.

Public ownership allows fans greater involvement with their team and increases civic pride. More than 18,000 shareholders attended the Packers' first annual "State of the Team" address in 1998 at Lambeau Field, where audience members engaged in a lively question-and-answer session with team management. A local ownership base means that the team cannot make a credible threat to leave town; in addition, requests for stadium improvements meet with healthy regional skepticism. As a result, the Packers are the least subsidized major professional sports team, and they are also an anomaly in a highly nomadic business: The team operates in a city with a population of just 100,000, the smallest market in pro sports. "I don't know if we appreciate how lucky we are to be in this little town with this team," comments Packers president Bob Harlan. "This is a great story and it will never happen again."[51]

Why can't the Packers formula be copied elsewhere? Because the sports leagues can be expected to block future public ownership initiatives. When Joan Kroc inherited the San Diego Padres from her husband, McDonald's founder Ray Kroc, she hoped to make a gift of the baseball team to the city and offered to throw in a $100 million trust fund to support operations costs. City officials were thrilled: Civic ownership would guarantee San Diego a permanent baseball franchise, and taxpayers would no longer face ransom demands from future owners. But the Major League Baseball owners' committee immediately shot down Kroc's proposal. Why? The prospect of a nationwide trend toward public ownership terrified them. If the marketplace ever tipped in favor of the fans, the owners would lose their most important bargaining chip: their all-too-credible threats to pack up and skip town.

As a result, communities are left to fend off owner threats one by one, and only rarely do they have much statutory support. In San Antonio, because of a Texas law that gives school districts a voice in proposed tax deals affecting land values, a local school board was able to stand up to the demands of the Spurs' owner for a $156 million arena. After the board of the North East School District voted against the arena, the Spurs had no choice but to abide by the decision. "If you have to choose between the National Basketball Association and children, it's no choice," declared school board president Bruce Bennett.[52]

At the federal level, Republican Senator Arlen Specter introduced a bill that would force Major League Baseball and the National Football League to contribute at least 50 percent of stadium construction costs for their new teams. The bill languished during the 1999 legislative session and is unlikely to be resurrected anytime soon; too many state representatives cling to the false belief that brand-new stadiums are a quick fix for their regions' problems. This is a shame, because a coordinated effort at the national level would be the most effective method of solving this social dilemma. As long as the temptation to create national competition exists, local efforts at fiscal restraint will suffer.

The Politics of Nonagression

Several politicians at the state and federal level have tried to eliminate the excessive public subsidies that states routinely dole out to corporations. Ohio State Senator Charles Horn, a vocal critic of these payoffs, has led a mini-revolt in his state. The Urban Center at Cleveland State University has been chosen to conduct a detailed investigation of the costs and benefits of Ohio's economic development programs, and it is clear that Horn expects the study's findings to lead to sweeping reform.[53] Changes in Ohio's tax credit program made in the early 1990s have already made the state a stand-out example of responsibility and prudence. Companies moving to Ohio do not receive up-front subsidies; rather, they earn tax credits only for the new jobs they create.[54] This practice, if adopted nationwide, would not eliminate state-to-state competition, but it would at least make the corporate world more accountable for its promises of jobs and economic growth.

A lack of cooperation with other states inevitably becomes a problem for a state that attempts to curb its competition unilaterally. Recognizing this pitfall, some communities and states have attempted to even the playing field through cooperative partnerships. In 1991, New York City and the states of New York, New Jersey and Connecticut signed a "nonagression pact" in which they agreed not to engage in bidding wars against each other. Before the year was out, the whims of corporate clients proved too great. When New Jersey could not resist trying to woo the New York Mercantile Exchange to Jersey City, New York City had to cough up an extra $30 million to convince the exchange to sit tight. Next, Connecticut managed to lure Swiss Bank Corporation from Manhattan to

Stamford with $120 million in incentives.[55] Needless to say, the contract has since become a worthless piece of paper that all parties look back on as idealistic folly.

In the cutthroat arena of incentive packages, it is unrealistic to expect that nonaggression pacts will persuade states to act honorably and rationally toward their neighbors. Because the stakes are high, the competition fierce and the political climate as variable as the seasons, it is all too likely that one or more of the parties will be tempted to stage a raid. Besides, alliances do not stop destructive bidding practices–they simply eliminate players from the game. The war is among economic regions rather than individual cities and states. For these reasons, we think it is time to identify ways for the federal government to enact laws that encourage cooperation and reduce dysfunctional competition between the states.

Melvin Burstein and Arthur Rolnick of the Federal Reserve Bank of Minneapolis argue that the United States Congress should enact legislation that punishes states for stealing companies from other states. For example, the federal government could place an embargo on federal grants to states that engage in destructive raiding. These disciplinary measures are not unprecedented; Congress has used them to bring states in line on issues ranging from speed limits to pollution levels. Yes, these laws reduce states' rights. But considering the resources states are squandering on corporate suitors, it would not be unreasonable for the federal government to find ways to ensure that they fulfill their responsibilities to their citizens.

Burstein and Rolnick have also proposed that Congress pass a law that imposes an excise tax on relocating companies equal to the value of the economic incentives promised by the state.[56] Under this scenario, after Rio Rancho, New Mexico, offered $114 million in incentives to Intel, the Feds would have socked Intel with a $114 million tax, thereby eliminating the value of the incentives–and eliminating the temptation for governments to bid against each other. While the tax may seem unduly harsh, it would in all likelihood never be collected; the very threat would deter corporations from shaking down states.

As long as corporations continue their nomadic ways, individual states will probably be unable to resist the temptations of destructive competitive bidding. By calling on Congress to help stamp out dysfunctional competition, we are not advocating big government but wise government.

Combating Dysfunctional Competition

Citizens, companies and government officials have many ways to combat dysfunctional competition to the benefit of their communities and society at large. Individuals, organizations and governments can all take steps to become part of the solution to the problem.

Individuals

Action at the personal level starts with awareness of the problem, which is a goal that readers of this chapter have already met. Now that you've been informed, here are some resolutions you should consider adopting:

- Vote against political candidates who encourage dysfunctional competition through extravagant deals for corporations and sports franchises. When your elected leaders propose giving tax revenues to rich business owners, lobby them to consider what the community is sacrificing in the process.
- When considering giving to a charity, find out what percentage of donations serve the mission of the organization. Charity watchdog groups post this information on their Web sites: National Charities Information Bureau, www.give.org; the Better Business Bureau, www.betterbusinessbureau.com; American Institute of Philanthropy, www.charitywatch.org. Reject telephone requests for charitable contributions if the caller refuses to put material in the mail or tell you whether he or she is a volunteer. Charity volunteers are usually happy to educate you about their organizations; the telemarketer has far less interest in doing so.

- If you discover that one of your favorite charities is mired in dysfunctional competition, educate the group's leaders about parasitic intermediaries. Instead of reaching for your checkbook the next time your favorite charity approaches you, think about contributing your unique talents instead.

Organizations

For-profit and nonprofit organizations alike can work to eliminate dysfunctional competition from their strategic repertoires:

- Charities must learn to stop chasing after the limited pool of charitable dollars and envision alternative forms of wealth such as talent, product donations and positive public relations. This process may lead them to reject the services of telemarketing agencies.
- School boards, neighborhood organizations and other community groups should strive to increase their voices in local decisions about tax abatements and incentive packages for corporations and sports team owners. This may require intense lobbying efforts, or simply a better knowledge of the local tax code.

Government

Politicians at all levels of government have launched efforts to end the destructive effects of dysfunctional competition; we are optimistic that, with time, the work of these individuals will lead to greater organization and connection on the issue. Here are some suggestions for building policies and legislation that foster cooperation instead of competition:

- Various legislators at the state and local levels have proved that corporate bullies can be tamed. Contrary to popular opinion, the result isn't political death; in fact, such a victory could turn the politician into a local hero.

- The U.S. Congress, with the support of the president, will have to take a more proactive role in ending the economic war between the states. Only federal legislation can stop dysfunctional competition once and for all.
- Laws should be enacted that will force charities to be more forthcoming about their fund-raising methods. One easy step would be to require that telemarketers reveal the true nature of their affiliation rather than allow for-profit firms to act as if they were charitable organizations.

4

Support Our Group

BECAUSE CERTAIN MEMBERS OF CONGRESS HAVE PORTRAYED THE tobacco crop as the only defense against the economic collapse of Kentucky, North Carolina and Virginia, tobacco farming is now one of the most coddled industries in the country. The American government currently spends at least $83.5 million annually to assist tobacco growers. Congress routinely votes down efforts to lower these subsidies. Most of this money ($67.3 million) pays for subsidized crop insurance; the rest is spent on administrative costs for price supports.[1]

Of the hundreds of crops grown in the United States, tobacco is one of a select few that receive USDA price supports.[2] This occurs even though tobacco is one of the most lucrative crops in the nation—receipts total $4,000 per acre—compared to $200 for an acre of wheat. Between 1974 and 2000, American exports of tobacco leaves and products jumped from $650 million to $6 billion.[3] Nonetheless, most of the USDA's crisis-era tobacco subsidies remain firmly in place.

Another factor distinguishes tobacco from other crops grown in the United States: Tobacco is a killer. Each year, approximately

430,700 American citizens die from lung cancer and other illnesses attributed to the consumption of tobacco.[4] Smoking is directly responsible for 87 percent of lung cancer cases and most cases of emphysema and chronic bronchitis.[5] The American Lung Association estimates that tobacco smoking costs the United States approximately $97.2 billion each year in health-care costs and lost productivity. The American government picks up the tab for at least 40 percent of smoking-related medical expenses—about $50 billion in 1993 alone.[6] In addition to paying the medical bills of those suffering and dying from the effects of tobacco consumption, the American government spends millions each year on ad campaigns, health programs and package labeling designed to convince its citizens to stop smoking or never to start.

In 1997, the attorneys general of more than forty states reached a settlement with major tobacco manufacturers, who agreed to repay $250 billion in state health care costs. Following the states' lead, the Department of Justice has taken the tobacco companies to court in an attempt to recover the billions of dollars the federal government has spent on treating sick smokers.[7] Meanwhile, Congress continues to dole out millions in insurance deals to tobacco farmers. Proponents contend that abolishing these perks would bankrupt small family farms and damage the economies of the rural South. Subsidies are not designed to promote tobacco use, the argument goes, but to keep America's family farms solvent.

Today, 58 percent of American farmers fit the government's definition of family farmers; yet these farmers produce only 4 percent of the total crop output, so they qualify for only 4 percent of the government's subsidy payments. The top 5 percent of farms produce 60 percent of the total output, which entitles them to 60 percent of the subsidy payments. Many of these farms are large agribusinesses—hardly needy mom-and-pop operations. The groups that profit the most from government tobacco subsidies are farms that already generate high incomes after meeting all their expenses.[8]

How can the same government that recognizes smoking as the number one preventable cause of death among its citizens also fund the growing of tobacco? The answer lies in the inordinate influence of special-interest groups in politics. This unprecedented power arises, in part, from fundamental human cognitive biases among politicians and voters; debates about special-interest groups rarely consider such biases, focusing instead on issues of power and incentives.

We use the term *special interest* to refer to groups that seek gains for their members without concern for the overall effect their proposals have on society, even when the gains to a group are much smaller than social costs. This action typically reflects an inability or unwillingness to recognize the potential for wise tradeoffs in which groups make small sacrifices in exchange for larger gains. We focus primarily on corporations because this sector of society relies on money as a tool to influence political decisions in its favor—often reducing the size of the pie for American citizens as a whole.

Not all political groups are exclusively self-interested. Activist groups have brought about many important social reforms that Americans now take for granted. Even when ideological and activist groups disagree with each other, they are fighting for what they believe is best for all. Interest groups can also educate politicians by giving them valuable advice and information about issues they may know little about.

In this chapter, we examine certain groups—such as the tobacco industry—that persuade elected officials to make bad decisions and squander resources. Why have most politicians been reluctant to change a system that compromises their integrity? We offer a psychological account to explain why citizens tolerate this corruption of politics. Next, we consider two more industries—mining and timber—that seem to have the magic touch when it comes to stalling reform and securing sweetheart deals. We then trace these deals back to their roots: the rampant use of money to buy political power. We will argue that a massive clean-up of election campaigns must be undertaken in the United States to curb the distortion of democracy.

Corporations in the United States are not the only group that tries to influence public policy. We will consider the social costs exacted by universities competing for research funding. We conclude the chapter with the story of a group of German coal miners who, as they made personal sacrifices on behalf of their union, ended up harming themselves and society at large.

The Basics of Corporate Welfare

For all the wrangling over the budget, there's a little-known truth that the politicians or the media don't readily acknowledge: The most expensive group of welfare recipients in the United States are not poor women and children, but corporations. Federal money spent on Aid to Families with Dependent Children, food stamps and Medicaid comes to about $85 billion annually. The total annual cost of corporate tax breaks and subsidies is conservatively estimated at $75 billion per year and may be as high as $167 billion.[9] It is difficult to put a price tag on corporate welfare because its definition can be slippery, depending, for example, on whether tax breaks are included in the equation.[10] No matter what the numbers are, when Congress makes its annual budget cuts, it is corporations, not the nation's poor, who find themselves sheltered time and time again. "We are in an era in which the Congress was able to find nearly a trillion dollars in cuts over seven years, the bulk of it from social services to the poor," noted Robert Shapiro, an analyst for the centrist Progressive Policy Institute. "But less than 2 percent of those cuts came from subsidies to industry."[11]

Tax breaks make up the bulk of corporate welfare. As the Congressional Budget Office noted in 1995, "The federal government's efforts to promote business are heavily weighted toward tax preferences, with spending and credit programs accounting for a smaller share of federal efforts."[12] In the 1950s and 1960s, corporate taxes provided roughly half of all federal government revenues. Over time, particularly during the 1980s, the tax code was rewritten to reduce corporate income taxes drastically. By 1996, corporate taxes matched only one-fourth the amount individuals pay.[13]

Corporate tax breaks resemble entitlements: Once added to the tax code, they are automatically renewed each year without review and are not subject to spending limits.[14] By contrast, direct spending on defense, roads, environmental protection and other programs must be approved every year through an appropriation bill passed by Congress and signed by the president. If such a program costs more than expected, it—or something else—must be scaled back to balance the budget. A direct spending program is listed in the official budget as a federal outlay, and the taxes that pay for the program are listed as revenues. But when an equivalent program of tax breaks is paid for by taxing people and companies that do not directly benefit from it, the combination shows up in the aggregate budget numbers as a wash—net taxes do not appear to rise, and neither does spending. In recent years, regardless of whether Democrats or Republicans control Congress, this formula has made tax expenditures the power tool of choice for many lawmakers.

The temptation to cater to special-interest groups is particularly irresistible when Congress is allocating government funds for the next fiscal year. Senator Ted Stevens of Alaska, chair of the 1998 Appropriations Committee, slipped the Interior Department $10.5 million in direct spending for projects designed to open up the Tongass National Forest to loggers.[15] These gifts, known as "earmarks" because they are designated for a specific use, are all too common in appropriations bills (typically hammered out quickly at the end of the legislative session by representatives anxious to get back home to begin campaigning for re-election). In this chaotic atmosphere, earmarks are easy to slip in uncontested, even undetected. Pro-tobacco members of Congress handed their benefactors a stealth $50 billion tax break by way of the 1997 balanced-budget bill—only to be forced to rescind it when the press and the public caught on.[16]

Corporate welfare is justified as an essential tool for creating jobs for Americans and for stimulating the economy. Little evidence is offered by either side of the political spectrum to support these claims. Basic economic theory suggests that, overall, society would be better off without subsidies.[17] One reason that certain subsidized goods, such as cigarettes, sell so well is that subsidies keep retail prices low. These goods sell much better than they would if they were not subsidized. Citizens have fixed budgets; therefore, if they spend their money disproportionately on subsidized goods, they will put companies that produce nonsubsidized goods at a disadvantage. Government money spent on subsidies ends up promoting consumption that would not occur if the price reflected the true cost of production. Thus, subsidies distort the marketplace and violate basic tenets of economic competition.

It's important to note that the government, like citizens, has only a fixed amount of funds to disburse. Money spent on subsidies is money that is not being used to fund government programs such as education or to reduce the national debt. Special perks impose a burden on all Americans for the sake of a chosen few. Citizens and companies that do not benefit from these preferences have a right to ask whether they are serving the public good, and why such practices persist when no one will admit to favoring them. We argue that an understanding of the psychology of decision making offers new insight into the motivations behind this wasteful system.

The Psychology of Special-Interest Groups

When politicians fight for restrictions against special-interest groups, the public tunes them out—even though these groups distort the will of the people across a range of critical policy areas. In the 2000 presidential campaign, neither Republican John McCain nor Democrat Bill Bradley was successful in building a majority voting bloc that would make this issue its top priority. We offer two psychological explanations for why most people remain passive on this issue. The first focuses on the effects of social dilemmas on political action; the second concerns the lack of salience of indirect issues.

Group Identification in Social Dilemmas
As we discussed in Chapter 3, a social dilemma is a situation in which an individual must choose between advancing her own self interest and cooperating with a group to which she belongs. If each

group member chooses to cooperate rather than compete, all members will be better off. Researchers have found repeatedly that cooperation is more likely when people identify strongly with a group.[18] Identification can result from such trivial properties as being assigned to the same group in a psychology experiment; or it can result from ingrained membership in groups such as families, schools, teams, corporations or nations. When people think of themselves as members of a group, they are more willing to sacrifice their self-interest for other members of the group than nonmembers.

Social dilemmas become more complicated when the group is competing with other groups. In this case, members "cooperate" by helping members of their own group and hurting members of competing groups. The usual result is that individuals end up hurting themselves; they gain no net benefit at all because each gain for the cooperator's group comes at the expense of an equal loss for those outside of it. In sporting competitions, cooperation with one's group is the goal: Each point you score for your own team hurts the other team. But the real world is not made up of teams engaged in harmless competition. In the real world, the sacrifices one makes for one's own group can inflict genuine harm on outsiders.

This dysfunctional self-sacrifice occurs in many forms of political action by special-interest groups such as executives in the same industry or workers in the same labor union. Executives in power-generation industries might cooperate to improve business by supporting research that questions the value of antipollution laws; hiring lobbyists to oppose antipollution regulations; making campaign contributions; and writing letters to congressional representatives. While these cooperative measures help the group, the benefits come at a cost to its members, who must invest huge amounts of money and time in such efforts. In addition, both members and nonmembers suffer harm from the increased pollution that is a result of the group's accomplishments. Thus, each group member is making a sacrifice that hurts himself, helps his group and hurts outsiders.

Meanwhile, 275 million American citizens have their own opinions about government policy. While citizens collectively own far more money than the dominant players in a specific industry, no citizen has the same level of concern or lobbying power as a group of corporate actors. It should not be surprising that politicians listen most closely to those who organize most effectively to win their attention. We argue that if members of special-interest groups understood that their self-sacrifice is for naught, they might choose to be more selfish, and paradoxically, contribute more positively to society.

Ignoring Secondary Effects

One way to reduce the destructive effects of special-interest groups is to weaken their political influence. As we discuss later in the chapter, campaign finance reform would be a start; yet such bills fail in Congress year after year, in good part because citizens do not press their representatives on this issue. Why doesn't the populace demand that the pie-shrinking influence of special-interest groups be stopped? Why don't we rally to the banner of those who fight for campaign finance reform? The reason is that campaign finance reform is an indirect issue that influences the vivid concerns of voters only indirectly. In other words, it's boring. A recent Pew Research Center poll found that just 28 percent of voters believed finance reform should be an important campaign issue, putting it sixteenth behind such goals as reducing crime and improving education.[19] Campaign finance reform may be more important than any other issue because it influences how all other issues are decided, but this fact doesn't register. Human judgment focuses on vivid issues and pays scant attention to boring ones. Small aircraft safety became a vivid issue only after the death of John F. Kennedy, Jr., even though statistics on such accidents are reported frequently in the news. Similarly, the issues affected by political action committees (PACs) overshadow the very issue of whether PACs exercise inordinate influence in a democracy. The problem is that we are accepting, without examination, a system that shrinks the pie.

Campaign finance reform is a process issue, not an outcome issue; it affects the process of politics, which in turn affects all other issues. People need to think through this process if they are to value campaign finance reform. But a significant amount of psychological research suggests that people do not intuitively think multiple steps ahead.[20] For example, most negotiators do not think about how their opponents will respond to their next move. Similarly, most negotiators do not develop contingency plans in the event their proposals are rejected. In the context of political issues, we argue that the skill of thinking multiple steps ahead is a necessary prerequisite of valuing campaign finance reform. For voters to become concerned about such initiatives, they must think through the effect this issue has on other issues. Initial evidence suggests that this is not an intuitive process for most voters.

Archaic Laws, Modern Losses

With 730 million acres of public land, primarily in the West, the federal government is by far the nation's biggest landlord. After the Civil War, the government devised a system of subsidies—including the Homestead Act, railroad rights-of-way and land grants—to induce people to relocate to its western lands. As the nation developed, most of these subsidies died a natural death. Others thrived. Many of the subsidies that contribute to today's tax burden are such leftovers (for instance, supports for tobacco farming, mining and timber); others (such as the sports stadium subsidies discussed in Chapter 3) are contemporary but misconceived.

Changing conditions have reduced the economic importance of extractive/natural resource industries such as agriculture, mining and timber. Extractive industries in the West, for example, are now far less profitable and employ far fewer people than do recreation, tourism, manufacturing and finance. As the Western economy diversified from 1982 to 1990, employment rose by nearly 50 percent—but during this time, employment in agriculture, timber and mining fell by 21 percent.[21] Although dollars are replaced more easily than natural resources, subsidies to these industries are passionately defended. History, lifestyles, even birthrights are said to be at stake.

The Granddaddy of Subsidies

> I consider [the 1872 General Mining Law] the most egregious thing that the
> Senate turns its back on every year. . . . It is so gross, so egregious, that people
> can't believe it is factual, that it is actually happening.
>
> —Former Senator Dale Bumpers

In 1872, the General Mining Law was enacted to regulate the extraction of hardrock minerals, which are nonfuel minerals such as gold, copper and silver. The law was intended to promote settlement of the West, and even by nineteenth-century standards, it provided generous opportunities to individual prospectors. One hundred twenty-five years later, it has never been updated. Believe it or not, the following provisions are still in place:

- Anyone discovering a "valuable mineral deposit" on open public lands has a right to mine it, no matter what other nonmineral values exist.
- Anyone proving the existence of "valuable mineral deposits" may patent (purchase) the land and minerals at 1872 prices–$5 an acre.
- No royalty is required for the value of ores taken from public lands.
- No environmental standards exist.
- No reclamation provisions exist.[22]

Labeled the "granddaddy of subsidies" by the Green Scissors organization and "a license to steal" by former Senator Dale Bumpers, this country's great mineral giveaways are perhaps the most outlandish waste of money and resources the government authorizes.[23] Every year, $2 to $3 billion worth of minerals is extracted from public lands for laughably small fees. Table 4.1 tells the story.

Since 1872, land and mineral values have risen considerably. Big corporations have displaced small prospectors, and some 3.5 million acres of federal land, containing $230 billion worth of minerals, have

TABLE 4.1   U.S. Mineral Giveaways, 1872–1993

State	Giveaways in Millions
Alaska	$ 9,333
Arizona	$ 71,016
California	$ 12,182
Colorado	$ 12,014
Idaho	$ 17,416
Montana	$ 18,000
Nevada	$ 41,183
New Mexico	$ 8,572
Oregon	$ 697
South Dakota	$ 727
Utah	$ 39,773
Washington	$ 688
Wyoming	$ 56
Total	$231,657

Note: Minerals extracted from public or patented lands

been purchased under the law—an area the size of Connecticut. When the claims staked by prospectors and speculators are added in, the amount of public land that has been either bought for $5 per acre, or staked for $25 and $100 in annual rent, adds up to more than 11 million acres.[24] Many of the mines on federal or patented land are literally billion-dollar giveaways, often to foreign companies.[25] In 1994, American Barrick Resources, a Canadian company, patented nearly 2,000 acres of public land in Nevada for less than $10,000; the land contains over $10 billion in recoverable gold reserves. In 1995, a Danish company paid $275 to patent land in Idaho containing more than $1 billion in minerals.[26]

In return, mining companies have left a vast legacy of polluted groundwater, unreclaimed ore pits and thousands of miles of ruined streams. It is not uncommon for millions of tons of land to be mined for a few ounces of gold. Runoff from mines has polluted more than 12,000 miles of rivers and streams and 180,000 acres of lakes and reservoirs; this contamination is a serious risk to underground aquifers.[27] The Mineral Policy Center estimates direct cleanup costs for the more than 500,000 abandoned mines on federal lands in the $30 to $70 billion range.[28] More than 52 of the mines have been declared Superfund sites and, according to EPA estimates, will cost more than $17 billion to clean up.

The powerful political lobby of the mining industry, which has put pressure on members of Congress from Western states, has blocked efforts to enact a mineral royalty, create an abandoned mine reclamation program and reform the 1872 Mining Law. Various initiatives, however, suggest that the tide is turning. The Western Governors' Association has entered into a cooperative agreement with the Department of the Interior and mining companies to accelerate cleanup at abandoned mines.[29] In 1994, Congress imposed a moratorium on patenting; but patents already filed continue to be granted and mining companies continue to work already claimed lands. At the regulatory level, in February 1999, the Bureau of Land Management proposed a rule that would prevent "unnecessary or undue degradation" of public land and its resources by the mining operations it oversees.[30] The Interior Department, led by Secretary Bruce Babbitt, banned hardrock mining on thousands of acres in Arizona north of the Grand Canyon.[31] The Clinton administration withdrew mining access to 430,000 acres of Montana's wilderness in an effort to preserve the area's grassland, forests and streams, an environmentally stable habitat for grizzly bears, elk and trout.[32] These changes signal that, in recent years, the U.S. Forest Service has attempted to change its traditional image as a tool of special-interest groups.

No matter what reforms presidents and government agencies enact, only the legislative branch of the government has the power to stop these handouts once and for all. A conspicuous form of corporate welfare and an enormous waste of taxpayer resources, the archaic 1872 law desperately needs a complete overhaul by Congress. The subsidies embedded in public lands create false incentives for miners and hinder sound land management; they distort the market, block the collection of billions in public funds and foster the environmental destruction of public rivers and lands.

The Great Timber Giveaway

> In terms of assets, the [Forest Service] would rank in the top five in Fortune magazine's list of the nation's 500 largest corporations. In terms of operating revenues, however, the agency would be only number 290. In terms of net income, the Forest Service would be classified as bankrupt.
>
> —Randal O'Toole, Thoreau Institute

Though national forests currently provide only 4 percent of the nation's timber, the government is still subsidizing this harvesting to the tune of about $111 million a year. The agreements the timber industry has managed to secure for decades have resulted in billions in lost tax dollars. Since 1992 alone, the U.S. Forest Service has lost $2.8 billion on its timber program. A Wilderness Society analysis of commercial logging sales in 104 national forests during fiscal year 1997 found that 83 of those forests lost money selling timber.[34] Although the Forest Service claims to have earned a $78 million net profit in 1996 from commodity timber sales, the agency did not include the $154 million redistribution of revenues to counties or the $128 million cost of timber road construction.

How does the Forest Service manage to rack up such huge losses every year? First, it follows an outdated subsidy program instated during a post–World War II construction boom; this program enables the Forest Service to offer timber harvesting rights on national forests to private companies at cut-rate prices far below the service's own administration and preparation costs. In addition, the service continually subsidizes the construction of an extensive network of logging roads. Every year, Congress appropriates taxpayer dollars to make up the difference. Even the most conservative analyses of commodity sales indicate that taxpayers are earning an abominably poor return on the sale of their resources.

The Forest Service simply does not incorporate a large enough share of overhead expenses into the minimum acceptable bid for timber sales. Why not? As with mining, old rules still on the books are partly to blame. In 1930, when it cost the Forest Service fifty cents per thousand board feet to hold a timber sale, it wrote a rule specifying that fifty cents be returned to the Department of the Treasury for every thousand board feet. The fifty-cents rule still applies–but today the average sale costs over $50 per thousand board feet.[35]

The Forest Service's economic operations are riddled with accounting gimmicks and unwarranted incentives. While the cost of timber sales (overhead, planning, road construction and so forth) is underwritten by congressional appropriation in the form of taxpayer dollars, the service is nonetheless permitted to keep the bulk of its timber sales revenues. In other words, there is virtually no direct connection between income and expense. Thus, the service's budgeting provides incentives to generate a large number of below-cost timber sales and to discount the value of recreation, wildlife habitat and environmental amenities. In the private sector, a business's income must cover expenditures or the business will face bankruptcy. But the Forest Service is not a business–it can always fall back on taxpayer dollars.

There is one more reason so many timber commodity sales occur. Out of 122 national forests in forty states, the U.S. Treasury is required to pay 25 percent of the proceeds of each timber sale to local communities. Not surprisingly, when local budgets are tight, state representatives put political pressure on the Forest Service to hold sales in their districts so that dollars can be funneled back home.[36]

The costs of timber subsidies to the American taxpayer are not only financial. More than 440,000 miles of timber roads–nine times the mileage of the interstate highway system–have been built on national forests.[37] Many old-growth forests have been eliminated, wildlife habitats destroyed in the process. Declines in the American grizzly bear population and the fragmentation of more common wildlife such as elk cannot be easily measured in dollars and may never be recovered.

In 1999, an unwarranted subsidy was eliminated when Purchaser Road Credits for the timber industry were defeated in both houses of Congress. And in the last days of his administration, President Clinton issued an executive order banning logging and logging road construction on 58.5 million acres of national forest land, nearly one third of all federal forests.[38] Whether these reforms reflect a turning of the tide against timber subsidies remains to be seen.

Special-Interest Groups in the United States

The fourth quarter of the twentieth century was a particularly trying time for the integrity of the American political system. From Watergate to the presidential election of 2000, many of the scandals that arose were rooted in the financing of political campaigns. Laws enacted to curb corruption invariably failed as politicians desperate to be elected—and the special interests that bankroll them—used lawsuits and loopholes to evade reforms.

Secret corporate slush funds, enormous contributions from wealthy individuals and the subsequent rewarding of ambassadorships to some of these donors were just a few of the unethical activities that the Watergate hearings uncovered in the 1972 campaign to re-elect President Richard Nixon. Through limits on donations and campaign spending, disclosure requirements and a voluntary system of public finance, the Federal Election Campaign Act of 1974 was a bold step toward restoring fairness and lawfulness to the electoral process. Although previous prohibitions of direct contributions from labor unions and corporations were upheld, these groups were allowed to set up PACs—segregated funds that solicit voluntary contributions from the group's employees and members for use in political activities. The act prohibited individuals from contributing more than $1,000 per year to a federal candidate, more than $5,000 per year to a PAC and more than $25,000 collectively per year to all

federal candidates, parties and PACs. PACs were limited to donations of $5,000 per candidate, per election.[39]

In the twenty-five years since then, legislative and legal actions
taken by and on behalf of special-interest groups have made the
1974 act virtually worthless. The Supreme Court's *Buckley v. Valeo*
decision tore the first holes in the 1974 act, primarily by striking
down campaign spending limits as a violation of the right of free
speech. *Buckley v. Valeo* loosened restrictions on personal spending
by candidates for their own campaigns, on congressional campaign
spending and on "independent expenditures," or spending by individuals and PACs not directly linked to a candidate or an election
campaign. It also created a loophole for the funding of political ads
on television and radio by making a new distinction between "express advocacy," or ads directly advocating a vote for or against a
candidate; and "issue advocacy," or ads that try to steer public opinion on candidates or issues without directly encouraging or discouraging a vote for a particular candidate.[40] By freeing up restrictions on
the funding of issue ads, *Buckley v. Valeo* has allowed labor unions,
corporations and ideological groups to flood the airwaves during
election seasons with ads that mention candidates by name—and
often ruthlessly attack them.

The most damaging reversal of post-Watergate reforms occurred
in 1978 with the creation of the "soft money" loophole by the
Federal Election Commission (an organization widely regarded as
an anti-reform tool for Congress).[41] This strategy lay dormant until
the 1988 presidential campaign, when the Dukakis campaign, followed quickly by the Bush campaign, opened the floodgates. Since
then, reformers have had difficulty closing them even slightly.
Technically, donations of soft money must be spent exclusively on
generic party-building activities at the state and local level, such as
voter-registration drives, party bumper stickers and television ads
supporting party platforms rather than a particular candidate. The
government places no limits on the amount of soft money that individuals and groups can donate—unlike donations to national campaigns. The myth of soft money is that it is spent strictly on state

and local party activities that have no influence on federal elections, a premise widely acknowledged as fiction.

Federal candidates solicit soft money from corporate and union treasury funds as well as from individuals. These funds are then funneled to state parties, which spend them on voter registration drives and on "issue ads" that often espouse a viewpoint toward a federal candidate. Although this spending occurs at the state level, it is controlled by or coordinated with federal parties and candidates. Because soft-money donations have no upper limits, they typically come from unions, corporations and individuals that have already reached their annual limit of hard-money donations. Soft money thus permits contributors and candidates to skirt funding regulations and frees up hard money for federal campaigns. Soft-money donations many times the hard-money limits—$100,000, $250,000 or even $1 million—are common. By the end of the 2000 presidential campaign, the Democratic and Republican national party committees had raised a record $457 million in soft-money donations—almost twice the $231 million raised by the two parties during the previous presidential election cycle.[42]

Corporations, ideological and citizens' groups and their PACs all hire experts to lobby for their agendas during meetings with members of Congress and presidential staff members. A recent reform, the Lobbyist Disclosure Act of 1995, requires people who spend more than 20 percent of their time lobbying Congress or the executive branch to register and reveal their expenses as well as the issues they advocate.[43] As a result, the huge amounts of money that special-interest groups spend to promote their agendas have become a matter of public record. Analyses by the Center for Responsive Politics, a nonprofit campaign reform group, show that the final years of the twentieth century were a time of rapid growth in the lobbying industry. About 15,000 registered lobbyists operated in Washington in September 1997; their ranks had increased to 20,500 by mid-1999. Expenditures by the special-interest groups that hire lobbyists (corporations, unions and ideological groups) have naturally risen as well, from $1.26 billion in 1997 to $1.42 billion in

1999. For each member of Congress in 1998, there were 38 registered lobbyists and $2.7 million in lobbying expenditures.[44]

Soft money and excessive lobbying corrupt for a simple and obvious reason: The corporations and other groups that donate and
lobby have learned to expect returns in the form of tax breaks, ear-
marked appropriations or action on legislation important to the
group. For these special-interest groups, donating soft money and
lobbying have become the price of doing business with the government. We believe these activities are especially insidious because
they exploit the human tendency to process information selectively.
When small groups spend money and time to secure relatively unre-
stricted access to the government, they limit the voices that members of Congress hear regularly.

Contributions and Votes: The Story Behind Corporate Welfare

> What Senator Lott and his colleagues have done today is public health malprac-
> tice, plain and simple. Ignoring the advice of every health professional in
> America, they have chosen to listen only to a handful of television ads and a lot
> of PAC committees.
>
> —Former U.S. Surgeon General Dr. C. Everett Koop, June 17, 1998[45]

Big Tobacco took a roller coaster ride in 1998. When the year
began, cigarette manufacturers were pushing hard for a "global settlement" to end their liability suits with more than forty states. When
Congress began considering a bill that added to the settlement, the
companies changed course and fought the legislation with all their
might. The antismoking bill sponsored by Senator John McCain of
Arizona would have settled all the states' smoking-related lawsuits and
included a landmark provision to allow the Food and Drug
Administration (FDA) to regulate nicotine as a drug. If this legislation
had passed, it would have been devastating to the tobacco industry.

In June 1998, Senate Republican leaders Trent Lott and Mitch
McConnell organized the votes needed for a filibuster to delay a

vote on the McCain bill indefinitely. Traditionally, a filibuster meant endless speechifying on the floor of the Senate by members trying to blockade a vote on a bill they expected would otherwise pass; it was not uncommon for legislators to set up cots on the Senate floor as they participated in all-night filibusters. These stalling tactics were successful if they eventually prevented the bill from reaching a vote. In recent years, there have been no actual filibusters; the mere threat of one is enough to provoke a vote of "cloture" to override it. Cloture is a vote to limit the debate on a bill; sixty senators must vote to end the filibuster for a cloture vote to be successful. In this instance, supporters of the McCain bill were three shy of the sixty votes needed. A minority of senators, forty-two, were able to kill the bill.

Senator McCain attributed the defeat in part to the tobacco industry's use of "protection money" in the form of campaign contributions.[46] Indeed, the statistics paint a powerful picture of donations followed by rewards. During the three most recent election cycles, the forty-two senators who voted to kill the bill received an average of $20,761 each from tobacco industry PAC contributions. The fifty-seven senators who voted for cloture received noticeably less— an average of $4,970.[47] All told, tobacco PACs and industry employees donated $1.6 million to Senate campaigns between 1993 and 1998. Also between 1993 and 1998, Senator McConnell, who fought the McCain bill so strenuously, was the third highest recipient in the Senate of contributions from tobacco PACs and individuals who work in the industry. McConnell was given $86,575 during this period; only Jesse Helms and Lauch Faircloth, the two senators from North Carolina and both stalwart tobacco supporters, received more ($118,950 and $117,486 respectively from 1993 to 1998).[48]

The link between tobacco donations and pro-tobacco votes is no less compelling in the House of Representatives. In July 1997, Representative Nita Lowey of New York proposed an amendment to the 1997 Department of Agriculture spending bill that would have eliminated crop insurance and noninsured crop disaster assistance for tobacco farmers. The amendment was defeated by a 216–209 vote. The top nine House recipients of campaign contributions from tobacco PACs and individual employees during 1997–1998 *all* voted against cutting these wasteful and unwarranted subsidies. The nine representatives all served tobacco-growing states (Kentucky, North Carolina and Virginia), and the amounts they received during this one election cycle ranged from $16,900 to $45,000.[49]

So far, we have been talking about hard money. In the 1999–2000 election cycle, the tobacco industry contributed $3.88 million in soft money to the Republican and Democratic national political parties. The Republicans received 88 percent of these funds.[50]

Attempts to sway congressional opinion don't end with political campaigns. The tobacco companies' 1998 lobbying bills shattered all previous industry records. When the McCain tobacco bill became a real threat, the industry spared no expense to protect its interests in Congress. Industry spending on lobbying increased 1.8 times from 1997 to 1998, from $38.2 million to $67.4 million; this moved the tobacco industry as a whole up from eighth place in 1997 to fourth in 1998. The industry leaders, British American Tobacco and Philip Morris, ranked nos. 1 and 2 as the biggest individual spenders among *all* industries in 1998. Tobacco's lobbying efforts were all the more notable given that the industry focuses on a much narrower set of issues than other highly active groups such as the American Medical Association and the Business Roundtable.[51] Congress is hit hard and often by the tobacco industry in the weeks leading up to an important vote.

The tobacco industry is hardly the only special-interest group that use campaign dollars and lobbyists to garner tax breaks and subsidies. The mining industry spent more than $12 million on lobbying and campaign contributions in 1997 and 1998. Of this amount, more than $2.5 million came in the form of soft-money donations to the national parties, with more than $2 million of this amount going to the Republicans.[52] This marks a considerable increase from the 1993–1994 election, when the industry gave a little over $500,000 to the Republicans. Hard money PAC contributions to individual federal candidates totaled nearly $1.4 million during the

1997–1998 election cycle.[53] The mining industry spent far more on lobbying than on campaign contributions–$9.2 million in 1998 alone. As with tobacco, this amount is particularly high given the limited scope of the industry's concerns. When these numbers are taken into account, it becomes easier to understand why every attempt to reform the Mining Law of 1872 has failed.

Concerning the timber industry, representatives of Western states have cited plenty of reasons for their steadfast support of logging interests, among them their desire to keep the local economy afloat and create jobs. An additional reason might be the big contributions they receive from the timber and paper industries' PACs each election cycle. During the 1997–1998 cycle, timber company PACs and individual employees contributed a total of $4,480,627 in hard and soft money to congressional campaigns and national parties. Timber companies also spent $11.7 million on federal lobbying in 1998.

When a vote to cut the funding for logging roads was proposed in the House in July 1997, pro-timber forces fought reform by passing an amendment to the bill that was much softer on industry. The top ten House recipients of campaign contributions from timber PACs and individual employees all voted to protect logging interests from large subsidy cuts. These representatives, primarily from Western states, received between $13,872 and $31,942 each during the 1997–1998 election cycle.[54] In the Senate, Democratic Senator Richard Brian of Nevada proposed an amendment to the Department of the Interior's 1998 spending bill that would have ended logging road credits for timber and paper companies. The amendment was defeated by a 51–49 vote. The top ten Senate recipients of timber industry PAC and individual campaign contributions *all* voted against ending logging road subsidies. These senators had received between $66,874 and $404,515 from logging special-interest groups from 1993 to 1998.

The strong correlation between campaign contributions, lobbying expenses and congressional votes on tobacco bills does not by itself prove that the votes are "bought." But it does appear that Congress is susceptible to making decisions based on the selective processing of information provided by a relatively few—but powerful—groups and individuals.

The cases of tobacco, timber and mining are just three examples of the ways in which money, once it enters the political system, has the power to corrupt everyone it touches. The system today is unfair to everyone involved. Many politicians are distressed by the amount of time they must devote to fund-raising, which they must carry out by making endless strings of phone calls to potential donors and attending countless dinners and other special events. While many candidates find such groveling demeaning, they realize that they can't get elected without the expensive television ads that have been so successful at influencing voters. Politicians are even more upset by the moral dilemmas that soft money donations create. "I continue to vote my conscience, but I realize that each vote affects your fund-raising," Senator Dick Durbin of Illinois told journalist Elizabeth Drew. "If the system isn't corrupt, it's corrupting. It forces you into compromising yourself."[55] By giving unfair advantage to incumbent candidates, the system is also antithetical to democracy. During the 1998 congressional campaigns, House incumbents received nearly ten times more money from PACs than their challengers, and Senate incumbents received almost nine times more than theirs. No surprise, then, that 98 percent of House incumbents and 90 percent of Senate incumbents were re-elected.[56]

Big business has grown weary of the incessant badgering for increasingly larger donations. A nonpartisan group called the Committee for Economic Development (CED), whose members include executives from companies such as General Motors, Xerox and Sara Lee, has endorsed stricter campaign funding laws. "The business community, by and large, has been the provider of soft money," said the committee's president, Charles Kolb. "These people are saying: 'We're tired of being hit up and shaken down.' Politics ought to be about something besides hitting up companies for more and more money."[57]

In September 1999, CED members were targeted by Senator Mitch McConnell in his fight against campaign finance reform. In a

letter sent to CED members, McConnell accused the group of trying to "eviscerate private sector participation in politics" through
"anti-business speech controls."[58] In another letter, McConnell told
an executive that his CED membership was damaging his company's reputation. McConnell reportedly scrawled "I hope you re-
sign from CED" at the bottom of yet another letter to a senior executive. Many of these executives work for companies that had
important issues pending before Congress at the time the letters
were sent, and they believed McConnell was trying to intimidate
them. But by attracting media attention, the letter-writing campaign
may have backfired. "I think most of the people at CED have figured out just how corrupt the campaign finance system is, and this
letter is just an example of what they already knew," commented
member Edward A. Kangas.

The group that loses the most under the present system is the one
group that cannot be considered a special interest—the American
public. Consider this: Fewer than 1 percent of Americans give more
than $200 to political candidates.[59] This means that the vast majority
of the $457 million in soft money raised by the national parties for
the 2000 election was donated by a tiny minority of American citizens and organizations.

In short, except for a small group of frightened legislators who
can't imagine how they will win a campaign without soft money, almost everyone wishes the system would change. The Senate's
McCain-Feingold bill (written by the deliberately bipartisan duo of
Republican John McCain and Democrat Russell Feingold of
Wisconsin) has called for bans on soft money, tightened limits on
PAC donations, restricted issue ads and free television time to congressional candidates who are willing to restrain their campaign
spending. When it seemed likely that the bill would pass, anti-re-
formers including Lott and McConnell worked furiously to sink it
through "poison pill" amendments they knew the other side could
not support. Filibusters on both sides caused the bill to be buried in
late 1997. This drama played out in an almost identical manner at
the end of 1999, when McConnell once again was able to rally all

but eight of his fellow Republicans behind a filibuster of McCain-Feingold. The House version of the bill, known as Shays-Meehan (under the sponsorship of Republican Christopher Shays of Connecticut and Democrat Marty Meehan of Massachusetts), passed in both 1998 and 1999; but because of the Senate defeats, no reform was passed.

In documenting the problem of special-interest groups that inappropriately influence government, we have focused primarily on the tainting influence of corporate money because these examples are so vivid and egregious. Corporations are not the only factions that try to rally politicians to their various causes. As professors, we are well aware of the intense lobbying efforts universities in the United States must undertake to gain research funding from Congress.

In 1999, members of Congress dedicated a record $797 million in earmarked funds for academic research.[60] These projects bypass the traditional sources of federal funding for research, the National Science Foundation (NSF) and the National Institutes of Health (NIH); each of these institutions conduct rigorous reviews in which scientists assess the merits of proposed projects and fund them accordingly. By contrast, federal earmarks are based on the ability of hired lobbyists to influence legislators. Many schools have found it easier to appeal to Congress for money than to have their faculties spend time writing detailed proposals for NIH and NSF funding. Thus many research projects are receiving funds based on influence rather than merit.

Members of congressional appropriations committees have been particularly successful at securing research funding for projects in their home states. Between 1980 and 1996, the University of Hawaii received $197 million in academic earmarks, more than any other school; Senator Daniel Inouye of Hawaii is a longtime member of the Appropriations Committee. The University of Pittsburgh, the alma mater of a longtime member of the House Appropriations Committee, Pennsylvania's John P. Murtha, received $151 million; the university was the second-largest academic recipient of earmarks during this period.[61]

Many of the projects funded by earmarks, such as a plan to harness the power of the aurora borealis in Alaska, are of dubious merit. Yet it is impossible to judge their importance because they are not subject to scientific scrutiny. The best way to fix this situation is to do away with academic earmarking altogether. If these research projects truly deserve the millions of taxpayer dollars being thrown at them, then the budgets of the NSF and NIH should be increased to accommodate them.

So far, our discussion of special-interest groups has been limited to their influence in the United States. We conclude the chapter by considering how the self-interested actions of a labor union have affected German society and the Earth's population as a whole.

The Case of German Coal

Between 1956 and 1980, employment in German coal mines went into a steep decline. With the goal of creating jobs and increasing reliance on a domestic energy source, the German government persuaded the country's electricity suppliers to burn expensive German coal exclusively instead of imported oil. To encourage electricity suppliers to use coal, the government subsidized coal mining. The cost of the subsidy was covered by a tax on electricity. By 1986, the mines had become so heavily subsidized that German coal was selling at three times the world market rate.

This situation is not unique; Mexico, Nigeria, Venezuela and Spain all subsidize coal in various ways. Aside from the questionable practice of using taxpayer dollars to favor particular energy sources, artificially low prices reduce consumers' incentive to save energy, resulting in increased emissions. When coal is burned, it releases carbon into the atmosphere; carbon contributes to the greenhouse effect, and ultimately, most experts agree, to the warming of the Earth's atmosphere (see Chapter 7).

During the early 1990s, under pressure from other European countries to create a more equitable and environmentally sound energy policy, the German government began to look for a way to cut its coal subsidy. The first problem was that if the subsidy were cut off completely, coal production would decline by 75 percent;[62] only 25 percent of production would be efficient enough to compete with other sources of energy (including imported coal). The number of coal workers would decline drastically, from 250,000 to 31,000. By 1992, the average coal worker earned the American equivalent of $36,000 per year—yet if the taxpayer subsidy had been funneled directly to workers, they would have been earning $92,000. The government could have saved money by switching to a cheaper form of energy and paying the coal workers $36,000 to do nothing.

After the electricity tax was declared unconstitutional in 1994, the coal subsidy was instead taken out of general funds (and from contributions of the coal-producing states of Saarland and North-Rhine/Westphalia). In addition, the Kohl administration proposed funding reductions that would cut mining jobs from 85,000 to 35,000 by the year 2005. In March 1997, led by their union, IG Bergbau, coal miners gathered in Bonn to protest Kohl's plan. They were willing to scale back jobs, but they refused to go lower than 45,000.

During the three days that Chancellor Kohl negotiated with the head of the union, up to 15,000 miners demonstrated in Bonn and about twice as many in Saarland, the heart of the mining region. On March 11, miners blocked the main road through the capital's government center, then traveled to the nearby city of Cologne to camp out in a stadium while negotiations continued. Their primary concern was the preservation of jobs: "Where will we work, when everything is closed?" asked miner Peter Kloss.[63] Descended from generations of miners, he and his colleagues knew no other means of survival.

A compromise sent the miners home victorious. The total federal mining subsidy through 2005 was increased from the government's original offer of DM 56.6 billion (about $34 billion) by DM 1.65 billion, and an additional DM 1.75 billion was pledged by the state government of North Rhine/Westphalia.[64] By 2005, annual subsidies were to be set at DM 5.5 billion. The miners did not get everything

they wanted: Mining jobs in 2005 were expected to decrease to between 35,000 and 45,000.

Were the demonstrations effective from the point of view of individual miners? Conservatively, we can estimate that each miner lost a
day of work during the protests. If the protesters had met their goal,
about 11 percent of the 85,000 existing jobs, or 10,000, would have
been saved. As it turned out, they gained only 6 percent of the jobs
over eight years. Some of the miners would retire or stop working for
another reason during this time, so the savings might be closer to ten
years saved for 5 percent of the currently employed miners. Thus the
benefit of the protest would amount to six months per miner, perhaps even as much as 200 days of work. That amount is certainly
worth a day or two of lost wages to attend the demonstration.

So far we have considered the impact of the group of protesting
miners on each miner. Now let's consider the impact of each individual miner on the agreement, under the assumption that the gains
of the protest were proportional to its size. (This must be roughly
true, as there would have been no gains if no one had protested.)
Did each miner benefit substantially from his own participation in
the demonstration, or would he have been better off staying at
home and letting his comrades protest on his behalf? If only 10,000
miners were involved in the Bonn protest (the actual number was
higher), then each protestor contributed one ten-thousandth of the
group's total gains. Similarly, each miner contributed one ten-thousandth of his personal gains from the protest, or one ten-thousandth of his extra 200 days of work. That works out to 2 percent of
one day, or about ten minutes saved.

Why the difference between 200 days and ten minutes gained?
From the perspective of the group, each miner's contribution was
worth the effort; by working together, the group gained 200 days per
miner. But each individual contributed only ten minutes per miner,
including himself. If a miner was concerned only about himself and
not about the other miners, the day or two spent protesting was a
waste of time. Better to let the 9,999 other miners earn his 199-plus
days for him and sacrifice the ten minutes he would earn for him-

self. He might as well take off work and go to a soccer game instead of camping out in a soccer stadium.

This is a classic social dilemma. While it is often in the best immediate interest of one member of a group to look out only for himself, the group as a whole will be better off if individuals choose instead to cooperate. In this case, each miner is better off staying home (and even going to work, if possible), but each miner who participates in the protest improves the lot of miners as a group.

When we consider the environmental and economic burdens of a continued reliance on coal as the dominant energy supply, we realize that all Germans—and all citizens of the Earth—are hurt by the actions of this special-interest group. This situation results in the curious coincidence of the narrow self-interest of the individual miner with the largest interest of society. It would have been better for everyone if each miner had acted selfishly and stayed home. Then the government, unmoved by political protests, might have spent less money subsidizing mines and more money on projects that would benefit society, such as researching alternative energy sources or investing in the development of the former East Germany.

Appeals to participate in organized activities often promote confusion about allegiance to the self versus the group. For example, the Newspaper Guild (affiliated with the Communications Workers of America) argues:

YOUR VOICE COUNTS!

Sometimes you may think that the voice of an individual doesn't count for much. "What does it matter if I join or not?"

While your membership in the Guild is confidential, management is very aware of the total number of members, so every member counts.

A union with more members can do: more. It's as simple as that.

There's more protection for our jobs, our salaries and our benefits.

That's why the Guild has joined with other media unions in the Communications Workers of America family of unions. Now print, broadcast and electronic media employees are coming together in one union.

It's the only way the voice of the employee can be heard and made stronger in this era of mega-mergers and media giants.

Check out what the Guild won—including 9 percent wage increases—what it lost, and what it protected you from when the current contract was negotiated.[65]

Notice the slippage from the question of self-interest to the issue of group benefit as the appeal moves seamlessly from "you" ("your voice") to "we" ("our jobs"). The danger of such appeals is that they encourage individuals to believe that self-sacrifice for the group is in their own self-interest.

The same dilemma occurs when company executives lobby against pollution regulations or donate to the political campaigns of those they hope will support their group. Their political action takes time and money away from other activities, thus hurting themselves and their company. They help the group of companies that pollute, but—as in any social dilemma—the harm to themselves is greater than the share of the pie received by the group. Because they also harm everyone who suffers from pollution, the net effect of their action is negative. If they were more selfish, or at least more concerned with the narrow interest of their particular company rather than the group it belongs to, we would all be better off.

We are not arguing in this chapter that people should be ruthlessly selfish. Rather, they should think about their membership in the largest group possible—the human race—when making individual decisions that have an economic, social or environmental impact. The more people who do this, the easier it will be to solve the problems that plague society as a whole, such as global warming.

Citizens must begin to support candidates who demand tightened regulations on election funding and lobbying activities. Only through these reforms can politicians fully meet their responsibilities as our representatives. This means they must create policies to benefit the populace that votes for them on election day, and avoid policies that benefit the special-interest groups who put money in their campaign accounts and whisper in their ears during the annual budget session.

5

Live for the Moment

IN JULY 1997, ONE HUNDRED CANADIAN FISHERS BLOCKADED AN
American ferry headed for Alaska. Three hundred passengers and
crew were stranded onboard the ferry for three days. This militaristic
action resulted from disputes between the two countries over
salmon harvesting levels. Negotiations between the Canadian and
American delegations to the Pacific Salmon Commission over each
nation's harvesting limits had recently broken down. In the absence
of agreed-upon limits, Alaskan fishers had gradually tripled their
catch of salmon; the Canadians retaliated with the blockade.

Two years earlier, a Canadian patrol boat fired machine gun shells
across the bow of a Spanish trawler and illegally seized the ship. The
Spanish ships had been legally harvesting turbot, a fish that used to
be unwanted bycatch (throw-aways), more than two hundred miles
off of the Newfoundland coast. The Canadians asserted that the
Spaniards' "theft" was depleting the fish stocks close to their coastal
waters. The Spaniards countered that it was Newfoundland's own
mismanagement that was causing shortages.

Canada is not a particularly militaristic society. Why then is it so easy to find examples of Canadians acting in such radical ways? It turns out that such aggressive behavior is not so rare when it comes to fish. In recent years, Vietnamese have shot at Thai fishers, the Malaysian navy has fired on a Thai trawler, Russians have shot at Japanese fishers, the Philippine navy has arrested Chinese fishers, Ireland has arrested a Japanese tuna-boat captain, Iceland has used force to exclude Danish trawlers from its waters, Australian forces have seized many Indonesian boats and a Portuguese naval ship has fired on a Spanish fishing boat.[1] In December 2000, fishers of spiny lobsters off the Galápagos Islands ransacked the Darwin Research Station's laboratory, where scientists monitor the effects of quotas. The director's dinghy was hijacked as he was commuting to work, computers were destroyed and the Ecuadorian navy's special forces had to rescue two employees who, "fearing for their lives, had taken refuge in mangrove swamps."[2] This behavior is part of the mounting economic and social disruption that will become increasingly common as the world over-harvests the oceans.[3] Fishers around the world are running into the manmade problem of overharvesting, the result of too many well-equipped boats chasing after too few fish. Species that were once plentiful have now disappeared, and people have adapted to lower-quality fish as a food source. Now even undesirable fish have begun to disappear. As this pattern repeats itself across the globe, 200 million jobs, a world resource and peace between nations are at risk.

Despite their assertions that they care about the long-term impact of their choices, decision makers often overweight present concerns; as a result, they demonstrate a shocking disregard for the effects of their behavior on future generations. This phenomenon results from selfishness and from the human psychological tendency to discount the future. In this chapter, we look at the worldwide fishing crisis, specifically the failure of the New England fisheries, as a vivid example of an intergenerational social dilemma. We will also explore how urban sprawl and other pressing policy issues have grown out of short-term thinking.

The New England Fishery

When the explorer John Cabot arrived at the Grand Banks off the coast of Massachusetts in the early 1500s, he described them as "swarming with fish that could be taken not only with a net but in baskets let down with a stone."[4] For the next 460-plus years, fishing was plentiful off the coast of New England. As humans developed better technology, fishers caught more and more fish. The oceans seemed limitless.

Limits were discovered in the 1960s, when factory trawlers from around the world began emptying the oceans with improved technology and higher fishing capacities subsidized by their respective governments. These trawlers destroyed one fishing area by clearing it of fish, then moved on to another. In 1974, more than 1,000 foreign trawlers captured 2.2 million tons of valuable groundfish off the New England coast, ten times the American catch. Debates arose over the ownership of the oceans. In 1976, the American government passed the Magnuson Fishery Conservation and Management Act, consistent with the worldwide Law of the Sea treaty. This act, like others around the world, cut back on competition between nations by extending coastal waters to two hundred miles and allowing countries to evict foreign fishers.[5]

Despite these improvements, the Law of the Sea did not eliminate competition *within* nations and did not lead to wise stewardship of the oceans. In 1977, the New England Council adopted fishing quotas on cod, haddock and yellowtail flounder; in 1982, the council dropped the quotas when pressured by fishers who insisted they were no longer needed. Another setback followed when the American government provided New England fishers with low-interest loans to increase their capacity so that they could keep up with consumer demand after the foreign boats departed. Between 1982 and 1986, the fishing capacity of the New England fleets grew—and yet the cod harvest on Georges Banks dropped 50 percent.[6] A fishery that had yielded over 50,000 tons of haddock annually in the 1960s gave a mere 880 tons in 1993. This was one of the first signs that something had gone drastically wrong.

In the past few decades, fishers have become amazingly effective at catching whatever fish are out there. They are less effective at making sure fish are there to catch. Fishers are quite capable of wiping out entire fish populations and then moving on, usually to less attractive species. As halibut, haddock and cod disappeared from the Grand Banks, fishers switched to dogfish, skate, monkfish and other species that used to be considered bycatch. Similarly, bluefin tuna fishers went after swordfish, then yellowfin tuna as swordfish stocks were depleted. Although some have argued that the evolution of jobs from one species to another is natural, it is important to note the consistent pattern has been lower quality and prices. Another important indicator of overharvesting is that the average size of the fish caught is shrinking. Anne McGinn of the Worldwatch Institute says that consumers are now down to eating the babies.[7] Without a change in policy, all commercially viable fish will disappear from the coast of New England.

Vaughn Anthony, a scientist with the National Marine Fisheries Service on Cape Cod, was among the increasing ranks of scientists in the 1980s who argued that overfishing was the root cause of the lower harvest. Anthony's warnings were not taken seriously. Meetings were held to discuss the problem, but at every turn, the fishers fought off regulation and denied that action was needed. Their irrational denial of the problem prevented them from seeing that their own livelihoods, not to mention their children's futures, were at stake.

By the early 1990s, more and more scientists and finally the American government accepted overharvesting as an undeniable reality off the New England coast, but the fishers continued to fight regulation of their right to earn a living. The dispute was positioned as fish versus jobs, and the jobs won. But the focus on jobs obscured the true debate. The real dispute was between short-term thinking and long-term thinking; unfortunately, the victory of short-term thinking may be permanent. Halibut and haddock are now commercially extinct. When Canada closed its cod fishery in 1993, 40,000 jobs were lost. American cod quotas were cut close to zero in 1994.

The ecosystem that supported the cod is irrevocably altered and the fish may never return.

The situation on the East Coast reflects the depletion of fish populations worldwide. Fishing has traditionally been regarded as an unlimited industry. As technology improved, the world's annual marine harvest grew dramatically in the twentieth century, from 3 million tons in 1900 to 21 million tons in 1950 to about 80 million tons in recent years. From 1970 to 1990, the world fishing fleet doubled, to 3 million vessels. These data create the appearance of a healthy industry, but they are deceiving. The boom is not sustainable; the candle is burning at both ends.

Eleven of the world's fifteen major fishing areas and nearly 70 percent of the most desirable species of fish are in decline. Atlantic cod harvests dropped 69 percent between 1968 and 1992, and West Atlantic bluefin tuna (one of the most valuable fish in the world) dropped by more than 80 percent between 1970 and 1993 as a result of fishers' ignoring the warning signs of depletion. Sharks off the southeast coast of the United States are now following the same path. Bluefin tuna of the South Pacific has declined by 90 percent since the early 1960s. The size of swordfish caught in the North Atlantic has shrunk by 65 percent in the last thirty-five years.

The pattern of devastation around the world has been predictable. First, improved technology and more funding allow capacity to increase. These advances typically result in unsustainable amounts of fish being caught. As a result, scientists note that populations are threatened; fishers dispute the evidence and fight the scientists. Then, as fish populations are ruined, fishers move on to less attractive species and other locations. Although world fish harvests have increased, the harvests of highly valued species have decreased by 25 percent since the early 1990s.[8]

The Causes of Intergenerational Dilemmas

Our literature has taught us to romanticize fishing as a fundamental battle between man and nature. Books such as Melville's *Moby Dick* and Hemingway's *The Old Man and the Sea* glorify the awesome ability of marine creatures to fight head-to-head with man. But such stories are outdated. Today, fish no longer stand a chance.

Government subsidies are arguably the leading threat to the world's fish populations.[9] Through tax incentives, low-interest loans and direct subsidies, governments have become key contributors to overharvesting.[10] Their aid encourages fishers either to remain in or to enter an overcapitalized fishery, "masking the true costs of overcapacity and postponing the day of reckoning."[11] Currently, fishers all over the world are operating at huge losses. For every American dollar earned worldwide from fishing in the late 1980s, governments, taxpayers and fishers spent $1.77. By 1989, direct and indirect subsidies came to $54 billion against revenues estimated at $70 billion.[12] In addition to distorting markets, these actions increase overcapacity and speed up the destruction of the fishing basin. Although the United States has eliminated incentives for fleet expansion, we still exempt fishing from fuel taxes and provide special tax deferment for fishers. More important, we allow fishers to benefit free of charge from a national and world resource. As a result, in good years, fishers expand their capacity. In bad years, they lobby for, and receive, government support. Half the world's fishing vessels could be eliminated without a reduction in potential harvest.[13] Too many boats are chasing too few fish. The result is an absurdly inefficient situation: Nations spend citizens' tax dollars to build numerous well-equipped boats, but the value of fish available to consumers steadily decreases.

In fields such as medicine, technological advances promise a healthier future for mankind and nature. This is not the case with fishing. While treaties in the 1970s limited the destruction caused by global competition, international organizations such as the World Bank fueled the problem by providing funds for more boats and better technology, thus increasing the capacity of humans to catch fish beyond sustainable levels. International aid created modernized fishing fleets with better equipment for tracking fish and better infrastructure for handling the fish at the docks. Schools of fish are tracked by radar, sonar, spotter planes and satellites. When fish are spotted, catching them is routine. Trawlers release long lines with up to 3,000 hooks and drift nets that carpet the ocean floor and destroy large swaths of sea-bottom ecologies. Trawlers are able to harvest all the fish in a given area, gathering unimaginable quantities by using a technique that is often compared to strip mining. Worldwide, however, trawling covers an area fifty times that of strip mining.[14]

Like other modern fishing techniques, trawling shrinks the pie of social resources through its massive bycatch. Every year, 27 million tons of bycatch are caught, against 80 million tons of regular commercial catch.[15] Bycatch—fish that are the wrong species, too small, damaged in the harvesting process or that exceed the boat's quota—are tossed back into the ocean, usually dead or dying. In the worst cases, 15 tons of bycatch are discarded for every ton of shrimp and prawn taken. Before a public outcry in 1990, 500,000 dolphins a year were killed as bycatch in tuna harvesting.[16] Because it is so obviously wasteful, bycatch is a particularly vivid result of the failure to enlarge the pie of societal resources. It parallels the waste commonly seen in shark harvesting: Fishers catch a shark, carve off its fins for shark-fin soup and then dump the animal back into the ocean to die a painful death. In this case, the fins are the target catch, and the shark's body is bycatch.

Because the wasteful intake of bycatch inflicts an inefficient harm upon the rest of society, it cries out for government intervention. The United Nations Food and Agriculture Organization argues that 60 percent of bycatch can be saved through changes to fishing gear, by greater cooperation between fishers and scientists and by new technology.[17] These changes would give the sea an opportunity to replenish itself and become much more productive for humans and fish alike.

The Decisions We Make

Many wise solutions to the fishery crisis have been proposed, but they are always defeated by fishers and other groups with a stake in continuing destructive overharvesting. Why are wise solutions so rarely accepted? We argue that flawed human decision making lies at the root of the world fishery crisis. These fundamental failures in judgment must first be addressed if we hope to develop a realistic plan to solve the problem.

Common sense tells us that if fishers would simply harvest fewer fish, the remaining fish would have the chance to reproduce, thereby regenerating their species and providing a healthy supply of catch for these and future fishers. Why do humans instead continue to behave so self-destructively? One answer, consistent with the social dilemma (tragedy of the commons) concept we introduced in Chapter 3, is that each fisher has the incentive to harvest as much as possible to maximize profits. When individual fishers act this way, all the fishers in the fishing basin end up worse off because together they have depleted the supply of fish. This is a classic social dilemma. Similarly, each nation can justify subsidizing its fishing fleet to gain a competitive advantage. But when all nations behave this way, they all end up worse off. Regulations and treaties may be reasonable strategies for solving social dilemmas, but special-interest groups have been very effective at blocking such common-sense solutions.

The fishing crisis is a unique type of social dilemma: an intergenerational dilemma.[18] While the benefits of fishing are immediate, the costs of overfishing accrue in the future. Some of these costs are borne by fishers who must work harder in the next season (often the same fishers who overfish) or by consumers who must pay more for fish. But when a fishery is depleted, future generations are deprived of the fish as well. The typical result of such intergenerational dilemmas is tremendous discounting of the future based on wishful thinking.

Discounting the Future.   A special aspect of the fishing dilemma, in comparison to many other social dilemmas, is that society should have the added goal of enlarging the pie over the long term. We should be motivated to preserve fish populations beyond the lives of existing humans, so that future generations will benefit from thriving oceans and an adequate fish supply. Yet the fishers who defect in the present social dilemma are gaining immediate benefits in exchange for long-term hardships for themselves and others, many of whom have not yet been born. The fishing problem is in part an intergenerational dilemma because ensuring a sustainable supply of fish for future generations requires sacrifices in the present: lower incomes for fishers, changing employment patterns, fewer boats. But according to Herman Daly, we are acting as if our oceans "were a business in liquidation."[19] Although people generally believe that we ought to pass on to future inhabitants the resources and systems of the natural environment in as good a state as we inherited them, our actions with respect to the ocean are highly inconsistent with this view.

Why do fishers so consistently resist coordinated efforts to reduce the total catch? Because decision makers have a general tendency to deny the long-term effects of their behavior. When they focus on the present, people are likely to discount the future, even if they would personally reap all the benefits of taking future interests into account. A high discount rate may work against an individual's own self-interest, or he or she may be myopic on an intergenerational, global scale.[20] When environmental issues are at stake, both aspects may occur.

The tendency to overweight the present at the expense of the future pervades human decisions. For example, homeowners often do not insulate their homes adequately and do not buy energy-efficient appliances if they are more expensive—even when the homeowner would earn the extra costs back in less than a year, save money in the long run and help conserve natural resources. A lack of information about energy efficiency is one factor in these decisions, but even well-informed consumers underinvest in the energy efficiency of their homes. Well-managed and well-informed organizations also overly discount the future. When one of the best universities in the world began an extensive effort to improve its infrastructure, it chose a limited construction budget over long-term cost-efficient products.[21] As a result, the university passed on returns of over 25 percent—returns that its investment group would have been thrilled to receive.

Members of the Financial Executives Institute view overweighting of the present at the expense of the future by investors and managers as the greatest threat to global competition.[22] Researchers Elizabeth Mannix and George Loewenstein blame high discount rates for the failure of business to invest in the long term, for a lack of concern for customer loyalty, and for low rates of investment in research and development.[23] According to this view, business decision makers are maximizing present gains at the expense of potential future benefits. Similarly, fishers grab as many fish as they can now—a relatively small amount compared to the much larger future catch they are sacrificing. It can also be argued that overweighting the present is not only foolish but also immoral, because it robs opportunities and resources from future generations. According to this view, we have a moral obligation to remember future inhabitants of the earth; we should consider them as parties at the negotiation table when we make decisions.

Wishful Thinking About the Future.   Much of our tendency to overly discount the future comes from wishful thinking in an uncertain environment. Psychologists have found that people view themselves, the world and the future in a considerably more positive light than reality can sustain. In one study, most subjects believed they had a better-than-average chance of living past eighty.[24] Psychologists have also found that subjects who bet on sporting events are likely to bet on the team they hope will win, even if the odds are stacked against them.[25] In these cases and others, people tend to believe that the future will be better and brighter than they should reasonably expect.[26] These positive illusions enhance and protect self-esteem, increase personal contentment, and help individuals persist at difficult tasks and cope with aversive and uncontrollable events. But wishful thinking has its drawbacks; it can lead decision makers to deny that a problem exists and requires their attention, often until it is too late.

Fishers are motivated to believe that the scientists are wrong—that the oceans are not being depleted and there is no need for tighter regulations. "You base everything you tell us on what you really don't know," one fisher said on the television show *Frontline.* "It kind of bothers us fishermen. We're going to be told we've got to do all this stuff, but nobody knows anything. Doesn't make much sense. You guys have got some jobs, but I don't think we're going to have any if you keep on. Save the fish, but what about the people?"[27] This complaint highlights a fundamental problem: Decisions made about the future will always contain some degree of uncertainty. Uncertainty leaves room wishful thinking, but unfortunately, reality is too often deaf to our wishes.

Wishful thinking is related to the status quo bias we discussed in Chapter 1. Fishers under pressure to change their behavior nonetheless try to hold onto the status quo, which they believe would allow them to maintain their current catch. Insisting that the scientists are flat-out wrong, the fishers cling to the positive illusion that they need make no adjustment to their behavior for the fish supply to improve. Small changes in their fishing practices now could prevent the serious changes that will undoubtedly occur—such as the loss of their jobs—if they continue to ignore the reality.

Finally, wishful thinking often reflects a desire to deny that you are part of the problem. When a problem becomes so big that it can no longer be ignored, wishful thinking leads us to blame others and let ourselves off the hook. After American fishers have managed to fend off efforts to regulate the domestic fishing basin and the fish have disappeared, they can then blame the government for handing out subsidies and for not instituting regulations earlier, or they can blame foreign trawlers for depleting the fish—all of which are true. The key issue here is that without taking responsibility and supporting new, constructive government policy, the American fishers will never admit that changes in their own collective behavior could help alleviate the problems they are creating.

Solving the Fishing Crisis

Because the seas have for centuries seemed limitless, they have historically been open to all. Fishers developed their own laws of the sea, which included maritime codes, traditional systems of cooperative management and communal codes of conduct. These rules often deterred overfishing. Modern fishing agreements have failed to address the ongoing conflict between open access and exclusive fishing rights. Now, more than ever, these conflicts must be resolved. The stakes are much higher because many populations of fish are in danger of extinction. McGinn argues that "without reforming the underlying causes of overfishing—namely, overcapacity and open access—fisheries and fishers are doomed to a desperate future."

Over the last half century, the world has terribly mismanaged the seas. "Countries are fighting over shares of a declining resource," argues Michael Sutton of the World Wildlife Fund. "What gets lost is the fact that the resource is disappearing."[28] Before this resource completely disappears, we must act quickly to find solutions.

Perhaps the most obvious of all recommendations is to work toward an international agreement to bar countries from subsidizing their fishing fleets. Currently, nations spend over $50 billion per year to destroy their own long-term fishing interests. A more sensible system would tax the fishing industry for the resources they are taking from common ownership than to continue to subsidize them for doing so. It would be insufficient for any one nation to singly eliminate subsidies, as other nations would continue to subsidize the long-term destruction of the resource. Only joint agreement allows the parties to take the action that will increase the long-term welfare of all nations. Because special-interest groups would fight such an agreement, restraints would have to be placed on their lobbying attempts.

The other main ingredient of a long-term solution to overharvesting is restricting access to fish supplies. We need to establish an appropriate harvesting level and identify strategies that encourage fishers to fish up to, but not beyond, this maximum sustainable yield.

The maximum sustainable yield is a fishing quota that sets an equilibrium between a fish population's ability to reproduce and the value of the fish harvested. Conceptually, this level balances current harvest against the future productivity of the species.

There are two general approaches to reducing harvests. One is to regulate or tax the behavior of fishers to prevent them from depleting the oceans. The political left usually prefers regulation and taxation. The alternative is to provide property rights to the ocean; owners would then have a greater incentive to manage their resources. The political right usually prefers property rights. But this is a secondary debate. Any sensible strategy that can predictably improve the condition of the oceans is superior to current mismanagement.

Regulation

If we choose the regulatory path, we must make sure that the regulations we adopt are strong and enforceable. Too often, weak regulations occur too late to save the resource and are the result of illogical compromises rather than the creative development of a workable plan. Again and again, compromise regulations have delayed overharvesting but have not stopped it. For example, the international agreement that created two-hundred-mile coastal zones in the 1970s decreased global competition for fish. Unfortunately, most countries, including the United States, did too little to regulate their own fishers within the two-hundred-mile zone; turning a blind eye led to the loss of halibut and haddock, and probably cod, swordfish, shark and many other valuable species.

To reverse the depletion of fish species, future regulations must be tough and must logically lead to a sustainable harvest. Whether regulations are based on tonnage, fishing time or location should depend on the fishing basin in question. Most important, the overall level should not be based on a political compromise that leads to harvesting above the sustainable level; such agreements simply delay the eventual collapse of the basin.

Regulations must also be enacted to stop the destruction of marine environments by the fishing industry. Vessels should be held accountable for the devastation they cause to fisheries, a marine equivalent of the "polluter pays" principle.[29] This means that when a trawler clears a fishing area of marine life, or pollutes it, the owners should be fined for the devastation they have caused to fish resources and the ecosystem. These penalties would motivate fishers to adopt environmentally sound technology. If the fishers don't pay for the losses, someone else must. In the case of effects on biological diversity, the payers are future generations as well as our own.

Many people find regulation comforting because this is how the problem has been approached in the past. At the same time, policymakers have been tempted to cut special deals and enact compromises that make past and present regulations ineffectual. Legislators, negotiators, environmentalists and the fishing community have failed to manage the oceans competently. Compromise regulation would be a long-term recipe for disaster. If we cannot adopt tough, conservative regulations, we will have to look for alternatives.

Taxation

Another way for governments to control the behavior of individuals and organizations is through taxation. Economists argue that taxes make the most sense when the actions of certain parties impose negative effects (or "negative externalities") on the rest of society. Thus, gasoline should be taxed at a level that would effectively pay society for the negative externalities of pollution and overcrowded highways. When taxes are imposed appropriately, they motivate economic actors to modify their behavior to the degree that maximizes the cumulative good to society. New taxes on the catching and sale of fish could lead to voluntary cutbacks by fishers and force consumers to pay for the full social costs of consuming fish.

Property Rights and Local Ownership

The alternative to tough government regulation and taxation is to create ownership over the fish in the ocean, so that fishing groups will care enough about their resource to manage it for the long term. If the oceans and coastal areas were under some degree of local control or ownership and not open to all comers, fishers would have more incentive to preserve their shares of the resource. If mobility is reduced across fishing basins, fishers in any one basin will be more accountable for their actions. The group would have to be made aware that the opportunity to manage its portion of the ocean comes with risk, and that mismanagement will not be followed by government relief.

Property rights are most commonly administered by a government's issuing tradable permits to existing fishers based on their current harvest; the total of all permits will add up to the maximum sustainable harvest. Obviously, setting the level of total permits is crucial to sustainability.

Property rights can take various forms. In some cases, a single fisher or company is assigned the rights to a part of a fishery within a country's jurisdiction. The most publicized of the schemes is "individual transferable quotas," or ITQs. An ITQ bestows the right to harvest a certain fixed volume or share of fish in a particular area and time. Because the quotas can be bought and sold on the market, inefficient fishers can sell their rights to others and leave the industry. This trading often creates a concentration of ITQs in the hands of the few who can afford them. ITQs exist in Australia, Canada, Iceland, the Netherlands and New Zealand. In the United States, ITQs are in effect in several American fisheries, including the Alaskan halibut and sablefish fisheries. ITQs have helped correct economic inefficiencies in fisheries by encouraging the withdrawal of excess vessels from the industry. While property rights solutions attract criticism, their overall record indicates an improvement in most fisheries.[30]

James Marsh, a specialist in ocean economics, extends the property rights solution by suggesting that a single organization or a small group of organizations could be granted ownership of the world's population of a certain species of fish. The money from the sale of fishing enterprises would be given to the groups that have given up ownership rights.[31] Shares in these new ownership organizations could then be publicly traded. Fishers, environmentalists and others would be free to buy the corporation's shares and thus influence the behavior of the fishing company as owners of stock. Although these organizations would be free to sell rights to fish, owners would be motivated to protect their species of fish.

Property rights can also be given to a local community. Sociologist Elinor Ostrom has noted that some communities manage social dilemmas over resources for long periods.[32] When fishers in Alanya, Turkey, faced a declining harvest, their local fishing cooperative developed a long-term solution by identifying all the fishers in the basin and assigning each a specific location for a specific day. The locations then rotate, and the fishers enforce the system through informal and formal penalties. As a consequence, the best locations are not overharvested. Similarly, Pacific Islander fish populations have succeeded through detailed, site-specific boundaries that define fishing grounds and enforce strict limits on how fishing is conducted. Community-based systems effectively deter overfishing because they encompass a broader belief system that values the sea not only for the food and sustenance it provides but for the role it plays in the community's history and cultural identity.

In Turkey, community-based management has been so successful that it is being rewarded by the government. The Turkish government has given the Alanya cooperative jurisdiction over local fishing arrangements, which lends credibility to its participants and helps legitimize traditional management systems. Similarly, the Filipino government devolved management of near-shore fisheries to municipalities and local fishing communities in 1991. The change has helped keep fishery management responsive to local development needs; in turn, cooperatives provide fishers with supplemental income projects and with credit, lending and marketing services. Ostrom argues that community-based solutions are most likely to be successful when they have definite boundaries, rules appropriate to the local conditions and culture, democratic participation, and mechanisms for monitoring, enforcement and conflict resolution.

Solutions to the problems of fisheries—the taxation of fishers, increased regulation and local ownership—are inherently political, but they need not be stereotypically left or right. The most important goal is the creation of policies that enlarge the pie of social resources over the long term. We encourage the parties involved to debate proposed solutions to specific depletion problems in specific areas. Rather than search for a compromise solution that passes off the problem into the future, the debate should take up multiple strategies that are expected to bring about positive change.

How can individuals contribute to the solution rather than remain part of the problem? First, do not eat declining species, such as East Coast haddock and cod, swordfish and red snapper from the Gulf. When one is standing at the seafood counter, it can be difficult to remember which species from which regions have been overharvested, but several conservation groups are trying to minimize consumers' confusion. The Marine Stewardship Council, an international not-for-profit organization that promotes responsible fishing practices worldwide, plans to help citizens select responsibly harvested fish by awarding a special product logo to well-managed and sustainable fisheries. In addition, the Monterey Bay Aquarium and the National Audubon Society have created detailed, up-to-date consumer seafood guides and posted them on their Web sites: www.mbayaq.org and www.magazine.audubon.org/seafood/guide.

Individuals can also write letters to fishery decision makers, including politicians, government officials in charge of fisheries, large commercial fishers and environmental groups. In addition, we can research the views of politicians toward the fishing crisis and vote accordingly. We can also create collective action. Not long ago, public outcry over dolphins being caught as bycatch led to a fundamental shift in the way tuna are caught. We hope the chefs who are currently refusing to serve swordfish, an overharvested fish, will draw attention to this cause. But deeper and broader collective action is needed.

Citizens can also play an important role in holding fishers responsible for their political actions. It is not reasonable to expect fishers to turn away from what they are legally allowed to take. But it is reasonable to hold fishers responsible for their efforts to stall wise systems that will manage the oceans in a sustainable manner. For too long, we have allowed those in the fishing community to fight and weaken regulation; then we have bailed them out when their destructive practices ruined their own livelihoods. We need a new system that calls on fishers to support sustainable management or else be considered an enemy that must be controlled.

The Connection Between Fishing and Commuting

The global fishing crisis and the act of driving from the suburbs to your job in the city may seem to be worlds apart. Yet each contributes to the devastation of the natural environment. The development of urban sprawl, its dysfunctional aspects and possible solutions to the problems it has created parallel the fishing crisis.

In recent decades, our living standards have improved dramatically in many ways. Commuting to work is not one of them. Traffic is getting worse as years go by: A higher percentage of workers drive to work, and more of them drive alone; fewer walk, bicycle or use public transportation; and average commuting time has increased.[33] Although the cars being built today are more environmentally sound than older cars, total air pollution from cars has not decreased substantially and has even increased in some cities.[34]

The problem is worldwide. Large cities in developing countries such as Sao Paolo, Bangkok and Cairo are plagued by massive traffic jams and deadly air pollution. Among highly developed countries, the United States may suffer most from traffic and its side effects because of the extensive development of its suburbs. In Atlanta, Georgia, most commuters spend more than half an hour getting to work; as that time increases, so does air pollution. Atlanta has been denied federal funds for highways because it is in violation of the Clean Air Act. "It's not just the commute," says Richard Skinner, president of Clayton State College, in Atlanta's southern suburbs. "It's that it takes so goddamn long to get anywhere. To go to a cocktail party in Atlanta on a Friday, you start early in the afternoon or you don't get there." As the governor of Georgia, Roy Barnes, put it, "People in Atlanta are just tired of sitting in cars."[35]

Are the side effects of urban sprawl a legitimate problem in the United States? Writer Gregg Easterbrook argues that they are not. "Everybody wishes there were fewer cars on the road, fewer strip malls, and less demand for living space or commercial square footage. But how do you discourage such things without denying a place at the table to those who have not yet been seated? . . . As an issue, sprawl can also sound awfully similar to exclusionary zoning and other pull-up-the-ladder ideas that comfortable communities have used in the past to keep out unwanted minorities and immigrants. One person's green space preservation is another's denied housing permit."[36]

This free-market argument is deceptive. Automobile travel is heavily subsidized by taxpayers, including those who don't own cars. The biggest subsidy is the building of freeways, which are far more prevalent than unsubsidized, user-funded toll roads. Although drivers do pay for their own fuel, the protection of oil imports has repeatedly been offered as a reason for maintaining large military forces. A portion of the military budget can be viewed as the cost of delivering cheap fuel to American consumers—a subsidy for fuel users.

The commuting problem is the same type of intergenerational social dilemma we saw in the fishing industry: Each driver, like each fisher, is achieving an immediate benefit at the long-term expense of society. The more people use the resource, the more they devalue it. Each additional driver on the road slows other drivers and increases the pollution to which everyone is exposed. While commuters exercise their political power to demand more roads, few lobby for increased public transport to make cities more livable. The situation becomes worse every day as drivers refuse to consider the future costs of their behavior and as the government continues to fund this destruction of the environment.

Like the fishing dilemma, the commuting problem benefits current users at the expense of future users. The choices we make today lock in our lifestyle for future generations by making it more costly for them to change. Roads, once built, last for decades or even centuries. Future generations will find it cheaper to maintain them and use them than to develop alternatives, such as public transportation or more livable urban areas. Thus, because of our decisions, many will continue to spend 15 percent of their waking lives sitting in traffic.

The commuting and fishing dilemmas differ in important ways. In the early stages of overfishing, the price of fish rises; this gives fishers an incentive to increase their catch. By contrast, as commuting increases, drivers face the adverse effects of overcrowding from the opening day of a new freeway. This difference means that drivers have a stronger motivation than fishers to alter their behavior in positive ways, such as switching to public transportation. Another difference is that the effect of overfishing is simply to deplete fish populations; the effects of driving are more complex. Driving creates air pollution, which has an immediate effect on everyone. In the long run, by reducing demand for public transportation, driving makes the construction of new transit systems less economical.

A Solution

We have discussed how private ownership of fisheries could encourage responsible behavior among fishers. Similarly, the private ownership of roads may be one useful solution for urban traffic and air pollution. If roads became private property sold on the open market, drivers would be expected to pay for use of the road; this would generate enough money for a return on the costs of buying the land and building roads. In the same way, if the purchase of oil were handled entirely by the market, consumers would have to pay for the troops needed to secure the oil supply, just as banks pay for armed guards.

Modern technology has made it practical for drivers to pay for the use of privately owned roads. This solution has been adopted in several foreign cities—including Singapore, Rotterdam and Hong

Kong—and even uses technology dating as far back as 1963.[37] Electronic devices could detect when a driver uses a certain road and send a bill from the road's owner or deduct the cost from a bank account. Like telephone usage, costs could be adjusted according to the time of day, thus speeding the flow of traffic during rush hours by encouraging people to drive at other times. The road's owner would use funds collected to maintain roads and build new ones. This proposed solution is similar to the notion of fisheries' being owned by groups of fishers who sell a limited amount of fishing licenses.

Under this proposal, road costs currently absorbed by nondrivers would be transferred to drivers. As a result, drivers would be forced to think more seriously about their commuting behavior. For many, it would become less expensive to rely on public transportation than to drive to work each day. The value of housing and parking near train stations would increase; and as public transit systems came closer to breaking even, they could use their increased revenues for more frequent trains and buses and better maintenance.

What are the objections to such a scheme? First, drivers balk at the notion of paying for roads. In a survey of people's willingness to pay tolls to decrease congestion, John Calfee and Clifford Winston found that commuters were willing to pay less than $4 for every hour of driving saved.[38] This amount depended only slightly on income, and it was not affected by how the money would be used. These results are consistent with commuters' responses to the Dulles Greenway toll road, which opened in October 1995; motorists pay a one-way toll of $1.75 between Leesburg and Washington Dulles International Airport and save as much as twenty minutes on the trip. When motorists complained that the toll was too high, it was cut to $1.00 to attract more of them.[39] Now it is back up to $1.75, and the idea finally seems to be catching on.[40] Creative incentives such as "smart tags," an electronic system that charges tolls to drivers' credit cards without making them stop at a toll booth, give drivers a twenty-five-cent reduction in the toll.

Drivers receive substantial benefit from these schemes, perhaps enough to make the payment worthwhile. First, pollution is reduced, which cuts back health risks to drivers. Second, because time spent in traffic is hard on cars and wastes gas, when commuting times are lowered, the extra expense of the toll is recouped through less spending on gasoline and car maintenance.

Despite these benefits, people resist such plans. First, they complain that their privacy would be infringed upon if data on their driving patterns were available on a computer. One might wonder why people are so opposed to this, yet accept that information about their credit card purchases, ATM transactions, airline tickets and telephone and Internet usage are all computerized. An additional slight invasion of privacy seems a small loss in exchange for larger gains. Perhaps because of the status quo bias, people exaggerate the effect of new losses.

Others complain that the cost of new tolls would be an unfair burden on the poor. This objection could be easily overcome by allowing the poor to pay reduced fees, as they do for electricity and other utilities. In this case, costs of public transportation should also be reduced to keep it an attractive option. The effect on the poor would be a small loss suffered in exchange for a larger gain. This loss is particularly small because many of the truly poor do not own cars and already rely on public transportation, or they are unemployed and do not commute at all.

The third objection comes from those who resist the idea of switching from driving to taking public transportation. In this case, the status quo bias also appears to be an important effect. Of course, some people live so far from reliable public transport that they cannot take advantage of its benefits. But many of those who do live nearby still get in their cars and slog through traffic every day. Those who balk at the notion of taking the train or the bus, citing inconvenience and reduced privacy, have often failed even to look at the benefits of public transportation. Being a passenger rather than a driver frees time to read or work during the commute. People also resist the idea of moving closer to where they work without considering such benefits as extra time and lower travel costs.

In sum, we believe that most people would prefer a system of privately owned roads and user fees if they were willing to give it a chance. This requires accepting various small losses in return for larger gains, both immediate and long term. In the long run, the availability of convenient public transport of the sort that exists in many European cities and in Singapore will lure people away from their cars. We are not asking people to change their preferences. We are asking that they support public policies that will, in the long run, improve most people's lives.

Beyond Fish and Commuting

Overfishing and automobile commuting both illustrate the broad human tendency to seek immediate benefits at the expense of long-term benefits for everyone. While we believe that both crises will cause great harm to future generations if they continue unchecked, we do see some encouraging signs that these trends can be reversed. An example of a successful response to air pollution is the Montreal Protocol of 1987. In 1974, chemists F. Sherwood Rowland and Mario Molina found that chlorofluorocarbons (CFCs) were transported to the upper atmosphere, where they broke down the ozone molecules that shield the earth from ultraviolet radiation and contributed to global warming (a topic we will explore in depth in Chapter 7). Because CFCs do not break down spontaneously, their effects are long lasting. In 1985, scientists observed a pronounced reduction of the ozone layer over Antarctica (the "ozone hole"), which was believed to be caused by the use of CFCs in aerosol cans, by plastic manufacturing and (as freon) by refrigerators and air conditioners. Many countries soon banned the use of CFCs.

In 1987, representatives of twenty-four nations and the European Economic Community met in Montreal and agreed to reduce the production and use of CFCs and other ozone-destroying chemicals.

The agreement made provisions for developing countries, which were allowed more time and given some assistance in converting to CFC substitutes, and also called for frequent reviews based on scientific evidence. These reviews have resulted in several more agreements and some speeding up of CFC reductions. The treaty is working: The production of CFCs has been replaced with alternative, less harmful chemicals.

The same approach can be applied to solve the problem of overfishing, and specifically to the attempts of the United States and Canada to solve their differences regarding the fishing of salmon on the Pacific Coast. Salmon stocks have declined as much as 96 percent over the past twenty-five years because of overfishing, climatic changes and habitat degradation in the North Pacific Ocean.[41] Decreased prices for wild salmon have in part resulted from the widespread use of hatcheries, manmade structures created for the harvesting of salmon eggs. Since the 1950s, nearly 2 billion hatchery fish have been released into Puget Sound tributaries in an attempt to stave off salmon extinction. Raised in captivity, hatchery fish often lack the survival instincts necessary to live in the wild, and they pass their weak genes on to wild fish.[42] As the quality of salmon decreased and supplies remained low, the pie over which both countries were fighting became quite small. The overall value of the Pacific salmon fishery had been reduced to just half its worth in 1996, when fishers received about $650 million for their catch.[43] In 1999, 25,000 naturally spawning chinook salmon were returning to Puget Sound rivers to spawn; a healthy population would be double in size.[44] It should not be surprising that this situation led to disputes between the United States and Canada over boundaries and harvesting procedures for salmon. These tensions culminated in the 1997 Canadian blockade of an American fishing boat.

To the pleasant surprise of many observers, the two countries were able to negotiate an unprecedented agreement that could very well resolve the Pacific salmon crisis. On June 3, 1999, the United States and Canada announced a pact that was expected to end the decades of dispute. The main tenet of the agreement was the establishment of a flexible fishing quota based on the abundance of fish rather than on fixed annual limits. This quota employs a technique that responds to large fluctuations in runs of the five species of salmon in the North Pacific. The agreement will permit larger harvests in years of abundance and smaller harvests in lean years. Experts predict that, overall, the salmon catch will be reduced anywhere from 5 to 50 percent, depending on the stock. The pact will also reduce the American share of the total Pacific salmon harvest to 16.5 percent, down from an average of 20.5 percent. This change reflects the historical tendency of American fishers to take more than their share of salmon. Because both countries acknowledge that Canada is owed compensation, the United States will solely finance the pact. Funds will be administered jointly by the countries to aid in the recovery of threatened salmon species and the management of fisheries.

Economic, environmental and political factors all contributed to this complex agreement, which makes use of the type of wise trades we advocated in Chapter 2. This agreement also confronted the past mistakes of overweighting the present and discounting the future. As a result, the agreement creates value for both nations over time. The new quota system means that fishers have an incentive to keep their catch low so that salmon populations have a chance to increase, allowing quotas to rise over time. The countries are also adopting unilateral environmental measures aimed at improving salmon stocks. Canada's fisheries minister, David Anderson, imposed a virtual ban on all fishing for coho salmon. Canada also undertook a $260 million program to preserve the salmon habitat, improve research and buy up fishing licenses. Similarly, the citizens of Seattle and the surrounding area have committed themselves to making small sacrifices so that the chinook, chum and sockeye salmon can be taken off the Endangered Species Act's list. Decades of habitat damage have been caused not only by fishers but by residents who have logged the headwaters and banks of rivers, dammed their flow, built on flood plains and polluted and developed estuaries. Taxpayers and utility ratepayers will have to pay hundreds of millions of dollars to correct some of this damage and help save these salmon species from extinction. The focus of the United States and Canada, as they commit to restoring healthy populations of salmon in the Pacific Ocean, is no longer on dividing the pie but on enlarging it.

Both the CFC and salmon initiatives suggest that once we, as a society, understand the severity of an environmental problem, we can overcome short-term thinking and enact long-term solutions. As these recent solutions begin to show signs of success, we hope that they will lead to more innovative solutions to the dilemmas of over-fishing and air pollution.

6

No Pain for Us,
No Gain for Them

WHEN THE WORLD TRADE ORGANIZATION (WTO) HELD ITS ANNUAL
meeting in Seattle in December 1999, it placed an upcoming series
of "Millenial Round" talks high on the agenda. A few years ago,
the WTO's summit entered the public consciousness, if at all, only
through the back pages of the *Financial Times* and the *Wall Street
Journal*. The Seattle meeting, by contrast, received front-page press
around the world, thanks to the thousands of people who turned
out to voice their opposition to free trade. The two-day demonstrations included a 25,000-strong march, a traffic-blocking sit-in
and the vandalism of numerous businesses in downtown Seattle
by self-described "anarchists." The protests brought the WTO to a
temporary standstill and trapped various dignitaries, including
U.N. Secretary-General Kofi Annan and U.S. Secretary of State
Madeleine Albright, in their hotel rooms. As protestors were

hauled off to jail, common thieves stepped in to loot the vandalized stores.

Though a long-time advocate of free trade, President Clinton arrived at the meeting and, taking his cue from the protestors, called on the WTO to increase its openness and set labor standards among its member countries—or face trade sanctions. Representatives from developing countries such as India, Egypt and Brazil were infuriated by Clinton's tough new line. When the delegates were finally able to congregate, their anger led to dissension and inaction. They returned home discouraged and exhausted, having accomplished none of their goals.[1]

Just who were these activists and anarchists who succeeded in bringing the world's largest trade body to a standstill? The protestors were a patchwork of special-interest groups and included environmentalists who accuse free trade of destroying nature, nationalists who fear the homogenization of world culture and labor union members and sympathizers who think free trade eliminates jobs in developed countries and exploits workers in emerging nations. While these special-interest groups, known as nongovernmental organizations (NGOs), often claim to represent the disenfranchised, they typically focus on only a small part of a larger social problem. For this reason, their programs may in the end harm those they seek to help.

The NGOs succeeded in placing the previously murky issue of free trade in the forefront of people's consciousness. Most of these activists were well meaning, and their causes are certainly worthy of our concern and attention. Still, we believe that most of these groups are looking at the issue too narrowly. By citing specific labor and environmental causes as reasons for blocking trade agreements, they have failed to recognize larger opportunities for gain. NGOs typically disregard what is perhaps the most important benefit of open trade: its ability to alleviate poverty worldwide. The goals of protecting American jobs and creating new environmental restrictions usually conflict with the preferences of poor countries that are eager to become active participants in the world market.

As we have seen in previous chapters, some social tradeoffs benefit all interested parties, but other wise policy changes hurt some groups or individuals while helping others. A change in policy or law can be considered good when its benefit is large relative to its cost. Effective government makes choices that provide large gains, even when these gains are accompanied by small losses to some. The losers will object to such changes, and even those who view the problem from the outside are often reluctant to impose losses on some for the benefit of others. We argue that if governments were organized to take full advantage of wise tradeoffs, rich and poor alike would be better off in the long run.

In this chapter, we will consider those difficult cases in which we as citizens are faced with an opportunity to help a large number of people, but not ourselves. Our assistance may instead require sacrifices. By recognizing that certain widespread social benefits inevitably require a smaller group to be harmed, we will become more willing to trade off small losses for large gains. We make such tradeoffs already; almost every policy change involves some harm. Government policies that are designed to redistribute goods will inevitably hurt some while helping others. Our goal is to identify what the economist Joseph Stiglitz calls "near-Pareto improvements"–changes that will harm only a small special-interest group while improving the lives of a much larger group of people.[2]

We make no judgments about how much sacrifice people should be willing to absorb. This chapter is concerned with efficiency, not altruism. Developed nations are engaged in many projects aimed at helping developing countries, yet too many of these activities are inefficient. Whenever society requires someone to make a sacrifice for the greater good, the goal should be to maximize benefit and minimize harm. In return for the costs we are willing to bear or impose on others, we must strive to achieve the greatest benefit.

We have explored examples of this principle already–such as industries and societies that accept small profit losses now to preserve natural resources for future generations. In this chapter, we focus on two important and related social initiatives–expanding global trade and reducing poverty—and show how rich rewards can be obtained for many people worldwide without requiring any more sacrifices than we are now willing to impose on ourselves and others. We will propose twelve relatively inexpensive ways of helping the poor and discuss the benefits that free trade brings them.

We look back on slavery as the great moral outrage of the nineteenth century. In the twentieth century, two outrages existed and now threaten to spill into the twenty-first century: genocide and the neglect of the world's poor by the rich. The twentieth century will go down in history as a time when people in rich countries acquired a standard of living beyond the wildest dreams of past utopians while doing little to share this wealth with the world's poor. Like genocide, poverty has been tolerated because of human beings' lack of concern for the suffering we fail to prevent—a phenomenon we have discussed throughout the book. By failing to recognize inaction on behalf of the needy as a harm, we have missed countless opportunities to reduce poverty at little cost.

Many efficient ways of helping the poor—from providing vaccines and vitamins to developing nations, to enriching the education of toddlers in the United States—have been neglected. Similarly, we have failed to take full advantage of the opportunities to be gained from relaxing trade regulations, subsidies and protections. Free trade prevents war, increases efficiency, cuts inflation through price competition and thus makes better goods and services available to everyone. While loosened trade restrictions will cause some people to lose their jobs, and may have environmental costs, free trade will bring about greater long-term benefits to all, including the creation of jobs for workers around the world and the eventual promise of a cleaner environment through improved technology.

Poor nations have begun to demand a voice in global trade negotiations, but they will not accomplish their goals without the help of the wealthy. Those who are better off must be willing to do two things to improve society as a whole. First, as they have learned to do already, they must accept small financial sacrifices, whether in the form of contributions or taxes. Second, they must take an interest in poverty, wherever it occurs, as a policy problem and voice their political concerns on behalf of the poor. When solutions to these complex problems are efficient, the loss to the rich will be much smaller than the gain to the poor; small amounts of money and other goods will have greater value to the poor, who now have so little. Much can be done to help the poor with no greater sacrifice than the effort required to initiate change.

An Argument for Free Trade

In 1993, upon invitation from Canada and the United States, Mexico joined the North American Free Trade Agreement (NAFTA), a pact that calls for the gradual elimination of tariffs and other trade barriers on most goods made and sold in North America. Since then, many trade barriers within and outside of Mexico have been lifted. Because Mexico suffered a major financial crisis and a deep recession soon after the agreement was passed, the effects of its membership in NAFTA were at first difficult to estimate. Now, almost a decade later, we can say with certainty that trade between the three countries has increased substantially and has led to an overall improvement in the Mexican economy.[3] There is evidence that the agreement has also benefited the American economy through lower prices, higher productivity and enough new jobs to replace those that were lost.

One big loser has been the American Brussels sprout industry. A small group with little political clout, the American Brussels sprout farmers, mostly Californians, can meet in a small office. Since NAFTA, Californian farmers have suffered as a growing percentage of the Brussels sprouts consumed by Americans has been imported from Mexico. "It's simple math," said Steve Bontadelli, one of the farmers. "In Mexico, they pay workers $6 a day. That's what we're paying per hour. We just can't keep up." Bontadelli formed the letter "L" on his forehead with his index finger and thumb. "That's me," he said. "Loser." Aside from the competitive advantage gained by Mexican Brussels sprout farmers following NAFTA, a major contributor to the slump faced by their American counterparts are low sales: The average American eats just three Brussels sprouts per year.[4]

The American government entered into NAFTA with the goal of improving the national economy. But what happens when an agreement of this kind results in lost jobs for local workers such as the Brussels sprout farmers? The effects of trade agreements on society and the economy are difficult but not impossible to measure.

The Costs and Benefits of Free Trade

Although theories about foreign trade date back to the fifteenth century, the current increase in global trade began after the end of World War II. In 1948, 23 nations actively engaged in world trade, including the United States, signed the General Agreement on Tariffs and Trade (GATT), which aimed to eliminate trade barriers. Between 1948 and 1995, as membership rose to 123 nations, GATT brought about the reduction of many tariffs worldwide. During its final series of talks, known as the Uruguay Round, GATT member nations committed themselves to eventually cutting existing tariffs by one-third and eliminating other trade restrictions. As the talks ended in 1994, GATT activities were taken over by the World Trade Organization (WTO), a new international body designed to promote and enforce trade laws and regulations. The WTO expanded GATT beyond merchandise goods to include trade in services and the protection of intellectual property, and also made its rules legally binding for member nations.

One of the primary costs of trade expansion is that it restricts the ability of governments to regulate business. For example, if a country passes a law that protects the environment or the rights of workers (through, say, a minimum wage standard), producers in that country will lose sales to those in countries without such laws, assuming that conformance to these laws raises production costs. These sales losses would not occur if the producers did not compete with foreign producers in any market. Thus, free trade sometimes forces governments to choose between the local regulation of jobs and the environment and local prosperity. Many of the activists at the 1999 Seattle meeting were protesting the WTO's ability to overrule the decisions of democracies on labor and environmental matters.

Another cost of imposing "new" free-trade agreements is the creation of short-term harm. As competition increases between nations, jobs are inevitably lost, such as those of the American Brussels sprout farmers. In theory, net losses of jobs from free trade are not great. Studies have found that the creation of low-wage jobs in poor countries does not depress wages in rich countries.[5] But the short-term effects of trade expansion can inflict real pain. A regimen of constantly expanding trade over a long period causes repeated job losses for specific groups such as American farmers and factory workers.

Free trade is most commonly supported by basic economic arguments. First, proponents argue that open trade affords citizens the opportunity to choose from a wider array of goods. According to this view, trade restrictions are unfair because they limit consumers' choices. Thus, if a producer in country A can make something that buyers in country B will want—because of its uniqueness, quality or price—the producer should be allowed to sell its product and reap the rewards. The theory of "absolute advantage," developed by the British economist Adam Smith, suggests that those nations best equipped to produce and sell a certain good should not be prohibited from doing so by artificial barriers such as tariffs and quotas. Both the importing and the exporting countries are hurt by such barriers—the exporter because it loses sales, the importer because it must now either replace the goods at a higher cost or do without. Free trade among nations allows each country to specialize in what it does best rather than waste labor and other resources by producing things that it produces relatively inefficiently.

Another British economist, David Ricardo, expanded Smith's notion of "absolute advantage" to the principle of "comparative advantage," one of the great insights of economic theory and a second argument in support of free trade. Acknowledging that some nations lack an absolute advantage in the production of any commodity, Ricardo argued that even these nations could benefit from free trade by producing and exporting those goods or services in which they have the smallest disadvantage. Each nation has an incentive to trade whatever goods it can produce and sell with the least cost in labor and resources, relative to other goods that sell for the same price. Even if a nation required substantial labor and other resources to produce anything at all, it would still choose to produce some goods over others. By selling these goods, it could make money to buy other goods, which would require even more labor to produce. The participation of less advanced nations in the marketplace also allows more advanced nations to concentrate on producing the goods in which their comparative advantage is greatest. As worldwide production increases, the wealth of all nations can be expected to increase as currency values—and hence prices—adjust themselves, and every nation establishes a valued role in the marketplace.

A third argument for free trade is that it is believed to prevent war among nations by creating a constituency of citizens who oppose war. This may be the most important argument. A particular trade agreement may be unlikely to prevent a war, but a worldwide régime of free trade may reduce the overall risk of war, thus reducing the enormous human and monetary costs of war. This is an old argument that has been recently supported by statistical analyses. The expansion of international trade in the last fifty years has corresponded with a marked decline of war among nations, especially among the more economically developed countries.[6]

Fourth, advocates of free trade argue that trade limits based on national borders are arbitrary. The main arguments against expanded free trade among nations—local autonomy and short-term harm—are just as relevant to contraction of free trade among states or provinces, yet they are not applied at these local levels. The economic success of the United States would have been impossible without free trade among the various states. This principle is enshrined in the Constitution, which gives the federal government the sole power to regulate interstate commerce. Because the arguments made against international free trade can be applied to states within a union such as the United States, does this mean that the United

States should allow states to erect internal trade barriers? On the contrary: The efficiency of trade within countries suggests that trade expansion between nations will be equally successful.

Most economists believe that the advantages of free trade outweigh the disadvantages. So much for the theories. What about the facts? Historical trends support the view that free trade is directly related to economic prosperity. The Smoot-Hawley Tariff Act of 1930, which inflated American tariffs of imported goods up to 59 percent, has been blamed for making the Great Depression far worse than it would have been otherwise. In Europe, protectionist policies during this era are believed to have turned a worldwide recession into economic disaster and to have played a part in the outbreak of World War II. Conversely, loosened trade restrictions in the second half of the century have been closely correlated with global economic growth. Trade expansion is credited with the phenomenal postwar recoveries of Germany and Japan. The WTO claims that trade liberalization since World War II has been a major factor in lifting an estimated 3 billion people out of poverty.

In recent decades, the standard of living in Asian countries such as South Korea, Singapore and Malaysia rose dramatically following their entrance into the world marketplace.[7] One study determined that open economies have grown an average of 2.5 percent faster than closed economies, with even greater differences observed among developing countries.[8] If current average tariff rates were halved, the result could be a global increase in output of $450 billion per year—an extra $75 per person, or more than a month's income in many developing countries.[9] Small wonder, then, that the World Bank, an organization whose primary goal is stamping out poverty, advocates the widespread liberalization of trade regulations.

Of course, it can be difficult to state definitively that certain trade agreements are chiefly responsible for such social and economic benefits. The main benefit of free trade—and its primary goal—is its ability to keep prices down. We can expect other benefits as well, but these are difficult to extricate from the effects of decisions made as a result of increased trade. For example, in the United States, free trade enables the Federal Reserve Bank to set interest rates lower than it would otherwise, with less danger of inflation, thus stimulating employment. Opponents of free trade can easily point to jobs lost when factories relocate to developing nations. It is more difficult to attribute free trade to the creation of new jobs at home because the effect of trade on jobs is indirect. Trade increases price competition, which keeps prices low. Thus, the central bank does not have to worry a great deal about inflation, and it can lower interest rates. If the bank keeps rates lower than they would be without free trade, new businesses can borrow money more easily and create more new jobs. Thus the correlation between increased trade, low interest rates and job creation appears quite strong.

In sum, history suggests that the short-term upheaval caused by international trade agreements is worth the long-term expected gain of increased peace and prosperity. Returning to the North American Brussels sprout farmers, here is what we can expect to happen. Because the Mexican crop costs less, Americans will continue to eat more Mexican than American Brussels sprouts. Steve Bontadelli and the other American farmers will eventually give up on Brussels sprouts and find a crop they can produce more efficiently than the Mexicans—or perhaps they will give up farming altogether and find other lines of work. Meanwhile, with the American farmers out of the market, the Mexican farmers will find their profits growing. As profits increase and more Mexican land is cultivated with Brussels sprouts, eventually the workers will demand, and receive, higher wages. Both the Mexican farmers and their employees will buy more goods, including American goods, with their higher wages. As the Mexican economy grows more prosperous, its businesses, consumers and government will demand and receive more goods and services from the United States, including such expensive high-tech products as airplanes and telecommunication systems, which American workers will be called on to supply.

Ultimately, almost everyone is likely to benefit from the more efficient delegation of Brussels sprout farming to the Mexicans. The path from here to there will inevitably cause some people to suffer, and some of those affected may not live long enough to reap the compensating reward. Although we will never be happy about imposing losses on people, preventing these natural processes would impose greater losses upon us all.

Why We Resist Beneficial Trade Agreements

Even when they understand that the benefits of increased trade outweigh its harms, many people still oppose new agreements. Why? Because they worry more about harms caused by action than about those caused by inaction. We have called this the omission bias, and in Chapter 1 we saw how it works against the introduction of beneficial drugs and vaccines.[10]

In an experiment designed to assess people's opinions about free trade, subjects opposed to NAFTA said that trade agreements should not be approved if they cause some people to lose jobs, even if the agreements prevent many more job losses then they cause. When asked whether they would approve an agreement that would "cause 10,000 job losses in the U.S. but prevent 11,000 job losses in the U.S. over the same time period" (with no other effects and with jobs of the same type), NAFTA opponents, more than others, tended to oppose the agreement.[11] This opposition reflects the irrational human desire to avoid harmful actions even when they produce overall gains.

The omission bias is particularly common when inaction harms people of other nations, whom we tend to consider outside our zone of responsibility. We can think of this as a second bias: nationalism. In psychological terms, nationalism is a type of parochialism, or narrow loyalty to one's group. Because it reflects a greater concern for one group over other groups, nationalism can be thought of as a prejudice. Now that racism and sexism are widely condemned, nationalism is perhaps the last type of prejudice to be widely tolerated. This bias often takes subtle forms. In the study described above, a later question asked, "Suppose that a trade agreement would cause job gains in Mexico and job losses in the U.S., and no other effects. The gains in Mexico would be ten times the losses in the U.S. The jobs in question would mean just as much to the Mexican workers as to the U.S. workers. Would you favor such an agreement?"

Three-quarters of the respondents (American students), including almost all of the NAFTA opponents, said no. A typical reason was "Because we should not enter an agreement where we lose jobs."[12]

Note the use of "we." This pronoun can refer to any group of which the speaker is a member, from a couple to the entire human race. In discussions of public policy, "we" usually refers to co-nationals. Why do we tend to limit our group membership to the country we live in? Because nationalism has become a hidden, unquestioned assumption of the way people think about policy questions. Nationalism allows people's moral obligations to others, as expressed in their political behavior, to end at the border. Some subjects in this study felt no discomfort over sacrificing ten Mexican jobs for every American job.

In the same study, subjects were asked if they would favor the hypothetical agreement if they were living in a third country. Three-quarters of them said yes. We also asked whether they would support an agreement involving Pennsylvania (where the study was done) and another state within the United States, in which Pennsylvanians would lose a certain amount of jobs but those in the other state would gain ten times as many. Most subjects favored this agreement. One said, "This agreement would hurt Pennsylvania, but it would greatly help the economy of the whole country, so I would support it. I realize the implications of this last question, and it makes a valid point: If different countries could work together and look out for the benefits of the whole world, as the states of America are united, then everyone would benefit."

This is our point exactly. To enlarge the pie of resources for humankind, American citizens and citizens of other prosperous countries must be willing to accept temporary costs at home. In the long run, we will achieve greater prosperity throughout the world by taking opportunities to expand trade in which benefits exceed harms.

Moral Objections to Trade

Not all opposition to trade agreements arises from protectionist impulses rooted in psychological biases. Nations sometimes boycott goods produced by a rogue state, goods manufactured in a way that harms the environment or goods made by companies that abuse their workers. Unfortunately, legitimate concern about the abuse of humans and the environment is often difficult to distinguish from a protectionist agenda. Once a sincere political movement builds in favor of the exclusion of foreign goods, those who profit from the exclusion will join the movement and obscure its true merit.

Institutions for mediating environmental and labor disputes between nations do not yet exist, but groups of nations with opposing interests have at times proved capable of negotiation. The recent battle over genetically modified organisms (GMOs), specifically crops bred with insect- and herbicide-resistant genes, is one example. Supported by environmental and consumer groups, the European Union and developing nations protested imports of genetically modified soyabeans and maize from the United States and five other nations—Argentina, Australia, Canada, Chile and Uruguay—known collectively as the "Miami group." The Europeans believe that GMOs could spread to wildlife and endanger biodiversity. The Miami group has insisted that their crops carry no ecological or health risks, and many scientists have backed this claim. Those opposed to GMOs are adhering to the omission bias. To prevent a minimal and entirely speculative risk, they are willing to forego the known benefits of better nutrition and reduced pesticide use.

The issue of GMOs raises an important question: Where does the burden of proof lie in matters of consumer health and safety? Governments whose farmers engage in bioengineering argue that genetically altered crops should be bought and sold freely until research shows evidence of potential harm. Governments whose farmers do not rely on bioengineering (and are thus at an economic disadvantage) demand that these crops undergo rigorous testing to determine their safety before they enter the world marketplace.

Within the United States, the FDA and the courts have presumed that evidence of health consequences should affect whether a product is approved or remains on the market, but mere suspicions should not. Internationally, the Codex Alimentarius Commission, which regulates food and safety standards worldwide, also looks for scientific evidence of harm before banning a product.

When American consumers began to express concern about GMOs, the Miami group was willing to compromise. In January 2000, ministers from 130 countries met in Montreal to create the Biosafety Protocol, which requires exporters to label shipments of bioengineered commodities and allows nations to block such imports in the absence of adequate scientific evidence about their safety.[13] Trade advocates worry that European and developing nations will use the new restrictions to protect inefficient farmers.

Should trade rules allow bans of a product that some large group believes to be immoral—for instance, simply because it interferes with Mother Nature—even if most scientists consider the product perfectly safe? Can we give consumers honest information about products without using false risks as an excuse to protect domestic producers? How can we reconcile the benefits of free trade with the desire of a nation to assert its moral principles beyond its borders? How do we respect national sovereignty without sliding down the slippery slope of protectionism? Almost any practice may be declared a cultural tradition and thus elevated to a moral principle.

Countries considering trade sanctions against companies or other nations should at least adhere to the principle that domestic goods be held to the same standards as foreign goods. In the late 1990s, the United States slapped a ban on shrimp imports from countries that used trawls without "turtle excluder devices" (TEDs), escape hatches for endangered sea turtles. India, Malaysia and other countries suffering from the ban complained to the WTO, which overruled the U.S. decision because the United States did not impose the same requirements on its domestic shrimp harvesters. In 1998, the WTO encouraged the United States to resolve its environmental

concerns by negotiating turtle protection agreements with other nations.[14] In October 2000, Malaysia complained to the WTO that the
United States was still banning imports of its shrimp. The American
trade delegate countered that, unlike countries such as Pakistan
(which restored its shrimp exports to the United States by adding
TEDs to shrimp fleets), Malaysia has rebuffed attempts to negotiate
import agreements.[15] Meanwhile, enforcement of domestic sea turtle
protection laws in the United States has been half-hearted at best. In
1999, for the first time, game wardens in Texas began issuing warnings and citations for TED violations to shrimpers. As a result, fewer
dead Kemp's ridley sea turtles, an endangered species, have been
found on Texas beaches; numbers are down from 138 in 1998 to 90
in 1999.[16]

Environmental disputes are best resolved internationally. A ban
by one nation may assuage its citizens, but the overall effect of such
actions is small. When overharvesting was destroying mahogany
forests in the Amazon, it did little good for one or two nations to
ban the import of mahogany. An international agreement in which
all nations agreed to a ban was necessary to save the forests. Similar
multilateral agreements have been attempted, with varying success,
for whales and bluefin tuna.

Various grassroots campaigns have grown into international
movements that have changed practices widely considered immoral.
Nestlé was criticized for its efforts to market baby formula in poor
countries on the grounds that poor women would dilute the formula with contaminated water to make it go farther, and that breast
feeding was generally a better option. Boycotts of Nestlé products in
several countries—although not cutting profits greatly—put enough
pressure on the company for it to change this practice.

Trade agencies such as the WTO could make it easier for activists
to present their case; for instance, in certain dispute resolution proceedings, activist groups could be given an official standing that
would allow them to testify about their labor and environmental
concerns. The possibility of such standing would discourage activist
groups from making irresponsible claims to draw public support.

The WTO could also become more actively engaged in assessing the effects of its trade policies on the environment. Despite the Seattle protesters' depiction of the WTO as a tool of money-hungry conglomerates, moderate green groups have found the WTO's new chief, Mike Moore, to be quite open to their concerns. Environmentalists, free-trade advocates and poor countries already agree on certain issues, such as the need to cut back ecologically harmful subsidies for farming, fishing and fuel. Unfortunately, powerful European Union lobbies (including a group we studied in Chapter 4, German coal miners) stand in the way of this potentially unifying issue.

In sum, while the worldwide expansion of trade has lifted millions of people out of poverty, opposition to trade initiatives within wealthy nations continues to prevent many populations from sharing in this prosperity. In the next section, we consider the problem of global poverty and suggest ways to alleviate it by trading small losses for greater gains.

Reducing Poverty

World poverty is an undeniable reality. Robert MacNamara, former head of the World Bank, coined the term *absolute poverty* to describe the condition of perhaps half a billion of the world's people:

> Poverty at the absolute level . . . is life at the very margin of existence. The absolute poor are severely deprived human beings struggling to survive in a set of squalid and degraded circumstances almost beyond the power of our sophisticated imaginations and privileged circumstances to conceive.

Compared to those fortunate enough to live in developed countries, individuals in the poorest nations have:

- An infant mortality rate eight times higher;
- A life expectancy one-third lower;
- An adult literacy rate 60 percent less;

- A nutritional level, for one out of every two in the population, below acceptable standards;
- And for millions of infants, less protein than is sufficient to permit optimum development of the brain.[17]

Since these words were written more than twenty years ago, there have been some improvements. The percentage of the Earth's population living in extreme poverty—less than $1 per day[18]—fell from 28 percent in 1987 to 24 percent in 1998. Developing countries have experienced per capita income growth of about 1.3 percent per year. From the early 1970s to the early 1990s, less developed countries open to trade grew at least twice as fast as nations that kept their tariffs high.[19]

Many populations have grown poorer because of high population growth, the AIDS epidemic, ethnic and political wars and natural disasters for which they were unprepared. Half the children in the poorest countries do not attend school, more than 1.5 billion people lack access to clean drinking water, and infectious diseases still cause one in every four deaths worldwide.[20] Asia, where most of the world's poor live, has made progress overall, yet more than 500 million people live in poverty in southern Asia. Poverty has risen dramatically over the past two decades in central Asia and the former Soviet-bloc countries, and it continues to rise in Latin America. The situation in much of Africa is desperate. About 147 in 1,000 African children die before age five, 91 of them before their first birthdays.[21] Across the globe, 33.6 million people are now estimated to be living with HIV, 70 percent of them (23.3 million) in sub–Saharan Africa and about 20 percent (6 million) in southern and Southeast Asia.[22] With 95 percent of those infected with HIV living in the developing world, AIDS is increasingly a disease of poverty.

Perhaps the most notable global trend in recent history has been the growing gap between the rich and the poor. Between the wealthiest 5 percent of countries and poorest 5 percent, the ratio of per capita income rose from 78:1 in 1988 to 123:1 in 1993.[23] Just as many industrialized nations were accomplishing unprecedented prosperity, genocide and AIDS were deepening poverty in many developing nations. This growing distance between the rich and poor has led to a vicious cycle of polarization and neglect.

The Psychological Basis of Neglect

The vast resources and distribution systems of wealthy nations are more than equipped to confront global poverty head-on. Nonetheless, the rich have refused to accept the elimination of world poverty as their moral imperative; instead, they dribble out aid to crisis points as they arise. Why do we ignore this huge issue? Some of the same psychological biases that make us resist free trade also prevent us from reaching out to the world's poor.

In the case of free trade, we saw how social gains might be accomplished by taking actions that prevent some great harm and, as a by-product, cause a smaller harm. People resist these actions because they are concerned more about harms caused by action than about harms caused by omission; the omission bias stands in the way of larger gains.

The logically consistent position is that the distinction between acts and omissions is always irrelevant, but this argument is surely too extreme. For example, is allowing the poor to die of illness and malnutrition as morally abhorrent as physically killing them? Of course not. There are several differences between neglect and murder. For one thing, the motives of someone who simply fails to write a check to the United Nations Children's Fund (UNICEF) are benign compared to the motives of a murderer; for another, we have limited opportunities to inflict harm through action (murder, theft, etc.), yet almost unlimited opportunities to do good through action (or harm through omission). We can hardly be blamed for not seizing every opportunity to help others. Still, neglect and murder lead to the same result—unnecessary death; this might cause us to wonder whether morality demands that we do more than we are currently doing, individually and collectively, to help the world's poor.

Another extreme view is that when deciding what to do with our time and money, each of us should always choose the option that does the most good for society. Thus, if giving another $100 to UNICEF would do more good for malnourished children than fixing your television set would do for you, then you should give to UNICEF and do without a television. According to this view, the poor should be a factor in every financial decision you make. The end result would be that each moral person would be living in a deprived condition, on an equal plane with the world's poorest inhabitants—quite a different lifestyle from that of most residents of developed countries.

Philosophers who have addressed the issue of poverty recently, among them Peter Singer and Peter Unger, have pointed out that it is unrealistic to expect this level of altruism. Instead, they have focused on two questions. First, what we can realistically expect each other to do for society, and what prevents us from doing it? Singer has argued for a guideline based on the idea of the tithe. If each middle- or upper-class person in developed countries donated a tenth of his or her income to UNICEF—not an unbearable sacrifice—the result would be a huge decrease in world poverty.

Second, if we assume that each of us has a moral obligation to help those less fortunate, what prevents us from recognizing and acting on this obligation? Peter Unger lists various psychological factors.[24] The first of these is the distinction between acts and omissions discussed above. For all sorts of reasons, people are willing to excuse harmful omissions, even in themselves. This tolerance has limits, of course. To use a well-known example discussed by Singer, suppose a professor, while rushing to class, passes by a pond in which a small child appears to be drowning. The professor knows he could easily save the child, but he would be late to class and would get his new suit wet. We would regard the professor as a complete worm if he didn't help the child (although in most states and nations his inaction would not be criminal). If we think badly of such a person, why do we fail to criticize one who buys a new Lexus and fails to donate to UNICEF? If we assume that the price difference between the Lexus and the next-most-expensive alternative would save several children's lives, then objectively, a similar amount of harm is being caused in both scenarios.

One reason we hold the professor and the Lexus buyer to different standards is proximity. In Stanley Milgram's classic psychological study, the experimenter instructed subjects to give electric shocks to a stooge who pretended to be another subject in a memory study. Most of the real subjects complied with the instructions, even when the experimenter told them to increase the shocks into the danger zone and even when the stooge complained of heart problems. The proportion of obedient subjects declined from 65 percent to 29 percent, however, when the subject had to press the stooge's hand onto the shock plate rather than simply push a button.[25] The same kind of proximity effect could be at work when we condemn the natty professor but not the Lexus buyer: The closer we are to human suffering, the more we feel obligated be to stop it.

A second factor in our neglect of world poverty is what Unger calls "futility thinking." People commonly think, "The problem is so huge. Anything I can do is just a drop in the bucket." The phenomenon is easily observed in hypothetical cases. In one questionnaire study, respondents were told about two programs to save Rwandan refugees from cholera by providing clean water.[26] The two programs cost about the same and both would save about 4,500 lives. One program would take place in a camp housing 250,000 refugees; the other, in a camp with 11,000. The same number of people would be helped in both cases, yet respondents showed a strong preference to provide aid to the program in the smaller camp. The difference is simply a matter of perception. When a camp is filled with 250,000 refugees, helping 4,500 seems like a drop in the bucket; the problem appears so big that attempts to alleviate it seem futile. This preference might explain why the citizens and governments of wealthy countries reflexively aid poor countries afflicted by short-term crises such as floods, while making only minimal efforts to diminish "everyday" poverty.

One method charities use to overcome futility thinking is to tell potential donors how their $100 might be spent in one village. This technique gives the illusion that the donor's money will be sent to that village by courier. The truth is that donations are simply added to the agency's bank account for disbursement as it sees fit.

A third psychological factor, which we encountered in our discussion of free trade, is nationalism, a form of parochialism or group loyalty. Citizens of wealthy nations often argue that "we" should "take care of our own poor first" before helping victims of poverty elsewhere. As Barry Goldwater put it in 1961, "The American government does not have the right, much less the obligation, to try to promote the economic and social welfare of foreign peoples."[27] Goldwater and other opponents of aid were also opposed to internal efforts to help the poor, but they found the idea of shipping money out of the country particularly galling.

Of course, many poor American citizens do need help. But the argument that we should eliminate poverty in our own country before sending funds abroad is weak. It assumes that the government has a fixed budget for helping poor people, such that any aid the United States gives to poor countries is taken away from poor Americans. The truth is that helping the poor abroad rarely conflicts directly with helping the poor at home. If sacrifices are required—and we argue that much can be done to help those in other countries with almost no sacrifice—it is self-serving to argue that the poor in the United States must make them. Helping the poor in Africa is just as compatible with helping the poor in Alabama as it is with building a new opera house in Arizona. Resources could just as easily come from other government expenditures (such as subsidies for sports teams) or from private expenditures unrelated to poverty relief.

In sum, the choice between "helping the poor abroad" and "helping the poor at home" is one that we do not have to make. We suspect that this attitude arises both from a general bias toward one's own group and from the notion of "responsibility" in which each group is expected to take care of its own problems. The problem with this notion of responsibility is that most of the world's poor neither consented to nor have any control over the political and economic systems that deprive them of the means to support themselves. Citizens of rich countries are free to direct their altruistic efforts wherever they choose; but we all have some altruistic concern about the world's poorest people. Because of this concern, for example, Americans would expect Japanese citizens to contribute to the alleviation of world poverty, and the Japanese would expect the same from Americans. We will be critical of each other's parochialism for the same reasons we oppose each other's selfishness.

A final psychological bias, faulty reference points, causes us to oppose aid that would enable developing nations to join the world economy. As we suggest later, such aid involves encouraging investment and trade. Both of these steps would lead to new businesses in poor countries, which would then export to rich countries. But when such ideas are suggested, many people cry "exploitation," on the ground that foreign workers would be paid far less than employees of industrialized countries to manufacture the same goods. Often, our faulty reference points cause us to label foreign labor as exploitative.

In calling this judgment an error, we must distinguish between real and perceived exploitation. When a boss or a government uses the threat of punishment to force people to work against their will or to prevent them from complaining or organizing, then a crime is occurring. Most countries have laws against such exploitation. Estimates of increases in this kind of crime must go into calculations of whether to loosen specific trade regulations. Concerned citizens can be vigilant in these matters by publicizing crimes that go unpunished. Consumer groups can urge citizens to boycott imported products made by such methods. The U.S. Department of State and groups such as Amnesty International and Human Rights Watch document cases of abuse.

Yet it is a mistake to assume that it is inherently exploitative to pay a worker a very low wage—just enough money to induce enough workers to do the job—when workers in one's own country would be paid much more for the same job. To call this exploitation is to adopt the wrong reference point, as if the employer had cut wages from a higher level. One of the attractions of investment in poor countries is that many residents are so poor that they will voluntarily, without threat of punishment, work for far less than the minimum wage of industrialized nations. Factory work offers them a substantial improvement in both wages and working conditions.

In San Pedro Sula, Honduras, some garment workers are employed by factories where they have few rights, are fired for becoming pregnant and are forbidden to unionize. Others work in air-conditioned factories with unions. Almost all employees in both situations prefer their jobs to the alternatives. Eber Orellana V'asquez worked on a dairy ranch before getting a job in what some American activists called a sweatshop. After three years of factory work, V'asquez said, "This has been an enormous advance for me, and I give thanks for it. My monthly income is seven times what I made in the countryside, and I've gained thirty pounds since I started working here."[28] If the economy develops overall, competition for workers will likely increase, and wages and working conditions will improve as a result.

One of the most egregious forms of worker exploitation is child labor. Hundreds of millions of children around the world are believed to be working under harsh, hazardous and largely unregulated conditions. In 1989, the United Nations adopted the Convention on the Rights of the Child, an international treaty guaranteeing basic human rights to children, including freedom from exploitative labor.[29] But local enforcement of such human rights laws has proved difficult, particularly in Africa, Latin America and Asia, where half of the world's child laborers live. One in three African children and one in five Latin American children work, primarily in homes as domestics, in the fields or on the streets.

Opponents of free trade often point to child labor in developing countries as a reason not to enter import-export agreements. They thus perpetuate the myth that most child laborers work in the sweatshops of industries that export goods to wealthy nations. In a 1997 report on child labor, UNICEF estimated that fewer than 5 percent of child laborers work for export industries; children are far more likely to be employed by informal local sectors, often as street vendors or domestics. UNICEF argues that trade sanctions and boycotts should not be used to combat child labor because such restrictions can have devastating long-term effects on the local economy and on the welfare of all children in the region under sanction. Because developing nations often respond to boycotts by cutting back on social services, funding for elementary schools may be the first thing to go. The increased poverty brought on by sanctions also means that more children will be sent to work as domestic help. As domestics, they are far more likely to suffer physical and sexual abuse than they would as factory workers.

According to UNICEF, child labor could be eliminated without increased hardship to poor families, if only wealthy countries were to make this a top priority. Improving schools worldwide is a key to solving this problem. In 1997, UNICEF estimated that it would cost $6 billion to put every child in school by the year 2000—an amount less than 1 percent of what the world spends each year on weapons. So far, wealthy countries have been unwilling to make this kind of investment, despite moral and economic incentives to do so.

Another crucial step is providing poor families with income alternatives once their children are taken out of the workforce and put in school. In Bangladesh, group "micro-credit" schemes have given the disenfranchised, particularly women, a lift out of poverty. The Grameen Bank has been a model worldwide for its success in providing small low-interest loans to the needy. Finally, from southern Asia to West Africa, activists have successfully pressured local employers to adopt codes of conduct governing child labor and are now pushing transnational corporations to follow these codes as well. These codes have been put in place without a detrimental effect on the welfare of poor families or the local economy.

In sum, citizens of wealthy nations hold a multitude of psychological biases that interfere with the search for real solutions to worldwide poverty. Once we become aware of these biases, it becomes our responsibility to alter our behavior.

What We Do Already

How have rich countries helped the poor abroad? First, we have largely ended colonialism and brought about a worldwide shift toward self-government. A gradual process lasting throughout the twentieth century, the end of colonialism was an important change of attitude on the part of citizens and governments of rich countries. National self-determination, a principle of Woodrow Wilson's "Fourteen Points" (conditions for ending World War I), was incorporated into the U.N. charter as a step toward encouraging the formation of new states, particularly in Africa. Self-government has shown uneven results. Countries such as Malaysia and Singapore are doing well; but others, such as Angola, appear to have been left with little ability to fend for themselves. Still other countries are struggling to realize the benefits of both their colonial and indigenous heritages.

One of the primary ways that citizens of prosperous countries such as the United States help the poor abroad is through direct donations of aid, which are used to fund disaster relief efforts, infrastructure improvements, health and education initiatives and other projects. Donations administered by international nonprofit agencies (such as UNICEF) and development banks (such as the World Bank) are known as multilateral aid. Another major source of funding is government-to-government aid, or bilateral aid. Much government aid is channeled through the very same NGOs that solicit private charitable donations.

Foreign aid funding has achieved glorious successes and miserable failures. The World Bank contributed to Vietnam's economic renewal by guaranteeing $2.9 billion in loans between 1993 and 2000; 40 percent has been disbursed to date. Thanks in part to this assistance, Vietnam has sustained remarkable development, with an average annual GDP growth of 8 percent from 1990 to 1997, although the financial crisis in eastern Asia and reform slowdowns have recently impeded growth.[30] Economic stabilization efforts by the International Development Association (IDA) and the International Monetary Fund (IMF) helped decrease inflation in Bolivia from a peak of 23,500 percent in 1985 to less than 4.5 percent by the end of 1998. But Bolivia proves that foreign aid is not a cure-all: The country is still one of the poorest in Latin America, with a per capita GNP of just $1,000 and education, health and nutrition conditions similar to those of sub–Saharan Africa.[31] Since the mid–1970s, sub–Saharan Africa has received an estimated $270 billion in net aid from foreign donors, and yet more than 40 percent of the population continues to survive on less than one dollar a day.[32] The World Bank and the International Monetary Fund, the two leading international lending agencies, have faced harsh criticism for their multibillion-dollar African aid programs. In a 2000 report, the World Bank admitted that it has wasted billions on ill-conceived projects in Africa since the 1960s; for instance, a Tanzanian project squandered $2 billion over twenty years on roads that disintegrated almost as soon as they were built.[33] Countries with highly inefficient or corrupt central governments have proved particularly incapable of using foreign donations to improve the lives of their citizens. Throughout the 1990s, billions of dollars in foreign aid to Russia simply evaporated, apparently into the hands of oligarchs operating the strings of the Yeltsin régime, while most Russians sank deeper into poverty.

Assessments of the nearly $1 trillion in foreign aid that has been distributed since the 1950s have led many charities and governments to the same conclusion: Financial assistance has the best effects on countries with sound management, low levels of corruption and a strong movement for government reform and stabilization. The World Bank estimates that a $10 billion increase in aid to governments with good economic management will lift 25 million people out of poverty. Yet if this sum is distributed across the board to developing countries, only 7 million will be helped.[34] The World Bank suggests that dual assessments of poverty and economic management should determine how finances are allocated, the greatest funding going to impoverished countries that have good policies already in place. Although it is difficult to argue that the poor of economically unsound countries are less deserving of aid, our primary concern should be doing the most good with finite resources—an argument made throughout this book.

Another important contribution by rich countries has been medical research. Medical breakthroughs in disease prevention discovered by scientists in developed countries have benefited the rich and poor alike. In 1967, after a smallpox vaccine was invented in the U.K., the U.N. World Health Organization (WHO) launched a global campaign against the disease. At the time, some 10 to 15 million new cases were reported each year; by 1979, smallpox had been stamped out worldwide. We are now winning a similar effort to wipe out polio; only a few new incidences are reported each year. Other medical research has led to successful public health programs that deal with malaria, cholera and tuberculosis, although these remain big killers.

Many of the treatments discovered by scientists in wealthy nations can benefit the poor at little cost. UNICEF estimates that "more than 12.5 million children under five in developing countries continue to die each year, 9 million of them from causes for which inexpensive solutions have been routinely applied in the industrialized world for half a century."[35] Most incidents of death, blindness and other handicaps among children in developing countries could be prevented cheaply through remedies such as oral rehydration salts for diarrhea, vitamin A capsules, iodized salt and vaccination against childhood diseases.[36] The World Health Organization estimates that, in some poor countries, a person can be cured of tuberculosis for $13.[37] These expenditures are one of the most efficient ways to use money to improve the human condition.

Agricultural research conducted in developed nations has also contributed to reducing poverty abroad. As a result of research carried out by Norman Borlaug and supported largely by the Rockefeller Foundation, wheat production tripled in Mexico in the 1940s and increased by 60 percent in India and Pakistan in the 1960s and 1970s.[38] The research was part of the "green revolution," a series of agricultural advances, investments and policies that allowed food production to keep up with population growth in some of the world's fastest-growing countries. Borlaug, who won the Nobel Peace Prize in 1970 for his contributions, has been credited with preventing 1 billion deaths.[39] The green revolution continues, although it has yet to reach much of Africa.

Research on new methods of energy generation and communication have also benefited the poor. It may be that the poorest countries will simply skip the installation of telephone wires and go directly to satellite communication with mobile phones. This technology will also allow access to the Internet and eventually put the smallest villages in touch with up-to-date information about weather and new crops, permit local doctors and nurses to learn the latest in medical diagnosis and treatment, and give school children access to libraries of information.

Rich countries also educate people in poor countries, directly and indirectly. We do it directly by accepting students from these countries into our colleges and universities, particularly at the graduate level. Although many of these students stay in the developed countries that educate them, others return and use their knowledge to improve their local communities and government. We educate indirectly by writing books that are used in schools and colleges throughout the developing world. Modern science has been the backbone of our own development, and we cannot expect the rest of the world to prosper without it.

As we saw earlier, another way that rich countries have helped is through trade. Japan, Singapore, Taiwan and South Korea all have used exports to move from poverty to (relative) wealth in a few decades. Japan is the most dramatic success story; other nations in Southeast Asia, such as Malaysia, Indonesia and Thailand, are following the same path. Bangladesh, though not yet prosperous, has used textile and clothing exports as a means of development. China is currently undergoing rapid development driven by exports. Mexico and other Latin American countries are trying to do the same, mostly with agricultural goods. The amazing increase in standard of living that some countries have enjoyed simply could not have happened without trade. If the experience of other regions is any indication, contrary to the arguments of Western environmental and labor groups, we can expect developing nations to find the benefits of free trade to be worth the costs.

A final, crucial benefit is investment, which gives a boost to poor countries that lack the ability to develop export enterprises. Private corporations and banks typically target a small number of middle-income countries where expansion opportunities are high; just 26 countries have received 95 percent of private donations; the remaining 140 developing countries split the 5 percent left over.[40] Private donations rose rapidly in the mid-1990s, then tapered off following the 1997 financial crisis in eastern Asia. Even though poor countries voice legitimate concerns about the effects of foreign ownership on their communities—such as loss of autonomy and the threat of cultural homogeneity—the nations that have been the most open to foreign investment have achieved the most rapid growth in living standards.

Twelve Measures That Will
Cost Little and Do a Lot of Good

During the 1990s, many wealthy countries cut back their direct foreign aid, and these spending reductions have hindered poverty relief. Active citizens must look for new opportunities to achieve better results.

When we look closely at world poverty, it becomes evident that we—citizens of rich countries and our governments—can do a great deal to help the poor at little or no net cost to ourselves. Many of the things we can do will help us, the privileged, directly. As we have discussed, nearly every economic or social change brings some harmful effects to some people, and in many cases these limited effects have aroused disproportionately strong opposition to the reform; however, such harms are generally a small price to pay for the large benefits achieved. The costs appear especially small when we think of foregone benefits as harms resulting from omission. Each of these twelve changes has the potential to provide great benefits at comparatively trivial costs.

None of our recommendations involves direct outlays of cash. Many of them call for taking advantage of untapped opportunities;

others require hands-on training and education in developing nations. In addition, each form of aid listed below carries an implicit contract: In exchange for increased foreign assistance, the governments and citizens of developing nations must be willing to assume responsibility for improving their society. They must prove that they are ready to lessen corruption, improve government efficiency and promote democracy. This is the type of wise trade we have advocated throughout this book, in which each side gets what it cares about. The poor receive more funds and new ideas and opportunities to improve their lives. In return, the rich gain the satisfaction of witnessing these improvements, as well as the assurance that newly stable governments will contribute to world peace and to the world economy.

1. Loosen Trade Barriers.   Throughout this chapter, we have seen examples of how free trade has helped poor countries gain wealth. Still, continued resistance to trade agreements has kept them from yielding as much benefit as they could. Workers and firms in rich countries have exerted political power to try to reduce foreign imports, which they view as a direct challenge to their livelihoods. The African Growth and Opportunity Act, which lowered tariff barriers to goods from forty-eight sub–Saharan African countries, took two years to pass through Congress because it was opposed by environmentalists, labor activists and representatives of textile-producing states. The bill finally passed, but only after being bottled up for months in a conference committee.

Even more promising was a measure that almost passed—but didn't—at the World Trade Organization's 1999 meeting in Seattle. The United States, Japan, Canada and the European Union considered a joint proposal to accept essentially all imports from the world's poorest forty-eight countries, duty free. These countries account for 0.5 percent of the world's trade, so the threat to wealthy countries was minimal; yet European countries such as France, which protects its farming as a national treasure, decided they could not sign the agreement. The Seattle meeting was an unfortunate example of a failure to reach a bargain that could have helped all nations involved. The deal fell through in part because each party refused to accept small losses in return for potential greater gains.

Setbacks such as this are particularly disheartening because so many of them have been supported or caused by activists professing a concern for the downtrodden. Within developed countries, almost all the lobbying in favor of trade comes from business and business groups; in the opposition are environmentalists, trade unions and traditional leftists. The leftists appear to take the view that anything good for corporations is bad for everyone else. The unions, in turn, adopt the rhetoric of the left to defend their protections. The opposition of most leftists to increased trade suggests a lack of awareness of the overall benefits that trade has brought to poor countries, and it is at odds with the left's traditional emphasis on reducing poverty. We argue that activists must take a closer look at what helps the poor and advocate measures that support positive change without being swayed by customary alliances or animosities.

2. Encourage Investment.   Without investment, poor countries can hardly take advantage of free trade or even develop at all. They need money to build transportation and communication systems, power plants and power grids. Locally owned firms need money for buildings and machines. For the poorest countries, this money usually comes from foreign investment by private companies; typically, few local investors are able or willing to assist to a significant degree. By guaranteeing loans and making small direct loans, rich countries can encourage good investments in poor countries at little cost. The 1995 bailout of Mexico by the United States and G7 other nations together with international financial organizations required no expenditures of funds. It required guarantees of $52 billion in loans, but the guarantees became self-fulfilling when they shored up investors' confidence in the future of Mexico's economy.

This strategy is not free of risk. If rich countries constantly make loans or guarantees, some will eventually fail. It is also questionable how much foreign investment should be undertaken. Excessive foreign intervention encourages private investors to become careless and dependent on foreign sources to cover bad investments. Too little investment could bring about major social disasters. Investments are most successful in democracies with sound management policies and low corruption; thus a policy of encouraging investments will also encourage these qualities in governments.

3. Using Loans and Debt Relief to Encourage Good Government. The World Bank is in the business of making and promoting loans from rich countries to the governments of poor ones. Lenders include governments, individual bond owners and funds that own bonds. As many of these loans will not be paid back, holders of government bonds do not expect large returns on their investments. However, many poor countries do spend substantial portions of their government budgets paying interest on these foreign loans and bonds. The World Bank estimates that in early 1999, the forty poorest countries collectively owed $200 billion.[41] In Tanzania, where one child in six dies before the age of five, the government spends four times as much on debt service than it does on primary health care.[42]

There is no easy answer to the question of whether to forgive the debts of poor countries. If they are forgiven, it will encourage lending and borrowing with little concern for the long-term use of the funds. In addition, wealthy lenders could seize on debt cancellation as an excuse to cut back future loans and direct aid.[43] If debt is not forgiven, governments have a much harder time digging their way out of poverty or attracting other investment.

One solution to the problem is to make a trade between the small loss of debt forgiveness and the large gain of government reform. The loss will be fairly small because foreign lenders have already written off some of these debts. In June 1999, leaders of the Group of Seven industrialized nations met in Cologne and agreed to make debt relief for poor countries contingent upon government reforms. A similar effort had failed to yield much relief, but this new plan would provide more: a cancellation of $70 billion of the poorest forty-one countries' debt (about a third of their total debt).[44]

Many reforms could be undertaken in exchange for debt relief, such as the elimination of costly subsidies. Like many rich countries, poor nations subsidize favored industries and goods, distorting the market and taking money from where it creates the most benefit. Venezuela, for example, subsidizes the price of gasoline, which leads to high local consumption of the country's biggest export. Because rich citizens consume much more gasoline than the poor, they benefit disproportionately from the subsidy. Reform will be difficult to enforce within developing countries because governments can be expected to promise one thing to their lenders and another to their constituents. Nonetheless, this is the direction that debt relief, as well as foreign aid in general, has to follow.

4. Decreasing Corruption and Promoting Civil Society.   Although corruption is rampant throughout the world, it tends to occur most often in the poorest countries. Civil servants in developing nations are typically underpaid and may resort to "petty" bribe-taking as a means of earning a living wage. In cases of "grand" corruption, public officials at the highest levels hide large bribes in overseas bank accounts.[45] Leaders and former leaders of the poorest countries in Africa collectively have stashed billions of dollars in Swiss banks. Russian bankers, oil magnates and other financiers close to the Yeltsin régime have been accused of bleeding the country dry throughout the 1990s.

Corruption inherently discriminates against the poor. When building or business permits are controlled by corrupt government officials, those who cannot afford to pay bribes are prevented from improving their lives. When elections or legislators are bought, the voices of the poor are not being heard. Corruption also prevents economic development. If governments award contracts to the cronies of those in power, investors cannot be sure that merely offering a better product at a better price will lead to profits. A "Bribe-Payers Survey" conducted in 1999 by Transparency International, a global coalition against corruption, found that the bribery of public officials by foreign companies from industrialized nations is rampant within developing nations. Payoffs breed a cycle of growing bribes that primarily benefits corrupt government officials. And although the bribe-payers may grumble about being ensnared in a corrupt system, the primary victims of this system are the poor.

In the 1990s, the governments of rich nations began to take important steps toward reducing bribery at a global level. The twenty-nine wealthy member nations of the Organization for Economic Cooperation and Development (OECD) and five other countries (Argentina, Brazil, Bulgaria, Chile and the Slovak Republic) signed an Anti-bribery Convention in 1997 that makes it a crime to "offer, promise or give a bribe to a foreign public official in order to obtain or retain international business deals."[46] A related measure outlaws tax deductions for bribes paid to foreign officials—a practice that, amazingly, has been perfectly legal in the United States. Members of the Organization for American States, a coalition of governments in North, Central and South America and the Caribbean, have signed a similar treaty, the Inter-American Convention Against Corruption.

Widespread monitoring and punishment will be necessary to enforce these agreements. The OECD sponsors nonmember outreach plans, including workshops and forums on combating corruption in Asia, Latin America and eastern Europe. Transparency International's seventy-seven national chapters lobby governments, keep the media informed and mobilize citizens in their anticorruption efforts.[47] International business groups may need to forge cooperation through the creation of anticorruption blocs.[48] Efforts to reduce corruption can generally be expected to reduce poverty. Since Nigeria's transformation from a military dictatorship into a democracy in 1999, poor Nigerians are finally able to gain access to gasoline at world-market prices. Together, governments and active citizens can pressure the governments of developing nations to join in the fight against corruption by passing laws and forging cooperative agreements.

5. *Reducing Armies and War Within Developing Countries.*   Poor nations experienced a steep rise in violence at the end of the twentieth

century. The cheap and unregulated weapons pouring into African nations as a result of military downsizing in eastern Europe has vastly increased the scope and death toll of internal conflicts. Since 1984, 15 million people have died in the ongoing Sudanese civil war. The United Nations estimates that as many as 300,000 children under the age of eighteen were serving as combatants throughout the world in 1998.[49] Much of the violence has been ethnic and political, such as wars in central Africa between the Hutus and Tutsis and an ongoing civil war in Angola. Although the military expenditures of developing nations make up only a small percentage of global totals, these countries spend a far greater percentage of their national budgets on weapons and armies than do wealthy countries. Sub–Saharan African nations spent upwards of $5 billion on their militaries in 1998; northern Africa spent $3.7 billion.[50] Ongoing conflicts have left many nations deep in debt and without funding for basic health and education services.

International donors may indirectly contribute to the military budgets of poor countries. As the Congo succumbed to civil war, the International Monetary Fund continued to lend money to at least three countries involved in the conflict: Rwanda, Zimbabwe and Uganda. In August 1999, the IMF approved a $193 million standby credit for Zimbabwe and made $24 million available immediately. By October, the IMF discovered that it may have been misled about the amount Zimbabwe spent on military intervention in the first half of 1999.[51] Zimbabwe told the IMF it spent $18 million to support Congo President Laurent Kabila's war against Rwandan and Ugandan rebels, but total expenditures were revealed to be closer to $166 million. At the time the discrepancy was revealed, inflation stood at more than 65 percent in Zimbabwe; the country's domestic debt more than doubled in 1999. In 1998, the war in Congo and internal unrest led Uganda to spend $230 billion on defense. Although Uganda's economy has made great strides in recent years, military outlays contributed to a rise in the budget deficit in 1999/2000 to 1.16 percent of GDP.[52] In June 2000, the International Rescue Committee estimated that two years of war in eastern Congo had caused the deaths of more than 1.7 million people, four times as many people as would have died in the area under normal conditions.[53] Two hundred thousand of these deaths were violent, and many of the rest were attributed to the wartime collapse of health services and food supplies; an estimated one-third of those killed were children under five.

Rich countries can do two things to contribute to peace in developing nations. First, we can work to cut off the flow of arms to these countries. A 1998 World Bank conference advocated several measures to bring about demilitarization in Africa: international arms exporting agreements and arms embargoes, conventions to curb the illicit trafficking of arms, arms destruction and buy-back programs.[54] The International Code of Conduct on Arms Transfers, endorsed by a commission of seventeen Nobel Peace Laureates, would ban arms sales to governments that are undemocratic, have poor human rights records or are engaged in aggression. The European Union has approved a comparable agreement, and efforts to adopt a similar policy in the United States are underway.[55]

Second, we can continue to contribute peacekeeping troops to trouble spots. The decision to launch a military intervention is always difficult; the results are unpredictable and may lead to loss of life. America's intervention in Somalia, for example, was considered a failure after 30 American servicemen were killed and 175 wounded, although the international relief effort is estimated to have saved 300,000 Somali from famine. A tension exists between multilateral intervention (carried out by a union of forces from different countries) and unilateral intervention (undertaken by a specific country). The process by which the United Nations decides whether to send troops to an area is often painfully slow. In East Timor, thousands were killed while the U.N. debated what to do; they finally sent in unarmed observers. Multilateral intervention, however, has the advantage of making clear that most of the world is concerned. At the other extreme is the rapid use of military power by one country, perhaps with the tacit consent of its allies, as happened in the Persian Gulf War. The trouble here is that the world may come to see such intervention as aggression rather than peace-keeping.

There is no rule of thumb that wealthy countries can follow when confronting conflicts in poor nations, although demilitarization efforts can be expected to create large benefits, and peacekeeping missions will often be a better choice than taking no action at all.

6. *Reducing Population Pressure.*   The world's population grew from 1.6 billion in 1900 to 6 billion by the end of the century, and is expected to reach 10 billion at some point during the twenty-first century. On the whole, the world is expected to be able to support all people who will inhabit it a hundred years from now. The trouble is that although birth rates are declining in most regions, the decline is uneven. In Russia, births declined from 1.89 per woman in 1990 to 1.17 in 1999.[56] Birth rates in most northern and western European nations hover around 1.7 per woman, and stand at 2.1 in the United States.[57] Rates are far higher in the world's poorest countries, particularly in southern and eastern Africa and the Middle East. The fertility rate in Ethiopia was 7.7 in 1990.[58] Rates remain high in Latin America and southern Asia despite considerable declines in recent years.

For many nations, high birth rates are unsustainable. Water that is free of both salt and disease is now the main environmental factor preventing further increases in either population or living standards. Africa and Latin America are currently not adapting quickly enough to sustain their own growth rates. The Middle East and southern Asia may have problems securing fresh water, especially if rising sea levels begin to cover Bangladesh. Egypt already has insufficient water for its increasing population, and Iran will reach the same point by 2020.[59]

Increased use of contraception is the most direct way to manage population size and thereby prevent future poverty and famine. Very small increases in the rate of contraceptive use can lead to significant effects on the rate of population growth.[60] A decline from three children per woman to 2.5 (16 percent) amounts to an approximate 50 percent reduction in the growth rate.[61] In Bangladesh, an increased supply of contraception caused birth rates to fall from an average of 6.3 children in the mid–1970s to 3.4 by 1993—an enormous reduction, and an important turnaround in a country with the highest population density in the world.

Worldwide, some 58 percent of married women were estimated to be using contraception in 1993, with rates as high as 72 percent in Europe and North America and about 55 percent in less developed regions.[62] The great statistical standout is Africa, where only one in five married couples uses contraception. Short-acting and reversible methods such as the condom and the pill are largely inaccessible to Africans. Although condoms can be distributed at little cost, the demand remains unmet. Surveys have found that 26.8 percent of married women in sub–Saharan Africa would like better access to effective birth control.[63] The unmet need is also high in northern and western Africa (20.8 percent), Latin America and the Caribbean (20 percent) and Asia (17.6 percent). Condoms are needed in these regions not only to prevent unwanted pregnancies but to slow the spread of sexually transmitted diseases, particularly AIDS.

In countries where large families are the cultural norm, campaigns that promote smaller families are one means of encouraging birth control, thereby managing populations and reducing poverty. China achieved huge declines as a result of government policy that put citizens under strong economic pressure to keep their families small; people with one child or none received benefits that others did not. These policies were coercive at first and have been abused in some cases by local officials, but eventually they shifted public attitudes away from a preference for large families. (Contrary to popular belief in the West, infanticide did not rise in China as a result of these policies.)

Other countries have accomplished important declines in birth rates as a result of such Western influences as television soap operas depicting glamorous women who have small families; advertising campaigns that associate large families with poverty; and better education for girls and women. Increases in education and health services led to birth-rate reductions in the state of Kerala, India, even while most of the population remains quite poor.

Foreign aid and charity can make great contributions to population control at a relatively small cost. Several NGOs, such as Pathfinder International (http://www.pathfind.org/), The Population Institute (http://www.populationinstitute.org/), and International Planned Parenthood Federation (http://www.ippf.org/) provide contraceptive services, counseling on safe sex, some medical services and carry out research on birth control in poor countries. In addition, some groups lobby wealthy governments for family planning and pro-choice initiatives and legislation. This is one area where rich countries can do a great deal to help the poor at little cost.

During his first week in office, President George W. Bush may have dealt a blow to such poverty reduction initiatives by reinstating a Reagan-era ban on federal funding of international family planning groups that support abortion. The "global gag rule" denies financial support to organizations that spend a portion of their non-U.S. funding on abortion (U.S. funding of abortions has been outlawed since 1973) or that discuss the availability of legal abortions with patients.[64] The International Planned Parenthood Federation (IPPF) predicted that programs aimed at preventing unplanned pregnancies, not abortion services and counseling, will suffer the most from the ban. "To place restrictions on family planning choices disempowers women and men and undermines their efforts to extricate themselves from poverty," said IPPF Director-General Ingar Brueggemann.[65] By focusing on the polarizing issue of abortion at the beginning of his administration, Bush may have imposed new hardships on the poor abroad, and at the very least overlooked opportunities to expand the pie of global resources.

7. Loosen the Borders of Wealthy Countries.   In principle, increased immigration to wealthy countries could help ease the plight of the poor. The gradual upward mobility of most immigrants suggests that leaving a poor country for a rich one is usually worth the risk. Some studies have suggested that new immigrants add to the overall well-being of others in the United States, despite the claims of anti-immigrant groups that newcomers either demand welfare or take jobs from "Americans" (i.e., those who got there first). Other researchers have argued that immigrants typically have little effect, one way or another, on the two countries involved.[66] It is debatable whether immigrants benefit their adopted homelands, but there is no evidence that they cause harm.

The world would surely be better on the whole if all immigration restrictions—like those on investment, trade and communication—were abolished. Restraints on personal freedom, without some major benefit in return, are bound to exacerbate poverty. However, immigration is such an emotional issue that the complete relaxation of borders is unrealistic.

It is possible that wealthy countries such as the United States could increase immigration considerably without much overall effect on society. Immigrants, their children and their descendents will face the main effects of immigration. For this reason, the costs and benefits of immigration for immigrants should become a part of the political debate over immigration in rich countries. Right now, it is largely absent from these debates in Europe and the United States. Although not a panacea, permitting more immigration would be a cost-free way for wealthy nations to help lift people out of poverty.

8. Increasing Education, Scholarship and Internet Access. The rich world already plays a strong role in providing higher education to students from poor countries, but we can do more at little cost. In particular, we can take advantage of the Internet as a medium for education at all levels. Educational Web sites abound in all areas of the sciences, and most of the classics in literature can be found online as well. As greater numbers of the poor gain access to the Internet, we can expect it to be used as a teaching tool for adult literacy.

At present, the poorest countries have few connections. In 1998, there were only two Internet hosts (computers with active Internet Protocol addresses) per 10,000 inhabitants of Africa, seven per

10,000 Asians and 9.6 per 10,000 Latin Americans–compared to 100 per 10,000 Europeans and 855 per 10,000 North Americans.[67] The disparity in access to personal computers is similar.

Private investors from industrialized countries have a vested interest in expanding technology to poorer nations. In countries undergoing rapid development, such as India and China, we can typically expect technology to first reach the most profitable economic sectors before trickling down to the working class. It will be tougher to convince private investors of the benefits to be gained by wiring the poor nations of Africa. The World Bank and other aid agencies are engaged in a variety of projects aimed at increasing Internet access to the poor, but these are generally humanitarian rather than investment activities.

A great deal of foreign aid is spent on elementary education in developing nations; yet little can be done to reduce such costs because teachers' salaries are already extremely low worldwide. By contrast, at the higher levels of scholarship, many things can be done to disseminate information at little cost. Scholarly journals are one example. Currently, journals concerned with engineering, tropical medicine, education, computer science, business and economics–all the journals that scholars in poor countries need to keep abreast with current research–are sold for profit, with subscription prices ranging from $50 to several thousand dollars per year. Because academic writers do not receive royalties from the publication of their articles (and often pay for publication), no one benefits from this system except the publishers. Several recent initiatives have attempted to make journals available to the poor by clearing the way for open publication of scholarly work on the World Wide Web. The benefits to scholars in poor countries will be immense.

9. Increase Environmental Protection.   Environmentalists who oppose efforts to increase trade and industrial production argue that these changes lead to greater pollution. Yet as long as poor nations are unable to house and feed their citizens, pollution reduction will remain a low priority in the developing world. As nations grow richer, they cut back the kind of pollution that has direct, local, perceivable effects.[68] Thus, we can expect that increased trade will lead to decreases in localized pollution, including soot, ozone and bacteria.

Efforts to reduce pollution in poor countries can provide direct benefits to rich countries. This applies to the pollution of rivers and oceans as well as air pollution, which drifts for hundreds of miles. Singapore, for example, recently found itself suffering from pollution caused by forest fires in Indonesia. In the next chapter, we will take a closer look at air pollution that crosses national borders as part of a discussion of global warming. One solution we will consider is the idea of giving rich countries credits for reducing pollution in poor ones. These credits reduce the rich countries' obligation to lower their own pollution levels.

Environmental pollution and degradation can often be confronted cheaply and efficiently through conservation, the efficient management of existing energy sources, and the exploration of new technologies. The World Bank asserts that environmental measures are one of the most effective ways to reduce illness and death in southern Asia, where about 20 percent of disease is attributable to environmental causes such as lack of water, contaminated water, air pollution and poor sanitation. In India alone, illnesses related to water and sanitation cause about half a million deaths of children under five per year; indoor air pollution from cook stoves kills another half-million Indian women and children annually.[69] As a result, the World Bank has shifted its focus in reducing air pollution from large sources such as power plants to smaller sources. Finally, wind and solar power are two "clean" sources of energy that are showing rapid growth worldwide, particularly in Asia.[70]

10. Increase Funding for Medical Research.   A 1993 report from the World Bank points out that the number of years of human life lost per person from communicable diseases is several times higher in the poorest countries than in rich countries.[71] Differences in disease incidence between rich and poor countries are found solely among communicable diseases; noncommunicable diseases such as cancer and heart disease do not differ. It is difficult for medical researchers to find funding to study tropical diseases—such as malaria, hook-worm and sleeping sickness—that do not afflict rich countries. An es-timated 23.3 million sub–Saharan Africans are currently infected with AIDS. The disease has orphaned 11.2 million African children, and the life span of the average African is expected to drop from fifty-nine to forty-five by 2010.[72] Although 95 percent of worldwide HIV cases occur in the developing world, the types of drug treat-ments being developed are designed for the 5 percent who live in rich countries. The small amount of research aimed at developing an HIV vaccine focuses on the viral strains common in the United States and Europe, not those found in Africa and Asia.[73]

Pharmaceutical manufacturers have no financial incentive to search for vaccines for diseases that primarily afflict the poor. If a firm did develop an effective malaria or AIDS vaccine, it could never hope to recoup the millions or even billions of dollars spent on research and development. Once the product entered the mar-ket, it would be hijacked by other firms and by international aid agencies; the original manufacturer would be forced to sell the vac-cine at prices that cover production only. This situation would cer-tainly benefit the poor, but it would put the manufacturer out of business.[74] Although manufacturers might be willing to sell their products to poor countries at prices close to their production cost, they fear that the products will be smuggled back into rich countries and thus cause them greater losses. There is room for a bargain here: Rich governments could promise increased enforcement of smug-gling laws (and seek agreements with the countries involved) in re-turn for greater production and distribution efforts from manufac-turers.

The World Bank has proposed that rich countries contribute $100 million per year to fund research on diseases such as AIDS, cholera and tuberculosis. In a rare instance of cooperation, the Clinton ad-ministration and the U.S. Congress championed the creation of a global fund to buy vaccines for poor countries. With the promise of financial compensation, pharmaceutical and biotechnology firms will finally be motivated to engage in neglected areas of research. New vaccines will also save lives in rich countries, as these diseases are still occasionally imported. The benefits will be small, to be sure, but so will the costs. The benefit new vaccines would bring to poor countries, of course, is almost unfathomable.

11. Increase Funding for Agricultural Research.   Since the beginning of human civilization, population growth has depended on the growth of agriculture. New methods of breeding and growing crops have allowed people to spread into new territories for many thousands of years. The latest great agricultural advance was the "green revolution," spearheaded by Norman Borlaug, which led to the creation of new varieties of rice that could be grown in southern and eastern Asia. Without this revolution, famines would have been widespread. Increased yields have been able to keep up with population growth, despite no growth in the amount of land under cultivation.[75]

Many of the poorer parts of the world have not kept pace with modern research. The green revolution has not expanded to Africa and Latin America, in part because environmental activists have persuaded funding sources such as the Ford and Rockefeller Foundations and Western governments that high-yield techniques will lead to irreversible damage to the environment. Borlaug scoffs at these concerns: "If they lived just one month amid the misery of the developing world, as I have for fifty years, they'd be crying out for tractors and fertilizer and irrigation canals and be outraged that fashionable elitists back home were trying to deny them these things."[76] With the help of former President Jimmy Carter, Borlaug has found funding for projects in Africa in recent years and has tripled yields of corn in Ethiopia, Ghana and Nigeria.

Even simple research projects can make a big difference. One example of what can be done with very little money is the International Center for Tropical Agriculture (CIAT) in Cali, Colombia.[77] Researchers at CIAT teach local farmers how to conduct agricultural experiments.[78] In one case, an agricultural engineer explained the meaning of a control group in Quechua, the language of the Incas, which previously had no words to describe such a concept. Farmers have formed local research committees that experiment with new methods. One such group found a variety of corn with short stature and high yield that could withstand mountain winds. When yields improved, they sold the seeds to other farmers. The farmers around Cali have stopped believing that only God determines their yield. CIAT is supported by an international consortium of agricultural researchers–CGIAR, the Consultative Group for International Agricultural Research–which itself runs on a shoestring budget.[79]

12. Increasing and Disseminating Economic Research.   If developed countries spent as much effort researching the most efficient way to reduce world poverty as they spend on streamlining routine medical care or the postal system, many more lives could be saved. We need more research on cost-effectiveness in reducing poverty. A keyword search of current research grants (March 2000) awarded by the National Science Foundation (NSF) produced 48 related to poverty and economic development; 10 of these specifically concerned poverty in poor countries. By contrast, 186 grants concerned financial markets and 165 dealt with retirement, pensions or inheritance.[80]

Part of the problem is that because research-granting agencies are funded by taxpayer dollars, they often consider themselves obligated to focus on national problems. We suspect that taxpayers would understand, though, if these agencies devoted more funds to global concerns, such as research on tropical diseases. Citizens already understand that they or even their grandchildren may not benefit from the medical research being carried out today. Vaccines are one example of research that, in the end, has helped the world. The increased funding for research on reducing poverty would result in only a small sacrifice of narrow national interests because developed nations would also benefit from reduced poverty, whether through greater opportunities for trade or through protection from epidemics of disease.

Western business schools have devoted greater attention to global issues in the past decade. Decision making and negotiation training helps business students become better managers, consultants and entrepreneurs. More students than ever from developing nations such as Russia and India now enroll in Western MBA programs and transfer their newfound knowledge to businesses and governments back home upon graduation. In addition, study-abroad programs give students the opportunity to use business plans in other cultures, including developing nations.

A New Activism

All the steps we have listed would impose small costs on people in rich countries, although many of these costs would be recovered over time or carry side benefits. Increased global trade will cause some citizens of wealthy nations to lose their jobs, but it will prevent losses of other jobs, create new ones, and increase options for consumers. Some of these steps require foreign aid or other expenditures of the sort we already make for moral reasons. It would be nice if we all became more altruistic, more willing to sacrifice our own interests for the well being of those who suffer. But our point is that issues of efficiency have too often been clouded by moral debates. When good, efficient ideas for helping the poor are on the table, they do not draw the same interest from citizens as issues that involve personal morality. We must learn to ask ourselves how we can get the most benefit for whatever sacrifice we are willing to make. We need a new political activism on behalf of the world's poor, founded on the understanding that reducing poverty benefits poor and rich alike.

This attitude needs more political support. When the proposal to end duties on goods from the world's forty poorest countries came before Congress, few citizens' groups in the United States lobbied to support it—even though eliminating these tariffs is one of the most effective things we can do to help the poor at essentially no net cost to ourselves. We cannot abandon these issues to the special interests that have a stake in them, such as corporations seeking export opportunities or unions trying to protect jobs. Nor can we entrust these issues to NGOs, many of which give more consideration to furthering their own narrow political agendas than to helping the poor. Those who protest any loosening of trade restrictions have been particularly detrimental to the fight against poverty, often purely out of ignorance of the overall benefits that free trade brings to the poor. We must become an informed citizenry that recognizes the elimination of global poverty not only as one of the great moral issues of our time, but as one we can alleviate most effectively with the sharp eyes of an accountant.

7

The Case of
Global Warming

THROUGHOUT THIS BOOK WE HAVE DESCRIBED SITUATIONS IN which politicians and special-interest groups have taken positions with little consideration for the overall impact of their actions. We argue that a thorough analysis of the costs and benefits of certain initiatives will give a better idea of their real effects. In addition, to increase resources for all, our government representatives must learn to overcome intuitive biases and integrate wise tradeoffs into their policy decisions.

The decision-making and negotiation strategies we advocate are widely used by executives of successful companies but have not yet reached the political arena. In this chapter, we argue that the cognitive changes that must underlie better political decisions will even help us solve the most difficult societal issues facing us today—for example, global warming. We will use the debate on global warming to demonstrate the connections among the six principles of enlarging the pie of social resources.

Global Warming

Many of the themes developed in this book are relevant to the lack of a decisive response to global warming. This problem is more complex than many of the others we have discussed. It affects almost all aspects of society: economics, science, technology, government, health, poverty and our deepest concerns for the future of the natural world. Efforts to solve global warming must put aside parochial interests.

To understand the scope of the problem, we first need to understand some basic facts about the earth's atmosphere. The sun's energy reaches the earth in the form of visible light, infrared and ultraviolet light, as well as in other forms such as radio waves and x-rays. Warmed by this radiation, the earth emits other radiation in turn, primarily infrared light. Much of this infrared light is absorbed by the earth's atmosphere, which grows warmer as it collects light and warms the earth's surface. The eighteenth-century physicist and mathematician Joseph Fourier called this phenomenon the "greenhouse effect," because greenhouses also absorb light and keep out cold air.[1] Because of the greenhouse effect, the earth is about fifty-eight degrees Fahrenheit warmer than it would be without an atmosphere. This warmth is essential to life as we know it.

Fossil fuels such as coal, oil and natural gas are composed of carbon and hydrogen. Burning these fuels means combining them with oxygen: In this process, hydrogen becomes water (H_2O) and carbon becomes carbon dioxide (CO_2). These two naturally occurring atmospheric gases are particularly effective at trapping infrared light as heat; thus they are called "greenhouse gases."

Carbon is neither created nor destroyed in the production of energy; rather, it moves from one place to another. Aside from the carbon trapped in rocks, carbon is found in four places. First, it is present in all living things; we can think of the land-based plant and animal carbon supply as one unit. An equal amount, another unit, is present in marine plants and animals. By the same measure, the earth's atmosphere contains 70 units of carbon in the form of carbon dioxide. The ground stores about 800 units in the form of fossil fuel, primarily coal but also natural gas and oil. An additional 4,000 units of carbon are dissolved in the oceans.[2]

When we burn fossil fuels to heat our homes or generate electricity, we release carbon into the air. There it enters a complex cycle that eventually sends it to the sea floor in the form of calcium carbonate (chalk, from the shells of plankton), where it slowly, over eons, re-enters the earth. In the meantime, as we keep pumping more and more CO_2 into the atmosphere, it slowly builds up there—going from approximately 250 parts per million (ppm) in the 1950s, when this concentration began to be measured consistently, to around 350 ppm today. This buildup makes the atmosphere a better absorber of infrared and so raises average temperatures.

The Global Warming Debate

Scientific attention to global warming began in 1896, when the Swedish physical chemist Svante Arrhenius pointed out that humans were causing CO_2 levels to increase by burning coal and oil. Arrhenius calculated that a doubling of CO_2 in the earth's atmosphere could raise the average temperature by about four degrees Celsius. This estimate was only one degree higher than that provided by the best computer models we have today.[3]

Political interest in the greenhouse effect began in the 1930s, when a warm spell led to doom-and-gloom predictions that global warming was upon us.[4] Once the weather cooled off again, interest in the issue subsided. Renewed concern began in the 1980s, after new computer models suggested that warming effects could be noticeable in a few decades. In 1985, the United Nations Environment Program, the World Meteorological Organization and the International Council of Scientific Unions met in Villach, Austria, to discuss global warming. The participants issued a statement warning that it could become a reality as early as the first half of the twenty-first century, much earlier than previous estimates. According to the statement, while "some warming of climate now appears inevitable, the rate and degree of future warming could be profoundly affected by governmental policies on energy conservation, use of fossil fuels and the emission of some greenhouse gases."[5] At hearings of the U.S. Senate Subcommittee on Toxic Substances and Environmental Oversight in 1985, Senator Albert Gore, Jr., took up the cause, urging international scientific study of the greenhouse effect.

James Hansen, a scientist at the National Oceanic and Atmospheric Administration (NOAA) declared in a 1988 congressional hearing that he was 99 percent sure that warming induced by human beings had already begun.[6] Although many of his colleagues believed his certainty level to be too high, more of them have come to agree with Hansen in recent years. While politicians have picked up this debate about current warming, scientists have been more concerned about the long-term predictions of computer models.[7]

Also in 1988, the United Nations and the World Meteorological Organization founded the Intergovernmental Panel on Climate Change (IPCC), a group of scientists and other scholars brought together to assess the situation and analyze policy recommendations. In recent years, IPCC reports have confirmed that human-caused global warming is almost certainly a reality.[8] It will increase in the future, and its overall effects will be negative. What, if anything, we can do about it is much less clear.

A series of world conferences have kept global warming in the political limelight. A 1992 conference in Rio de Janeiro produced a preliminary global treaty. In a 1995 conference in Berlin, most nations committed themselves to a general agreement to reduce greenhouse gases. A more detailed "protocol" was adopted in Kyoto, Japan, in December 1997. Under the Kyoto Protocol, the developed, industrialized countries committed to reduce their collective 1990 levels of greenhouses gas emissions by at least 5 percent by 2012. In November 1998, a meeting in Buenos Aires, Argentina, adopted specific deadlines for carrying out the Kyoto Protocol.

What We Can Expect

Although we are uncertain about how much warming is occurring, we can expect the pre-industrial level of carbon dioxide in the earth's atmosphere to have doubled by 2050 if we continue to burn fossil fuel at current rates. The expected warming will have many consequences, a few of them positive but most negative. As glaciers melt and oceans rise, coastal areas and low-lying countries such as Bangladesh will be particularly hard hit. Some islands and coastal areas will become uninhabitable. Dikes will be needed to protect cities and some agricultural land. Changes in weather patterns that make some land drier and other land wetter will force populations to relocate. Current predictions suggest that the net change will hinder food production; at the very least, the reorganization of agriculture will be a long and complicated process. Potential effects on agriculture are exacerbated by other trends, particularly increases in population. At present, the production and distribution of crops is barely keeping pace with population growth. Global warming could upset this balance.

Some of the biggest effects of global warming may be on the distribution of plant and animal species. In the United States, for example, as the temperature warms, northern regions will become better suited to trees and plants that now grow in the south and to the animals and birds that depend on these trees. In principle, this problem will solve itself when plants and wildlife migrate. In practice, though, a great northern expansion of forests seems unlikely, as many trees and plants produce seeds that travel only a limited distance. If a road or town blocks the forest's path, migration will prove impossible. Thus, because of human habitation, we can expect global warming to cause an overall decrease in forests and plants. Some models predict that warming, by affecting ocean currents, could make some regions such as western Europe markedly colder, and thus less productive agriculturally.

One factor that contributes to global warming is the growing economic prosperity of China, India and nations in Southeast Asia. This trend is to be welcomed because it allows millions to rise out of poverty; however, industrialization requires increased use of fossil fuels. Most future growth in carbon emission is likely to come from the fast-growing economies of developing nations; China in particular relies for development on its vast deposits of coal. Without any intervention, emissions are expected to rise from 7 billion tons of carbon per year in 1990 to 20 billion in 2100.[9] If this happens, the concentration of greenhouse gases in the atmosphere would double by 2030 and triple by 2100.

If developed countries had followed the Kyoto Protocol when it was first created in 1997, they would have returned their greenhouse gas emissions to 1990 levels by the year 2000, thus postponing the date of CO_2 doubling by almost five years. The United States has not ratified the protocol and probably never will. Without participation from the United States, the protocol will not do much good. But let us imagine that the United States does ratify it. Will it do the trick? Freezing global emissions at current levels would delay the doubling until 2100. Although this proposal is far beyond anything now being considered, it still would not be enough to prevent greenhouse gas concentrations from continuing to rise far beyond the year 2100. If we wanted to stabilize CO_2 at double its 1950s concentration of 250 ppm sometime in the twenty-second century, growing populations and an expanding world economy dictate that emissions would have to be cut worldwide by 70 percent or more.

These estimates involve enormous uncertainties, not only about the weather but about the future of energy technology. Some new forms of energy, such as hydrogen fuel cells for cars and solar and wind power for homes, may become competitive with oil products more quickly than anticipated, thus leading to a massive reduction in the burning of fossil fuel.

What Should We Do?

Given these facts and predictions, we have several options, and some could be combined. First, we could do nothing special now to prepare for global warming. When the oceans rise too high, we will build dikes. When land becomes arid, we will move to wetter regions.

When population outstrips food production, we could stave off mass starvation by switching from meat to grains, which might give us time to control population. Given the uncertainties, and given that the warming may be slow, ignoring the problem might turn out to be the best approach. This would be a risky strategy, however, because it would leave us unprepared to cope with sudden change.

Second, we could prepare for the consequences of global warming. We could direct new development away from regions likely either to flood or to dry out and plan for the gradual resettlement of those who would have to vacate these areas. We could also try to reduce population growth. Of course, the very uncertainties that make the first approach attractive make this approach unappealing. We may end up wasting resources by taking the wrong steps; even planning would require considerable time and money. There are also political obstacles: Will the developed countries be eager to welcome 50 million refugees from Bangladesh who face no immediate crisis?

Third, we could reduce the production of greenhouse gases. Compliance with the Kyoto Protocol would cost the world $53 billion per year (in 1990 dollars), according to a model developed by William Nordhaus.[10] Given our uncertainty about the future, this is the most we can expect nations to spend; it is also about ten times more than we spend on family planning assistance, another global initiative aimed at preventing future harm.

Some actions taken to reduce greenhouse gases could be beneficial for reasons other than reducing global warming, and thus will be worth the effort. For example, increases in energy efficiency could be cost-effective in their own right. We would expect such beneficial steps to be taken eventually, regardless of global warming concerns, but it might be worth allocating resources to speed them up. However, we can expect that special interests would slow this transition. In addition, the resources required, such as incentives and taxes, are not trivial. But a "no regrets" strategy would be beneficial even if global warming turns out to be a lot of hot air.

Other steps are more expensive. Substantial reductions in carbon production can be expected to weaken the economy of any country that tries it. Large amounts of resources would be necessary to re-build and redesign everything from automobiles to factories to en-tire cities, and changes in social behavior would be required as well. For example, a society could realize substantial energy savings by al-tering residential patterns, with more people living in highly con-centrated developments (perhaps surrounded by nearby "green belts") linked by convenient systems of mass transportation. This step would require overcoming citizens' reluctance to live in urban areas, many of which currently suffer from social decay.

A fourth option would be to remove CO_2 from the earth's atmos-phere. We could do this by "natural" methods such as planting trees, thereby rebuilding the massive forests that people have destroyed in the past few hundred years. We could also reduce CO_2 through "fer-tilizing" the Antarctic Ocean with iron, which would allow marine phytoplankton to grow in abundance and suck CO_2 out of the at-mosphere. This proposal, known as "the Geritol solution," after the iron supplement, was identified by the U.S. National Research Council panel as a potential solution to global warming but has been largely scorned by politicians. Early scientific testing suggests that the amount of iron deposits that would be needed to produce lasting at-mospheric CO_2 decreases may be impractical. Even so, many scien-tists believe that the potential benefits are worth further research.[11]

Fifth, we could try to change the course of development of coun-tries where the use of fossil fuels is increasing. The international community could try to induce these countries to develop in other ways, particularly through trades in which wealthy nations offer some benefit in return for cooperation. For example, developed countries could provide aid dedicated to technologies that increase the efficiency of fossil fuel usage or that require the use of alterna-tive fuels. The developed countries would benefit from a decline in the effects of global warming. The developing countries could con-tribute other benefits to the trade, such as reductions in fossil fuel subsidies and increased monitoring of environmental effects.

All these options (except the first) require accepting wise trade-offs. People would have to swallow the idea that some agreement is better than no agreement, even if it seems unfair and even if it threatens national and individual autonomy. All the elements for an impasse are in place.

Psychological Biases That Prevent Action

Several of the psychological biases we have discussed in this book affect political decisions—or, more often, indecision—about global warming. As with the global fishing crisis, some of these cognitive mistakes are based on our faulty assessments of the effects of future actions.

The magnitude and nature of global warming are highly uncertain. We know that increased CO_2 correlates with warming, that CO_2 has been increasing and that warming will change sea levels, rainfall patterns and the habitability of many regions. We do not know how fast this will happen, or whether the warming effect might be countered by the cooling effects that caused past ice ages. Quantitative predictions rely on computer models of the global climate, but most still do not work well. Sometimes they predict that greater warming should have occurred than has been measured, so they appear to be taking insufficient account of some factor that is slowing things. The models also fail to incorporate various mechanisms that could lead to a sudden increase in warming.

People use this uncertainty to support whichever side they take on the issue. Like many political conservatives opposed to international agreements or government intervention, radio talk-show host Rush Limbaugh has argued that disagreement among scientists is proof that we need do nothing about global warming.[12] Notably, Limbaugh's evidence came from opinion polls of scientists that showed considerable disagreement on the question of whether human-caused warming has *already* occurred—a less important question than whether it *will* occur. On the other side of the debate, environmentalists argue that we should prepare for the worst-case scenario—widespread disruption of life on Earth.

In a wise essay about global warming, economist Thomas Schelling argues that we should be preparing for effects that are larger than those predicted by scientific models. He points out that "there isn't any scientific principle according to which all alarming possibilities prove to be benign upon further investigation."[13] Thus the best strategy may be to take a middle course but also to make sure we can adapt quickly if the worst happens.

Even if compelling scientific evidence of global warming emerges, we can expect the public and its representatives to remain skeptical about the need for action. The human preference for the status quo will hinder effective solutions. We might pay more to avoid significant social change than we would pay to accept major changes aimed at improving the environment and our own lives. This tendency could lead us to pay excessive amounts of money to maintain aspects of our current way of life that we would be better off without, such as detached one-family houses with large green lawns, or commuting to work by private automobile. We might be willing to spend more on dikes that temporarily stave off flooding than on resettlement and new construction. Losses of present conveniences and possessions loom larger than the great economic and environmental gains we could achieve (or the losses we could prevent) through relatively small sacrifices.

The status quo bias could also inhibit negotiated agreements by making governments reluctant to trade. For example, a country that is offered assistance in developing solar energy in exchange for a promise to reduce its use of fossil fuel might choose to view the reduction as a loss and thus refuse the offer. The same country, if it already had the assistance, might prefer to reduce fossil fuel than to give up the development aid.

The omission bias is another important factor in decisions about global warming. Throughout the book, we have discussed instances in which people act according to a general desire not to cause harm through their actions, yet they ignore the harm caused by inaction. The omission bias makes us reluctant to take actions to reduce global warming, even when we know that inaction will lead to changes in the status quo. Like other biases, this one can operate in citizens evaluating their government's policies or in government officials themselves. At the individual level, the omission bias permits us to deny responsibility. We excuse ourselves from changing our energy consumption habits or lobbying our representatives, even when such neglect exacerbates global warming. At the government level, legislators often oppose trade deals that will help many of their representatives but hurt a few—especially if these few are vocal in their protests.

The Search for Fair Solutions

Identifying the biases that cloud our perceptions is an important first step toward making wise decisions about global warming. An awareness of these flaws will make us more willing to confront the problem and consider solutions. Dealing with global warming effectively could require coercion—a kind of harm—and a move away from the status quo. Sometimes, the coercion infringes on what some view as their personal rights; for instance, the right to fell trees on private property. International agreements on carbon standards may interfere with national sovereignty by placing sanctions on violators. Most people will benefit from reforms that require coercion, though they would not normally cooperate with reforms in the absence of compulsion.

The various options for dealing with global warming will distribute costs and benefits in different ways among individuals, nations and generations. This leads to the question, What is fair? Fairness will be a matter of constant debate as solutions to the problem are considered worldwide. The application of different fairness criteria could lead to endless recrimination and breakdowns of the cooperation we will need to prevent a crisis.

One basic equity issue concerns the industrialization of developing nations. Countries such as China and India want the opportunity to develop as the West developed, through reliance on fossil fuels. These countries and others hope to accomplish the kind of benefits for their citizens that people in the United States enjoy—including heavy reliance on the private automobile. Requiring these countries to reduce carbon dioxide emissions would surely thwart some of their dreams. It does not seem "fair" to tell these countries that they cannot develop as we have.

Cost is another important equity issue. Who should pay for solutions to global warming? At the international level, several criteria have been proposed:

1. *Ability to pay.* The hardships imposed by expenditures could depend on individuals' income. As the average after-tax income per person is about $10,000 per year, $100 billion in contributions from the United States would come out to about $400 per citizen. If this burden were distributed according to income level, the contribution could be met without creating great harm to American citizens. But in Bangladesh, where the average annual income per person is about $250, a tax of even $40 per person would substantially increase the death rate from starvation and disease. The distribution of the total burden of controlling global warming should take into account the various countries' ability to pay.

2. *Causal responsibility.* When a bad situation requires a costly solution, we often assign responsibility according to perceived causation. In the case of global warming, the principle of causal responsibility would lead us to assign payment to the countries that have produced the most CO_2, including the United States, Canada, western Europe, Russia and other former Soviet states, Korea and Japan.

    When this principle agrees with the principle of ability to pay, which we have assumed to be relevant, it can be considered fair. But efforts to extract contributions from nations that have recently become poor could cause unfair hardships. For example, the U.S.S.R. was one of the world's top carbon producers; but emissions dropped and poverty rose sharply following the breakup of the Soviet Union. Should Russian citizens be required to pay for environmental damage caused by a régime whose downfall they overwhelmingly supported? Because of such complications, it appears unlikely that causal responsibility alone will determine who will pay.

3. *Deterrence.* Another reason for requiring polluters to pay for the harm they cause is that these costs may prevent them from inflicting similar harm in the future. While the principle of deterrence corresponds closely with the notion of causal responsibility, its application to global warming is not clear. Deterrence implies that punishment will deter future undesired behavior. But if countries are punished for actions that were well-intentioned and not yet known to be environmentally harmful, what lesson will they learn—that they should always listen to environmentalists? Global warming did not even become part of environmentalists' agenda until the 1990s; most of the buildup of greenhouse gases occurred earlier. Most likely, no lesson would be learned at all. If this is true, then deterrence is not a useful principle for allocating the burden of alleviating global warming.

Perhaps the most basic equity issue of all is whether we should pay some of the costs of reducing global warming now or leave potentially larger costs to future generations. This can be the easiest question to overlook, as no members of future generations are clamoring to be heard.

One major stumbling block in negotiations is that people tend to make egocentric determinations of fairness—they decide what is fair based on their own self-interest. In a social dilemma simulation based on the fishery crisis in the northeastern United States (described in Chapter 5), participants were assigned to one of four roles as representatives of different fishing groups, with different claims on the scarce resource. The stakeholders were informed that although they were responsible for maximizing their associations' profits, they had a shared motivation to negotiate a combined harvesting level that would preserve a sustainable amount of shark. The researchers asked the participants to allocate harvesting cutbacks among the four groups. The dilemma was designed so that several principles could be used to allocate cutbacks among the four parties: splitting profits equally, reducing harvests by equal numbers of metric tons, reducing harvests by equal percentages of current harvests and reducing harvests in proportion to how much each person depended on the long-term future. Each subject tended to think that the fairest method was whatever imposed the least cost on his or her group. The desire to maximize profit led subjects to justify (to themselves) their attempts to claim as large a share of the limited resource as possible.[14]

This experiment suggests that people are not simply selfish. They may sincerely desire to be fair, but their unique perspectives in a negotiation leads them to believe they are behaving justly when in truth they are not. Nations engaging in difficult negotiations over the costs of reducing global warming need to keep this fact in mind. Citizens and politicians are well advised to try to consider alternative views of what would constitute a fair solution.

Negotiating Tradeoffs

We have examined the biases that affect perceptions of the global warming debate and discussed the role that fairness concerns may play in negotiations about potential solutions. These biases combine to breed dysfunctional competition in which parties try to claim the greatest amount of resources for themselves—or try to shirk as much responsibility as they can. When parties are able to recognize and overcome these biases, they will become more willing to search for wise trades that require small costs in return for large gains.

One innovative solution to the global warming crisis is a set of mechanisms, collectively called "flexibility mechanisms," aimed at reducing greenhouse gas emissions by promoting creative cooperation among nations. The three mechanisms most often discussed are: (1) joint implementation, or international cooperation on emission reduction; (2) emissions trading between industrialized nations; and (3) the clean development mechanism, or efforts to allow rich nations to receive credit for helping poor nations to develop in ways that emit less CO_2. Incorporated into the Kyoto treaty and its subsequent elaboration in Buenos Aires in 1998, these mechanisms allow countries to reach beneficial trades on the issues that matter most to them. Because these three mechanisms are related, and because the Kyoto treaty may be revised further if it is ever implemented, we shall discuss them collectively as "flexibility mechanisms."

Suppose countries U and V both produce the same amount of carbon and must reduce their emissions by 10 percent. As a wealthy country, U is already fairly efficient in its use of energy. A 10 percent reduction would cost it $100 billion. Country V, on the other hand, is energy-inefficient and poor. It can meet its required reduction at a cost of $25 billion through relatively inexpensive initiatives that richer countries have already undertaken, such as replacing aging power plants with newer ones. But $25 billion is a much larger share of its total budget than $100 billion is of country U's budget, and this expenditure would impose great hardships.

The stage is set for a beneficial trade. Both countries must reduce carbon emissions, but V's emissions can be reduced at a much lower cost. V cannot afford even this relatively small amount, but U can. U might be able to buy its carbon reductions from V. For just $50 billion, U could fund a 20 percent reduction in V's emissions–the same total reduction as if U and V had each reduced emissions independently by 10 percent, but at a saving of $75 million. If either country were able to contribute greater funds, the reduction could be greater still and even more money could be saved.

This creative trade involves the negotiated cooperation of two countries, one of the outcomes being a low-cost reduction in carbon emissions. From our point of view, flexibility mechanisms are beneficial trades that help everyone. Many economists also think they are wonderful, and the Clinton administration insisted that they be included in the Kyoto agreement. Even so, environmentalists have resisted the idea of making small sacrifices for larger gains in the context of such negotiations.

This situation is not a fantasy. To reduce its use of coal and oil, the United States might have to replace coal-burning power plants with wind power or nuclear power, both of which cost more than coal in most areas. In Russia, great quantities of methane (a greenhouse gas like CO_2) escape from holes in pipelines. For the same reduction in greenhouse gases, repairing Russian pipelines would be an inexpensive alternative to building new power plants in the United States. Similarly, if the United States funded a new power plant in a poor country to "work off" its obligations under the treaty, it would save money and the other country would enjoy a new, more efficient plant. If the other country didn't expect to benefit from the trade, it could reject it.

In a recent test of the notion that emissions levels can be measured accurately, residents in the Mexican cities of Monterrey and Guadalajara replaced ordinary light bulbs with energy-saving bulbs that are 75 percent more efficient and last ten times as long.[15] The objective of the project was to lower electricity use and thus reduce carbon emissions from power plants. Det Norske Veritas, a Norwegian institute acting as an impartial observer, confirmed that the lighting helped reduce the equivalent of 171,168 tons of CO_2 from the atmosphere between 1995 and 1998. With the costs of the installation paid by the World Bank as part of an experiment, Mexicans can expect to save money from this plan in the long run. Most important, the experiment shows that carbon levels can be measured, thus suggesting that nations can be accurately credited for declines in emissions.

It is possible to make flexibility mechanisms part of the treaty for every nation. In this case, a system of "tradable quotas" develops: Each nation would have a quota for CO_2 emissions, but the quotas could be bought and sold in the marketplace. A country such as the United States could purchase some amount of a poor country's quota, thus allowing the United States to retain something closer to its current level of emissions. The poor country would be left with a smaller emissions quota, which it could meet by using the money it received from the United States. For example, the poor country could use funds from the quota sale to increase the efficiency of its power plants. This trading is highly efficient because poor countries can adopt energy-saving measures much more cheaply than rich ones can. A variation on this idea, "tradable permits," occurs within one nation, among firms that emit carbon into the atmosphere. Under this scenario, firms that could reduce emissions inexpensively would sell their permits to firms that cannot. Many firms would thus reduce their pollution more than they would otherwise. The total cost of a given level of emission reduction would therefore be lower, making it easier for government to demand greater reductions.

Estimates suggest that such trading can save the rich countries as much as 30 percent of what they would otherwise pay to meet Kyoto standards for CO_2 reduction.[16] The United States could save a great deal more—up to 90 percent.[17] Past experience bears out these estimates. In the Clean Air Act Amendments of 1990, the American government set up a trading system for sulfur dioxide emissions, the major cause of acid rain. Emissions of sulfur dioxide were cut, as required, and for far less than the cost originally predicted. Part of the credit for the lower cost must go to the new trading system.[18]

Flexibility mechanisms are not a cure-all. If they are extended worldwide, we can expect the relationship between trading and retroactive credits to complicate matters. To encourage nations to begin cutbacks immediately instead of waiting for the treaty to be ratified, the Kyoto treaty gave countries credit for cuts made since the initial signing. Since then, Russia has undergone a major economic collapse; this makes it fairly easy for a country such as the United States to pay Russia for the "reductions" resulting from the collapse. The situation is not all bad—it increases foreign aid to needy countries—but it does undercut the purpose of the treaty. Still, this problem is easily solved: Rather than scrapping the notion of flexibility mechanisms completely, governments should limit them to emissions reductions that come from improvements to infrastructure, not from declines in economies.

Opposition to flexibility mechanisms is fierce. Environmental groups typically argue that they are just a way for rich companies to buy out of their obligations. At the 1998 meeting held in Buenos Aires to flesh out the Kyoto treaty, European countries argued strenuously for limits on the amount of trading that could be undertaken; they disliked the idea of letting rich countries "off the hook." Michael Sandel, a professor of government at Harvard University, argued that "turning pollution into a commodity to be bought and sold removes the moral stigma that is properly associated with it. If a company or a country is fined for spewing excessive pollutants into the air, the community conveys its judgment that the polluter has done something wrong. A fee, on the other hand, makes pollution just another cost of doing business, like wages, benefits and rent."[19]

But should a moral stigma be attached to carbon dioxide? CO_2 is abundant in nature and essential for the growth of plants. It is more similar to water than to soot or sewage. The emission of carbon is a byproduct of economic growth, which is not an inherently immoral process. Rather, assuming that global warming is a reality, we simply need to find ways to reduce its production. Trading is an efficient means of doing so.

Many critics of flexibility mechanisms have made fair criticisms of particular projects. Technical difficulties do exist, particularly in measurement, and some plans for emissions reduction may not work. But we can expect obstacles to emerge in any sort of new global trading system, and we can assume that these problems will be resolved over time.

The real objection to flexibility mechanisms seems to come from moral intuition. And intuition, in turn, seems to result from an unwillingness to trade small losses for larger gains. In the case of tradable quotas, the loss is that the buyer country reduces its own carbon emissions less than it would if it had undertaken to comply with new standards on its own soil. The gain is that the seller country reduces its CO_2 more than the buyer country could for the same amount of money. The gain outweighs the loss, or the trade would not take place. We saw in Chapter 6 that "moral" objections to free trade often fail to account for the benefits that increased trade brings to the poor. Similarly, "moral" objections to flexibility mechanisms ignore the reduced costs that the solution provides to rich and poor alike as well as the decreased odds that the poor will suffer disproportionately from future warming. Active citizens need to show their support for government officials who understand that these innovative solutions are beneficial to everyone.

Changing Our Thinking

In asking citizens to change the way they think about politics, we are not suggesting that disagreement should disappear on such issues as education, crime and the environment. We are asking them to think broadly about the costs and benefits of political decisions and to advocate policies that will do the most good overall. Activism may be a struggle among competing conceptions of the overall "good," or among different beliefs about how to accomplish utopia. But political activism should not be a war between competing interests in which the gains of one group necessitate the losses of others. This kind of divisional activism fosters stalemate and inaction.

The six simple principles of this book can move us toward a more unified activism based on maximizing resources. All six of these principles apply to the specific issue of reversing the dangerous trend toward global warming.

First, individuals must learn to develop a more rational outlook toward political decisions by identifying the cognitive biases in their own decision making. This training, now a standard part of managerial education, should be made available to citizens and politicians alike. Identifying biases means becoming aware of the most common mistakes that affect our political judgment.

The behavioral decision literature has categorized a range of biases that affect judgment. We have discussed those most relevant to global warming: the omission bias, the status-quo bias, egocentric perceptions of fairness, and unwillingness to help solve social dilemmas. These biases cause resistance to beneficial changes that require losses as well as gains. Costs might include new technologies for reducing atmospheric CO_2, the expansion of public transportation networks or the funding of major research programs to explore new energy technology. By accepting small losses voluntarily, we can expect to accomplish an eventual decrease in the rate of climate change.

Second, we can break the fixed-pie approach to negotiation by searching for mutually beneficial tradeoffs. The fixed-pie mindset is the most widespread and detrimental mistake made within the two-party political process in the United States. When members of Congress seek to strengthen or weaken legislation, they should call a temporary truce to search for efficient trades. Parties who recognize that they value different components of the same decision will be in a position to search for creative agreements. Once again, this knowledge base is readily available: Eliminating the mythical fixed pie is now a standard component of managerial education.

Parties engaged in debates and negotiations about global warming must also learn to break the fixed-pie mindset. In the case of international negotiations, this may involve drawing on the differences between nations' needs and capabilities. When rich nations have already developed and used technologies to increase energy efficiency, they should be able to reduce their own global warming debt by sharing this expertise with the poor countries that need it. Flexibility mechanisms are logistically challenging, but the potential rewards are priceless.

The search for efficient trades can begin even before negotiation when we choose what to advocate in the political domain. Activists who try to wage war on all issues relevant to their cause are likely to dilute their efforts and lose on all fronts. For example, an environmental group may give the appearance of being equally concerned about such varied issues as global warming, the decline of biodiversity, the genetic engineering of soybeans and the safety of nuclear power. It seems likely that genetic engineering and nuclear power are relatively minor risks to humans and the natural environment, but biodiversity and global warming are more serious problems. Activists who take a hard line on all fronts will be perceived as rigid and insensitive to other concerns, such as the reduction of poverty. Like the boy who cried "wolf," they will be ignored when they should be heard.

Third, we can avoid the waste that results from dysfunctional competition. When state and local governments compete to see who can make the greatest sacrifice to win some prize, the winner typically offers more than the prize is worth. The human desire to want to "beat" the other side keeps the narrow goals of all parties in the forefront of negotiations and, in turn, prevents wiser and more cooperative decision making. Reducing dysfunctional competition means finding the most efficient means to a beneficial end, regardless of what "side" you are on.

When contemplating means of reducing global warming, we must decide on an overall goal and try to reach it at minimal cost. If our goal is to reduce the warming itself, methods of removing carbon from the atmosphere may be more efficient than reducing the burning of fossil fuel. Politicians who try to fend off all costs to an efficient solution are standing in the way of wise resolutions to the conflict. Citizens must learn to support officials who advocate solutions that will benefit the rich, the poor and the natural environment alike.

Fourth, we can recognize that loyalty to a small group is not always a virtue. A great deal of unnecessary harm occurs when people fight for "their" group at the expense of others. When individuals choose to ally themselves with a nation, a labor union or an industry, they often fail to recognize that their group membership is arbitrary.

We have advocated flexibility mechanisms as types of negotiated agreements based on wise trades, but special-interest groups will always try to block such pie-enlarging solutions. It can be tempting for members of pressure groups to feel noble when they make a personal sacrifice on the group's behalf. They need to realize that their "selflessness" may be exacting an even greater sacrifice from society at large. Seen in this light, it becomes clear that many special-interest group behaviors are inefficient and even unethical. If the

German coal miners described in Chapter 4 had recognized the destructive effects of the continued subsidization of coal on society and the environment, they might have accepted the need for layoffs and lobbied instead for job training in other sectors.

Fifth, we can do a better job of considering the effects of our decisions on future generations and adjusting our behavior accordingly. Although most people claim to be concerned about the effects of their actions on others, we often try to solve current problems by passing along costs to the young or to people not yet born. The devastation of parts of the natural environment is one undeniable example of this common behavior. We need to accept our responsibility to bequeath a healthy world to those who do not yet have a voice to demand it.

We can expect that global warming will have the greatest impact on those not yet born. Thus, global warming involves a tradeoff over time, in which people presently alive make sacrifices for the benefit of future generations. A compelling argument can be made that such sacrifices are not necessary and may even be unfair. After all, over the past hundred years, life on earth has steadily improved for human beings throughout the world, despite population increases, with the exception of southern Africa. Infant mortality has declined, people live longer, we enjoy more amusements and conveniences and we perform less backbreaking work than our forbears. Thus, assuming this trend continues, it is quite likely that future generations will be better off than we are, on average. But global warming could have devastating effects on millions at the bottom of the economic ladder. Why should we make sacrifices for those who may not need our help?

This brings us to our sixth principle: Sometimes great benefits can be accomplished for many at small or no cost to a few. We can apply this insight to attack some truly large problems, such as global poverty. Although most citizens of wealthy nations recognize a responsibility to help the poor abroad, they think of such help as a direct transfer of money or food. In other words, they tend to believe they must sacrifice goods so that these goods can go to others.

Citizens need to recognize that they can help the poor more efficiently. They can do a great deal of good at little or no cost to themselves, and sometimes even with mutual benefit.

Global warming is a good instance of a dilemma in which we, the
citizens of wealthy nations, must learn to recognize the needs of
those distant from us, whether in space or time. Despite expected
worldwide gains in wealth across time, global warming will almost
certainly have the most devastating effects on the poor. Thus, although most of the costs of dealing with global warming will fall on
the developed countries, most of the benefits will accrue to countries that are now poor and will still be relatively poor well into the
twenty-first century.[20] The abatement of global warming's effects can
be considered a cost that rich countries take on now to benefit poor
countries later.

The needs of the poor and the requirement of efficiency may require us to reassess our overall objective with regard to global warming. We may find that it would be more efficient to give aid to poor
nations that will need to cope with increased warming than to focus
on the long-term goal of preventing global warming in general. If so,
we might focus on protecting those whom we can expect to suffer
the most harm, such as the residents of Bangladesh. In general, our
high level of uncertainty about future global warming and its effects
on the environment should lead us to creative alternatives that
might help people more efficiently now and in the future. This
means carefully studying the long-term effects of continued reliance
on fossil fuels and exploring options such as flexibility mechanisms
and the Geritol solution.

These six strategies can help citizens think critically and rationally
about their own decisions and those of their elected officials.
Modifying our own thinking and behavior can be difficult. Most efforts at change fail. The psychologist Kurt Lewin suggests that for
change to last over time, an individual must go beyond mere awareness of his imperfections. For significant change to occur, people
must "unfreeze" their existing decision processes, specify workable

alternatives and create the conditions in which they can "refreeze" these new processes.[21] The same applies to organizations and governments.

Maximizing the pie of social resources requires such stages of change. In this book, we have tried to begin the unfreezing process by specifying numerous government inefficiencies that have led to unnecessary losses and sacrifice. The political decision-making principles we have described offer an alternative based on accepting small losses to gain large benefits. Once citizens have adopted this mindset, politicians will need to meet these expectations if they hope to gain power. At this point, citizens must "refreeze" their new decision processes and hold politicians accountable for their actions. By changing what citizens value, we can change what politicians endorse.

Taking Action

In his book *A House Divided*, Mark Gerzon argues that the American populace has been divided in an unhealthy manner between six dominant groups: the religious state, the capitalist state, the disempowered state, the media state, the transformation ("new age") state and the governing state.[22] Most citizens, he finds, focus on their membership in one of these states and make most of their political judgments accordingly. While it is easy to debate this particular delineation of citizen groups, we agree with Gerzon's argument that most of us use a limited lens for making political judgments.

The goal of this book has been to encourage citizens to adopt a new way of thinking about political issues that will inspire them to work for positive social change. Specifically, we have advocated a central objective: creating as much benefit as possible through wise trades. Just as we must overcome the parochialism that leads us to fight for specific issues, we must use our political power to lessen each country's dysfunctional competition with other nations. We must actively seek out opportunities to provide efficient aid to those in need, both within and beyond our borders. Individuals and governments will doubtless embrace different visions for the world, but in many areas we can find agreement. Eliminating poverty, decreasing warfare and protecting the environment for future generations will benefit us all.

Once citizens have adopted this mindset, what can they do to contribute to solutions? The first step is to seek out and vote for politicians who seem dedicated to enlarging the social pie through cooperative and creative strategies rather than engaging in wasteful partisan battles. In a representative government, politicians are often tempted to cater to the most vocal and financially generous special-interest groups. In the United States, however, the electorate seems increasingly supportive of the "boring" issue of campaign finance reform. We hope that more politicians will recognize that their support of such causes may increase their chances of being elected (and, more important, will not destroy their chances of being re-elected).

Many nonprofit organizations rate politicians based on the degree to which they are pro-union, pro-business, pro-environment, liberal, conservative, and so forth. We need more organizations and media groups that assess the degree to which politicians expand, rather than shrink, the social pie. We encourage the formation of more activist groups such as Common Cause and the League of Women Voters, which derive their advocacy from a set of basic principles about the political process itself rather than from a point on the political spectrum.

Activism does not end on election day. Whether working on their own or within groups, citizens must monitor the activities of their government and voice their concerns to elected officials and bureaucrats (who are usually not "faceless" but concerned citizens trying to do a difficult job). This includes calling or writing members of Congress or other civil servants about the issues you care about, particularly those that affect future generations and the world's poor—groups typically neglected in political decisions.

Citizens can work to improve government decisions in many other ways. Some actions are easy. For example, few costs are associated with choosing to avoid eating depleted fish. Grassroots activities, including boycotts of products such as tuna fish, have been successful in creating important social, economic and environmental legislation. We further encourage good citizen behavior, such as buying products from companies that act responsibly and becoming an advocate for the world's poor by helping out with one of the twelve areas we discussed in Chapter 6.

Notice that the activities we have advocated fall into two groups. One is individual action that has some small effect, such as buying energy-efficient light bulbs. The other is political action, which individually has no immediate effect but cumulatively can have a big effect. This action might include volunteering for political candidates who will support research on energy-efficient light bulbs or fund programs to supply these bulbs to nations where they have been unavailable. Because we have limited time and energy for self-sacrifice, it is important to choose the right type of action. It may feel inconsistent to use regular bulbs while writing your representative about how the government might encourage the use of fluorescent bulbs, or to take every legal tax deduction while advocating politically that some deductions be eliminated. Political actions, even when combined with the actions of others, have a only small chance of being effective; but when they are, the result is much larger than nonpolitical actions such as conservation efforts.[23] Your choice of action requires as much thought about costs and benefits as your choice of which policies to support.

Most readers of this book are already engaged in their communities in some manner. It is easy to imagine that there are good people on both sides of issues such as the Vermont school system dispute we described in Chapter 2. But when communities battle against other groups to gain the most for themselves, the common goal can get lost. The battle in Vermont has not improved the quality or the equity of schooling for the state's children. Although our activism may arise out of membership in a particular group, we have a responsibility to advocate solutions in which the interest of the small group and society as a whole coincide rather than conflict.

Many citizens are well-informed about the benefits of democracy, the role of advocacy groups, the political process and the logic of key actors in the system. But most citizens do not have access to the type of decision making and negotiation training that pervades management schools. There is a dramatic difference in how most of us make political decisions compared to how we make personal and business decisions. Many more forces are pushing against rationality in the political process, including our own intuitive biases, the voices of special-interest groups and the combative rhetoric and actions of political and economic rivals. Every time citizens and politicians succumb to these forces, we reduce the resources available for healthcare, education, defense and tax reduction—or whatever issue concerns us most. Thinking and acting more rationally about politics is a worthwhile goal for everyone. We hope the ideas in this book make a small contribution toward this goal.

Notes

Introduction

1. G. Allison (1971), *Essence of Decision: Explaining the Cuban Missile Crisis* (Boston: Little, Brown); J. Stiglitz (1998), "The Private Uses of Public Interests: Incentives and Institutions," *Journal of Economic Perspectives* 12, no. 2:3–22.

2. Stiglitz, "Private Uses," 3–22.

3. Ibid., 4.

4. C. M. Sennott (1996, July 7), "The $150 Billion 'Welfare' Recipients: U.S. Corporations," *The Boston Globe*, 1.

5. R. E. Nisbett and L. Ross (1980), *Human Inference: Strategies and Shortcomings of Social Judgment* (Englewood Cliffs, N.J.: Prentice Hall), xi–xii.

6. J. Baron (2001), *Thinking and Deciding*, 3d. ed. (New York: Cambridge University Press); M. Bazerman (1998), *Judgment in Managerial Decision Making* (New York: Wiley); R. Dawes (1988), *Rational Choice in an Uncertain World* (New York: Harcourt Brace Jovanovich).

7. I. Ritov and J. Baron (1990), "Reluctance to Vaccinate: Omission Bias and Ambiguity," *Journal of Behavioral Decision Making* 3, no. 4:263–277.

8. M. A. Neale and M. H. Bazerman (1991), *Cognition and Rationality in Negotiation* (New York: Free Press).

9. D. M. Messick and K. Sentis (1985), "Estimating Social and Nonsocial Utility Functions from Ordinal Data," *European Journal of Social Psychology* 15, no. 4:389–399.

Chapter 1

1. M. Angell (1996, June 6), "Shattuck Lecture: Evaluating the Health Risks of Breast Implants: The Interplay of Medical Science, the Law, and Public

Opinion," *New England Journal of Medicine* 334, no. 23:1513–1518; J. T. Rosenbaum (1997, June 6), "Lessons from Litigation Over Silicone Breast Implants: A Call for Activism by Scientists," *Science* 276, no. 5318:1524–1525.

2. It was always known that the implants could cause local irritation and could rupture; but women were informed of these risks before surgery, and they were not an issue in the major lawsuits.

3. J. Kaiser (1999, June 25), "Panel Discounts Implant Disease Risk," *Science* 284, no. 5423:2065–2066.

4. Angell, "Shattuck Lecture."

5. H. Farlie (1989, January 23), "The Six Million Dollar Man," *New Republic,* 18.

6. Ibid.

7. I. Ritov and J. Baron (1990), "Reluctance to Vaccinate: Omission Bias and Ambiguity," *Journal of Behavioral Decision Making* 3, no. 4:263–277; J. R. Meszaros, D. A. Asch, J. Baron, J. C. Hershey, H. Kunreuther, and J. Schwartz-Buzaglo (1996), "Cognitive Processes and the Decisions of Some Parents to Forego Pertussis Vaccination for Their Children," *Journal of Clinical Epidemiology* 49, no. 6:697–703.

8. D. Kahneman, J. L. Knetsch, and R. H. Thaler (1990), "Experimental Tests of the Endowment Effect and the Coase Theorem," *Journal of Political Economy* 98, no. 6:1325–1348.

9. From a respondent quoted by W. Kempton, J. S. Boster, and J. A. Hartley (1995), *Environmental Values in American Culture* (Cambridge: MIT Press), 109.

10. D. Kahneman, I. Ritov, K. E. Jacowitz, and P. Grant (1993), "Stated Willingness to Pay for Public Goods: A Psychological Perspective," *Psychological Science* 4, no. 5:310–315; D. Kahneman and I. Ritov (1994), "Determinants of Stated Willingness to Pay for Public Goods: A Study of the Headline Method," *Journal of Risk and Uncertainty* 9:5–38.

11. J. Baron and I. Ritov (1993)."Intuitions about Penalties and Compensation in the Context of Tort Law," *Journal of Risk and Uncertainty* 7: 17–33.

12. B. N. Ames and L. S. Gold (1990, September 28), "Too Many Rodent Carcinogens: Mitogenesis Increases Mutagenesis," *Science* 249, no. 4976:970–971.

13. W. K. Viscusi (1995), "Carcinogen Regulation: Risk Characteristics and the Synthetic Risk Bias," *American Economic Review* 85, no. 2:50–54.

14. Ames and Gold, "Too Many Rodent Carcinogens."

15. P. Huber, (1991). *Galileo's revenge: Junk science in the courtroom* (New York: Basic Books).

16. *Harvard Medical School Health Letter* (1989), "Whooping Cough: The Last Gasp?" 15, no. 2:3 ff.

17. Joint Committee on Vaccination and Immunization (1981), *The Whooping Cough Epidemic, 1977–1979* (London: Her Majesty's Stationery Office); M. H. Smith (1988), "National Childhood Vaccine Injury Compensation Act," *Pediatrics* 82, no. 2:264–269.

18. C. Bowie (1990), "Viewpoint: Lessons from the Pertussis Vaccine Court Trial," *Lancet* 335, no. 8686:397–399; C. P. Howson and H. V. Fineberg (1992), "Adverse Events Following Pertussis and Rubella Vaccines: Summary of a Report of the Institute of Medicine," *Journal of the American Medical Association* 267:392–396.

19. A. R. Hinman and J. P. Koplan (1984), "Pertussis and Pertussis Vaccine: Reanalysis of Benefits, Risks, and Costs," *Journal of the American Medical Association* 251:3109–3113.

20. J. Cohen (1994), "Bumps on the Vaccine Road," *Science* 265, no. 2:1371–1373; C. Johnson (1993, July 15), "New Vaccine Technologies Boost Children's Health," *The Reuter Library Report.*

21. J. K. Inglehart (1987), "Compensating Children with Vaccine-Related Injuries," *New England Journal of Medicine* 316, no. 20:1283–1288.

22. E. Marshall (1995), "Tamoxifen's Trials and Tribulations," *Science* 270, no. 5238:910.

23. J. Sachs (1997), "Nature, Nurture and Growth," *The Economist* 343, no. 8021:19–22.

24. L. Mastroianni, Jr., P. J. Donaldson, and T. T. Kane (1990), *Developing New Contraceptives: Obstacles and Opportunities* (Washington, D.C.: National Academy Press).

25. This figure cannot be calculated precisely. The difficulty of matching donors and recipients will limit the benefits of an increase in donors.

26. K. Griffin and M. Macchetti (1995, January/February), "A Boy's Gift," *Health,* 50.

27. L. A. Smirnoff, R. M. Arnold, A. L. Caplan, B. A. Virnig, and D. L. Seltzer (1995), "Public Policy Governing Organ and Tissue Procurement in the United States," *Annals of Internal Medicine* 123, no. 1:10–17; A. J. Wing (1996), "Organs for Transplantation: Should the UK Follow Belgium?" *Journal of the Royal Society of Medicine* 89, no. 12:661–662.

28. A. C. Klassen and D. K. Klassen (1996), "Who Are the Donors in Organ Donation? The Family's Perspective on Mandated Choice," *Annals of Internal Medicine* 125, no. 1:70–73.

29. Ibid.; M. E. Young (1998, March 14), "New Program Aims to Boost Organ Donation," *Dallas Morning News,* 6A.

30. C. Nickerson, J. D. Jasper, and D. A. Asch (1998), "Comfort Level, Financial Incentives, and Consent for Organ Donation," *Transplantation Proceedings* 30, no. 1:155–159.

31. G. R. Hardin (1968), "The Tragedy of the Commons," *Science* 162:1243–1248.

32. M. F. X. Gnant, P. Wamser, P. Goetzinger, T. Sautner, R. Steininger, and F. Muehlbacher (1991, October), "The Impact of the Presumed Consent Law and a Decentralized Organ Procurement System on Organ Donation: Quadruplication in the Number of Organ Donors," *Transplantation Proceedings* 23, no. 5:2685–2686.

33. D. J. Schemo (1998, January 15), "Death's New Sting in Brazil: Removal of Organs," *New York Times*, A3.

34. T. G. Peters, D. S. Kittur, L. J. McGaw, M. R. Roy, and E. W. Nelson (1996), "Organ Donors and Nondonors: An American Dilemma," *Archives of Internal Medicine* 156, no. 21:2419–2424.

35. Schemo, "Death's New Sting."

36. One religion that does inhibit donation is Buddhism, which holds that the soul does not leave the body for several days after death; at this point, it is too late for organs to be removed. Other religions forbid the integrity of the body to be violated after death.

37. J. J. Skowronski (1997, December), "On the Psychology of Organ Donation: Attitudinal and Situational Factors Related to the Willingness to Be an Organ Donor," *Basic and Applied Social Psychology* 19, no. 4:427–456.

38. The AMA admits that this group would be a small minority.

39. Council on Ethical and Judicial Affairs, American Medical Association (1994), "Strategies for Cadaveric Organ Procurement: Mandated Choice and Presumed Consent," *Journal of the American Medical Association* 272, no. 10:809–812.

40. M. F. Anderson (1995), "The Future of Organ Transplantation: From Where Will New Donors Come, to Whom Will Their Organs Go?" *Health Matrix: Journal of Law-Medicine* 4:249–310.

41. Council on Ethical and Judicial Affairs, American Medical Association, "Strategies for Cadaveric Organ Procurement."

42. E. Rosenthal (1993, May 11), "Parents Find Solace in Donating Organs," *New York Times*, C1, C11.

43. U.S. Food and Drug Administration (1981, June), "The Story of the Laws behind the labels," *FDA Consumer*:206–207.

44. National Press Club Address, October 29, 1974, cited in H. G. Grabowski and J. M. Vernon (1983), *The Regulation of Pharmaceuticals: Balancing the Benefits and Risks* (Washington, D.C.: American Enterprise Institute for Public Policy Research), 5.

45. W. M. Wardell and L. Lasagna (1975), *Regulation and Drug Development* (Washington, D.C.: American Enterprise Institute for Public Policy Research), 73.

46. Editorial (1987, June 2), "Human Sacrifice," *Wall Street Journal*, 30.

47. B. A. Brody (1995), *Ethical Issues in Drug Testing, Approval, and Pricing: The Clot-Dissolving Drugs* (New York: Oxford University Press).

48. R. Ueno and S. Kuno (1987, June 13), "Dextran Sulphate, a Potent Anti-HIV Agent In Vitro Having Synergism with Zidovudine," *Lancet* 1, no. 8546: 1379.

49. R. Loth (1988, October 12), "AIDS Protestors Close FDA Headquarters," *Boston Globe*.

50. L. K. Altman (1993, April 6), "AIDS Study Casts Doubt on Value of Hastened Drug Approval in U.S.," *New York Times*, C3.

51. J. D. Donahue, ed. (1999), *Making Washington Work: Tales of Innovation in the Federal Government* (Washington, D.C.: Brookings Institution Press), 159–173.

52. S. G. Stolberg (1999, May 11), "Drug Review Is Effective, Agency Says," *New York Times*, A16.

53. W. L. Pines (2001, January 11), FDA's New Mantra for Drug Approvals: "Safety (Yes!) First," WebMD Medical News, http://www.webmd.com.

54. D. Reissman (1999), "MCO Drug Review: How Soon Is Too Soon?" *Drug Benefit Trends* 11, no. 2:20, 22.

55. Anonymous (1995, June), "FDA Reform and the European Medicines Evaluation Agency," *Harvard Law Review* 108:2009–2026.

56. A. Alger (1999, May 17), "Trials and Tribulations," *Forbes*.

57. K. Eichenwald and G. Kolata (1999, May 16), "Drug Trials Hid Conflicts for Doctors," *New York Times*, A1, A34–35; K. Eichenwald and G. Kolata (1999, May 17), "A Doctor's Drug Studies Turn into Fraud," *New York Times*, A1, A16–17.

58. J. Moreno, A. L. Caplan, and P. R. Wolpe (1998), "Updating Protections for Human Subjects Involved in Research," *Journal of the American Medical Association* 280, no. 22:1951–1958.

59. T. O. Tengs, M. E. Adams, J. S. Pliskin, D. G. Safran, J. E. Sielgel, M. E. Weinstein, and J. D. Graham (1995), "Five-Hundred Life-Saving Interventions and Their Cost-Effectiveness," *Risk Analysis* 15, no. 3:360–390.

Chapter 2

1. J. Baden (1995, October 25), "The Adverse Consequences of the EPA," *Seattle Times*, B5.

2. Ibid.

3. R. L. Stroup (1995, April), "Endangered Species Act: Making Innocent Species the Enemy," Political Economy Research Center Policy Series, Issue PS–3, http://www.perc.org/ps3.htm.

4. A. Pandya, F. Rosenfeld, and V. Caffee (1998, March 11), "A Strong Superfund Law Is Crucial to Make Polluters Clean Up Sites," *Asbury Park Press*, 13.

5. M. H. Bazerman, J. Gillespie, and D. Moore (1999), "The Human Mind As a Barrier to Wiser Environmental Agreements," *American Behavioral Scientist* 42, no. 8:1277–1300.

6. N. Walley and B. Whitehead (1994, May-June), "It's Not Easy Being Green," *Harvard Business Review*, 46–51; K. Palmer, W. Oates, and P. Portney (1995), "Tightening Environmental Standards: The Benefit-Cost or the No-Cost Paradigm?" *Journal of Economic Perspectives* 9, no. 4:119–132.

7. Defenders of Wildlife (2000, April 20), "Top 10 Lies About the ESA," http://198.240.72.81/esatop.html.

8. A. J. Hoffman, J. Gillespie, D. Moore, K. A. Wade-Benzoni, L. L. Thompson, and M. H. Bazerman (1999), "A Mixed-Motive Perspective on the Economics Versus Environment Debate," *American Behavioral Scientist* 42, no. 8:1254–1276.

9. A. Gore (1992), *Earth in the Balance* (Boston: Houghton-Mifflin); M. Porter and C. van der Linde (1995, September/October), "Green and Competitive: Ending the Stalemate," *Harvard Business Review:* 120–134; M. Porter and C. van der Linde (1995), "Toward a New Conception of the Environment-Competitiveness Relationship," *Journal of Economic Perspectives* 9, no. 4:97–118.

10. Gore, *Earth*, 342.

11. Hoffman et al., "A Mixed-Motive Perspective."

12. Ibid.

13. R. E. Walton and R. B. McKersie (1965), *A Behavioral Theory of Labor Negotiations: An Analysis of a Social Interaction System* (New York: McGraw-Hill).

14. R. Stegemeier (1995), *Straight Talk: The Future of Energy in the Global Economy* (Los Angeles: Unocal).

15. D. Lax and J. Sebenius (1986), *The Manager As Negotiator* (New York: Free Press).

16. C. Solomon (1993, March 29), "Clearing the Air: What Really Pollutes," *Wall Street Journal*, 1.

17. Greenwire Environmental News Service (1997, December 26), "Today's Issue," http://www.eenews.net/Greenwire.htm.

18. A. Marcus (2000), "Cooperative Regulation: Setbacks and Accomplishments of Project XL" (paper presented at the Association for Public Policy Analysis and Management 22nd Annual Research Conference, November 2–4, Seattle, Washington), 3.

19. C. Skrzycki (1997, January 24), "The Perils of Reinventing: Critics See a Playground for Polluters in EPA's XL Plan," *Washington Post*, D01.

20. M. Kriz (1998), "A Kinder, Gentler EPA Environment," *The National Journal* 30:34.

21. W. H. Miller (1997, August 18), "Washington Wreck," *Industry Week,* 116.

22. Ibid.

23. Skrzycki, "The Perils of Reinventing."

24. M. B. Powers (1996, December 9), "Project XL Begins to Crumble As Some Firms Say, 'No Thanks.'" *Engineering News* 7, no. 4:1, 14.

25. Ibid.

26. Skrzycki, "The Perils of Reinventing."

27. P. Fairley (1995, November 1), "Feeling the Crunch," *Chemical Week* 157, no. 17:22–24.

28. Ibid.

29. National Academy of Public Administration (NAPA) (1997, September 1), *Resolving the Paradox of Environmental Protection,* National Academy of Public Administration Report (Washington, D.C.: National Academy of Public Administration), Report no. 97-11.

30. A. Blackman and J. Mazurek (1999), "The Cost of Developing Site-Specific Environmental Regulations: Evidence from EPA's Project XL" (Resources for the Future Conference Discussion Paper, Washington, D.C.), cited in Marcus, "Cooperative Regulation," 3.

31. Based on a data sample of eleven Project XL projects proposed during the first six months of the initiative.

32. J. P. Cohn (1997, September 1), "Clearing the Air," *Government Executive Magazine,* http://www.govexec.com/features/0997s5.htm.

33. Anonymous (1997, August 18), "Turning Rhetoric into Specifics: Project XL's New Head Talks of His Challenge," *Industry Week,* 118.

34. Anonymous (1999, April 19), "One Foot in the Future," *Industry Week,* 20.

35. L. Ross and C. Stillinger, "Barriers to Conflict Resolution," *Negotiation Journal,* no. 4:389–404.

36. R. Mnookin, S. Peppet, and A. Tulumello (2000), *Beyond Winning: How Lawyers Help Clients Create Value in Negotiation* (Cambridge: Harvard University Press).

37. D. H. Gruenfeld (1995), "Status, Ideology, and Integrative Complexity on the U.S. Supreme Court: Rethinking the Politics of Political Decision Making," *Journal of Personality and Social Psychology* 68, no. 1:5–20; P. E. Tetlock, R. Peterson, and J. Lerner (1996), "Revising the Value Pluralism Model: Incorporating Social Content and Context Postulates," in C. Seligman, J. Olson, and M. Zanna, eds., *Values: Eighth Annual Ontario Symposium on Personality and Social Psychology* (Hillsdale, N.J.: Erlbaum), 25–51.

38. S. Chaiken, D. H. Gruenfeld, and C. M. Judd (n.d.), "Persuasion in Negotiation," in M. Deutsch and P. Coleman, eds., *Handbook of Constructive Conflict Resolution: Theory and Practice* (San Francisco: Jossey-Bass), forthcoming.

39. J. Stiglitz (1998), "The Private Uses of Public Interests: Incentives and Institutions," *Journal of Econnomic Perspectives* 12, no. 2:3–22.

40. H. Raiffa (1982), *The Art and Science of Negotiation* (Cambridge: Harvard University Press); D. Lax and J. Sebenius (1986), *The Manager as Negotiator* (New York: Free Press); M. H. Bazerman (2002), *Judgment in Managerial Decision Making*, 5th ed. (New York: Wiley).

41. Stiglitz, "The Private Uses."

42. J. Zicconi (1998, January 22), "Court Throws Out Act 60 Lawsuit," *Stowe (Vt.) Reporter.*

43. J. Zicconi (1999, March 11), "'Gang of 10,' Rep. Marron Take Aim at Act 60," *Stowe (Vt.) Reporter.*

44. J. D Donahue (1999), *Making Washington Work* (Washington, D.C.: Brookings Institution).

Chapter 3

1. E. Almond, D. Schaefer, R. Seven, and S. Clutter (1996, December 15), "Mariners Put Up for Sale," *Seattle Times*, A1.

2. Seattle Mariners Board of Directors (1996, December 15), "Excerpts from Statement by Mariners Board of Directors: Owners: Last Out for Baseball in Seattle," *Seattle Times*, A23.

3. E. Pryne, C. Corr, and D. Schaefer (1996, December 25), "Seattle Holding Firm on Stadium Deal," *Seattle Times*, A1.

4. T. Egan, (1999, July 17), "What Price the Most Expensive Diamond of All?" *New York Times*, A8.

5. Ibid.

6. D. Schaefer and D. Postman (1997, January 14), "Cram Course for Stadium Panel–Group Ponders Financing Options," *Seattle Times*, A1.

7. Senate Committee on the Judiciary (1995, November 29), *Hearing Before the Subcommittee on Antitrust, Business Rights, and Competition*, 104th Cong., 1st sess.

8. M. S. Rosentraub (1997), *Major League Losers: The Real Cost of Sports and Who's Paying for It* (New York: Harper Collins).

9. J. Quirk and R. D. Fort (1997), *Pay Dirt: The Business of Professional Team Sports* (Princeton: Princeton University Press).

10. Rosentraub, *Major League Losers.*

11. Egan, "What Price?"

12. Ibid.

13. D. V. Baim (1990, November 26), *Sports Stadiums as "Wise Investments": An Evaluation*, Heartland Policy Study #32 (Chicago: The Heartland Institute), 6.

14. Rosentraub, *Major League Losers*.

15. Ibid.

16. K. Hartley and N. Hooper (1992), "Tourism Policy: Market Failure and Public Choice," in P. Johnson and T. Barry, eds., *Perspectives on Tourism Policy* (New York: Casell Mansell).

17. R. Fitzgerald, trans. (1998), *The Odyssey* (New York: Farrar, Straus and Giroux), 134–137.

18. T. C. Schelling (1984), *Choice and Consequence: Perspectives of an Errant Economist* (Cambridge: Harvard University Press), 290.

19. M. H. Bazerman, A. E. Tenbrunsel, and K. A. Wade-Benzoni (1998), "Negotiating with Yourself and Losing: Understanding and Managing Conflicting Internal Preferences, *Academy of Management Review* 23, no. 2:225–241.

20. M. H. Bazerman and W. F. Samuelson (1983), "I Won the Auction but Don't Want the Prize," *Journal of Conflict Resolution* 27, no. 4:618–634; J. H. Kageland and D. Levin (1986), "The Winner's Curse and Public Information in Common Value Auctions," *American Economic Review* 76:894–920.

21. M. H. Bazerman (1998), *Judgment in Managerial Decision Making* (New York: Wiley), 142–144.

22. L. B. Ward (1993, June 27), "Rio Rancho, N.M.: Atop a Mesa, a City Just Grows and Grows," *New York Times*, Section 10, 5.

23. V. Santillanes (1995, February 2), "Rio Rancho 'Desperate' for Funds," *Albuquerque Journal*, A1.

24. C. Farrell (1996, June), "The Economic War Among the States: An Overview," *The Region*, 4.

25. J. Mattey and M. Spiegel (1996, June), "On the Efficiency Effects of Tax Competition on Firms," *The Region*, 50–51.

26. K. S. Chi (1989), *Economic Development in the States* (Lexington, Kans.: Council of State Governments), 5.

27. KPMG (1995, September), *Business Incentives and Tax Credits: A Boon for Business or Corporate Welfare?* KPMG Survey, http://www.kpmg.com.

28. L. W. Reed (1997), "Time to End the Economic War Between the States," *Regulation* 19:2.

29. Ibid.

30. State of Washington, Secretary of State and Office of the Attorney General (1997, November), *How Much for Charity? How Much for Profit and Expenses?* http://www.secstate.wa.gov.

31. State of California, Office of the Attorney General (1997), *Report on Charitable Solicitation by Professional Fundraisers,* http://caag.state.ca.us/press/charit.htm.

32. Consumer Protection Report (1997, December), Washington, D.C.: National Association of Attorneys General.

33. State of New York, Office of Attorney General Eliot Spitzer (1998), *Pennies for Charities 1998,* http://www.oag.state.ny.us/charities/pennies98-2/penintro.html.

34. A notable exception is the state of Louisiana, where two attempts to pass legislation requiring telemarketing firms to register with the state, post bond, and file copies of their contracts have failed. Major charitable organizations successfully lobbied against the bills on the grounds that they would add a layer of bureaucracy and enforce government control of operations.

35. J. S. Greenlee and T. P. Gordon (1998, September), "The Impact of Professional Solicitors on Fund-Raising in Charitable Organizations," *Nonprofit Voluntary Sector Quarterly,* no 3:277–299.

36. M. Arena (1995, December 6), "Perils of High-Tech Charity," *New York Newsday,* A24.

37. Ibid.

38. E. Hayward (1995, August 27), "Where Your Charity Dollars Really Go," *The Boston Herald,* 1.

39. R. Franklin (1996, July 23), "Charity for Police Sees Most of Money Go to Telemarketers," *Minneapolis Star Tribune,* 1B.

40. Ibid.

41. E. Stark (1996, November), "Which Charities Merit Your Money," *Money.*

42. T. Crawford (1994, April 3), "Charities bid for dollars playing high stakes game," *Toronto Star,* A1.

43. Greenlee and Gordon, "Impact of Professional Solicitors."

44. B. Shore (1995), *Share Our Strength* (New York: Riverhead Books), 63–64.

45. Ibid., 77.

46. B. J. Wolfson (1998, July 29), "It's Official: Pats Reject House Plan," *Boston Herald,* F24.

47. J. Battenfeld and E. J. Silberman (1998, November 19), "Goodbye and Good Luck–Defiant Speaker: Don't Blame Me," *Boston Herald,* 37.

48. J. Battenfeld and E. J. Silberman (1998, November 20), "Krafting a Deal: Hartford Deal Leaves Mass. Pols' Hands," *Boston Herald,* 6.

49. T. Cassidy (1999, May 18), "Lawmakers Expected to OK Stadium Bill," *Boston Globe,* B4.

50. M. Vaillancourt (1999, April 29), "The Tough Stand by Finneran Might Pay Off If Deal Is OK'd," *Boston Globe,* A29.

51. M. Cunningham (2000, January 27), "Leap of Faith," *Milwaukee Journal Sentinel,* 10Z.

52. R. C. Johnson (1999), "Texas School District Blocks NBA Team's Arena Deal," *Education Week* 18: no. 21:6.

53. R. DiRossi (1997, May 21), "Ohio Economic Development Study Committee Selects Final Contractor," Press release, Ohio, Office of State Senator Charles Horn, http://www.senate.state.oh.us/horn/csu.htm.

54. W. Fulton (1996, December) "Costing Out the Smokestack Chase," *Governing Magazine,* 70.

55. Anonymous (1998, November 30), "There Are Solutions to the Corporate Welfare Mess–but Who Goes First?" *Time,* http://time.com.

56. Ibid.

Chapter 4

1. "Up in Smoke: Tobacco Program" (1999), *Green Scissors '99: Cutting Wasteful and Environmentally Harmful Spending* (Washington, D.C.: Friends of the Earth, Taxpayers for Common Sense, and the U.S. Public Interest Research Group), 75.

2. Since 1986, tobacco price support formulas involved a five-year moving average of prices and changes in a cost-of-production index. The secretary of agriculture has had the discretion to set the price support between 65 and 100 percent of the calculated yearly increase or decrease.

3. M. Kaufman (2000, September 12), "Tobacco Exports Get Aid in Bill Set for House Vote," *Washington Post,* A20.

4. American Lung Association (1999, July), http://www.lungusa.org.

5. Ibid.

6. Centers for Disease Control and Prevention (1994, July 8), "Medical Care Expenditures Attributable to Cigarette Smoking–United States, 1993," *Morbidity and Mortality Weekly Report* 43: no. 26:469–472.

7. "Tobacco Probe Yields No Charges Yet," (1999, July 27), Associated Press.

8. D. Watson (1998, January 8), "End the Subsidies," *Ventura County Star,* D8.

9. C. M. Sennott (1996, July 7), "The $150 Billion 'Welfare' Recipients: U.S. Corporations," *Boston Globe,* 1.

10. The Cato Institute's conservative estimate ($75 billion as of the 106th Congress) considers only government programs that provide direct subsidies to individual industries. Ralph Nader's Center for the Study of Responsive Law defines the term more broadly, to include federal tax breaks that funnel money to specific industries, arriving at $167 billion. S. Moore and D. Stansel (1996, May 15), *How Corporate Welfare Won: Clinton and Congress Retreat from*

Cutting Business Subsidies, Cato Institute Policy Analysis No. 254, http://www.cato.org/research/fiscal.html.

11. Sennott, "The $150 Billion 'Welfare' Recipients."

12. P. Webre (1995, October), *Federal Financial Support of Business* (Section 10), The Congress of the United States, Congressional Budget Office, http://www.cbo.gov.

13. Sennot, "The $150 Billion 'Welfare' Recipients."

14. Joint Committee on Taxation (1995, September 1), *Estimates of Federal Tax Expenditures for Fiscal Years 1996-2000,* Document JCS-21-95, 2.

15. M. Goozner (1998, October 25), "Budget Bill Gives Businesses Big Break," *Chicago Tribune,* http://www.chicagotribune.com.

16. Center for Responsive Politics (1998, June 18), "Tobacco Legislation Going Up in Smoke," http://www.opensecrets.org/pubs/tobacotally.htm.

17. H. Varian (1987), *Intermediate Microeconomics: A Modern Approach,* 2d ed. (New York: Norton); A. de Moor (1997), *Subsidizing Unsustainable Development: Undermining the Earth with Public Funds,* Earth Council, http://www.ecouncil.ac.cr/rio/focus/report/english/subsidies.

18. J. Baron (2001), "Confusion of Group-Interest and Self-Interest in Parochial Cooperation on Behalf of a Group," *Journal of Conflict Resolution 45;* 283-296 M. B. Brewer (1979), "In-Group Bias in the Minimal Intergroup Situation: A Cognitive-Motivational Analysis," *Psychological Bulletin* 86, no. 2:307–324; L. R. Caporael, R. M. Dawes, J. M. Orbell, and A. J. C. van de Kragt (1989), "Selfishness Examined: Cooperation in the Absence of Egoistic Incentives," *Behavioral and Brain Sciences* 12, no. 4:683–739; P. Schwartz-Shea and R. T. Simmons (1991), "Egoism, Parochialism, and Universalism," *Rationality and Society* 3:106–132.

19. K. Q. Seelye (1999, July 23), "Bradley Proposes Revamping Federal Campaign Finance System," *New York Times,* A19.

20. M. H. Bazerman (1998), *Judgment in Managerial Decision Making* (New York: John Wiley and Sons), 106.

21. Office of Management and Budget (1997, February 10), *Refining the Role of Government in the U.S. Market Economy* (Chapter 6), Economic Report of the President, Executive Office of the President of the United States (Washington, D.C, Government Printing Office), 221.

22. Mineral Policy Center (1999), "What Is the 1872 Mining Law?" http://www.mineralpolicy.org.

23. "Granddaddy of Subsidies: 1872 Mining Law" (1999), *Green Scissors '97: Cutting Wasteful and Environmentally Harmful Spending* (Washington, D.C: Friends of the Earth, Taxpayers for Common Sense, and the U.S. Public Interest Research Group), 38.

24. Editorial (1999, February 10), "Mining Laws Cheat Taxpayers," *USA Today,* 14A.

25. M. Satchell (1991, October 29), "The New Gold Rush," *U.S. News and World Report,* 44.

26. R. Nader (1999, June 30), *Testimony of Ralph Nader Before the Committee on the Budget,* U.S. House of Representatives, http://www.house.gov/budget/hearings/nader63099.html.

27. Mineral Policy Center (1999, August 12), "Mining's Environmental Impacts," http://www.mineralpolicy.org.

28. Ibid.

29. Western Governors' Association (1999, November 11), "Abandoned Mine Cleanup Partnership," http://www.westgov.org/ wga/initiatives/aml/aml.htm.

30. L. Finfer and B. Anderson (1999, February 9), "BLM's Proposed Mining Rule Would Update '3809' Regulations, Enhance Protection of Public Lands," Bureau of Land Management News Release, http://www.blm.gov/nhp/news/releases/pages/1999/pr990209.html.

31. Editorial (1999, February 8), "Mr. Dombeck's Vision," *New York Times,* A22.

32. Editorial (1999, February 10), "Mining Laws Cheat Taxpayers," *USA Today,* 14A.

33. "The Price Isn't Right: Money-Losing Timber Sales" (1999), *Green Scissors '99: Cutting Wasteful and Environmentally Harmful Spending* (Washington, D.C: Friends of the Earth, Taxpayers for Common Sense, and the U.S Public Interest Research Group), 42.

34. The Wilderness Society (1998, February 8), "Commercial Logging in National Forests Lost $45 Million of Taxpayers' Money in 1997," http://www.wilderness.org/own/tsprs_1997.htm.

35. J. A. Baden (1993, January 26), "Pork-Barrel Economics Thwart Forest Service Reform," *Seattle Times,* A11.

36. J. Armstrong (1998, October 15), "Perverse Incentives Fuel Chainsaws" *Chicago Tribune,* 22.

37. "The Great Tree Robbery: Timber Roads Construction" (1999), *Green Scissors '99* (Washington, D.C: Friends of the Earth, Taxpayers for Common Sense, and the U.S Public Interest Research Group), 41.

38. P. Reinert (2001, January 6), "Executive Orders to Face Scrutiny," *Houston Chronicle,* A6.

39. J. E. Cantor (1997, January 10), *Soft and Hard Money in Contemporary Elections: What Federal Law Does and Does Not Regulate.* Congressional Research Service Report, Library of Congress, 1–6.

40. E. Drew (1999), *The Corruption of American Politics: What Went Wrong and Why* (Secaucus, N.J.: Birch Lane Press), 51–52.

41. Ibid., 54.

42. Common Cause (2000, December 15), "National Parties Raise Record $457 Million in Soft Money," http://www.commoncause.org.

43. Common Cause (2000), "What We Are Working On: Glossary," http://www.commoncause.org.

44. Center for Responsive Politics (1999), "Influence Inc.: Summary," http://www.opensecrets.org/pubs/lobby98/index.htm.

45. Public Citizen (1998, June 22), "Tobacco PAC Contributions and 1998 Tobacco Votes," http://www.citizen.org.

46. Public Citizen (2001, January 19), "Soft Money Hurts Consumers and Taxpayers," http://www.citizen.org/congress/reform/soft$hurts.html.

47. Common Cause (1998, June 19), "Tobacco Money Continues Its Death Grip on Washington," http://www.commoncause.org.

48. Center for Responsive Politics (1999), "Top Tobacco Money Receipts," http://www.opensecrets.org.

49. Ibid.

50. Common Cause (2000, January 15), "Soft Money Laundromat," http://www.commoncause.org/laundromat.

51. L. Sweet (1999, July 29), "Tobacco Industry Knocks AMA from Top Lobbying Spot," *Chicago Sun-Times*, 26.

52. Common Cause (2000, January 15), "Soft Money Laundromat," http://www.commoncause.org/laundromat.

53. Center for Responsive Politics (1999), "Mining: PAC Contributions to Federal Candidates, 1997–98," http://www.opensecrets.org.

54. Center for Responsive Politics (1999), "Top Timber Industry Money Recipients," http://www.opensecrets.org.

55. Drew, *Corruption of American Politics*, 23–24.

56. Ibid., 265.

57. D. Van Natta Jr. (1999, August 31), "Executives Press for Political Finance Change," *New York Times*, A1.

58. Ibid.

59. Common Cause (1997, February), Editorial Memorandum: "McCain-Feingold Legislation Offers Bipartisan Opportunity for Comprehensive Campaign Finance Reform in 1997," http://www.commoncause.org.

60. T. Weiner (1999, August 24), "Lobbying for Research Money, Colleges Bypass Review Process," *New York Times*, 1.

61. Ibid.

62. M. Radetzki (1995), "A Scrutiny of the Motives for Hard Coal Subsidies in Western Europe," *Resources Policy* 21, no. 2:99–106.

63. J. Kahl (1997, March 13), "Ein Kumpel ist kein Kumpan," *Suddeutche Zeitung* (Munich), 3.

64. Anonymous, "Kohl Boosts Subsidy Offer–69 Billion Marks Coal Aid Through 2005" (1997, March 13), *Deutsche Presse-Agentur.*

65. The Newspaper Guild (1998, July), "Time to Join," http://www.timeguildnet.org/timetojoin.html.

Chapter 5

1. T. Zimmermann (1996, October 21), "If World War III Comes, Blame Fish," *U.S. News and World Report,* 59–60.

2. D. Ferber (2000, December 15), "Galápagos Station Survives Latest Attack by Fishers," *Science* 290, no. 5499:2059–2061.

3. A. P. McGinn (1998), "Promoting Sustainable Fisheries," in L. Brown, C. Flavin, and H. French, eds., *State of the World* (New York: Norton), 59–78.

4. C. Safina (1994), "Where Have All the Fish Gone?" *Issues in Science and Technology* 10, no. 1:37–43.

5. J. K. Sebenius (1984), *The Law of the Sea* (Cambridge: Harvard University Press).

6. J. Baron (1998), *Judgment Misguided* (New York: Oxford University Press), 21–22.

7. McGinn, "Promoting Sustainable Fisheries," 62.

8. Ibid, 67.

9. G. Porter (1996, May), "Fishing Subsidies, Overfishing, and Trade," United Nations Environmental Program draft paper, http://www.unep.org.

10. McGinn, "Promoting Sustainable Fisheries," 68.

11. Ibid.

12. Zimmermann, "If World War III Comes, Blame Fish."

13. McGinn, "Promoting Sustainable Fisheries," 65.

14. J. Raloff (1996, October 26), "Fishing for Answers: Deep Trawls Leave Destruction in Their Wake–But for How Long?" *Science News* 150, no. 17:268.

15. D. Russell (1996, July/August), "Vacuum in the Seas," *E Magazine,* 29–35.

16. Ibid.

17. Ibid.

18. K. A. Wade-Benzoni (1999), "Thinking About the Future: An Intergenerational Perspective on the Conflict and Compatibility Between Economic and Environmental Interests," *American Behavioral Scientist* 42, no. 8:1393–1405.

19. A. Gore (1992), *Earth in the Balance: Ecology and the Human Spirit* (Boston: Houghton Mifflin), 191.

20. K. A. Wade-Benzoni, A. E. Tenbrunsel, and M. H. Bazerman (1996), "Egocentric Interpretations of Fairness in Symmetric, Environmental Social Dilemmas: Explaining Harvesting Behavior and the Role of Communication," *Organizational Behavior and Human Decision Processes* 67, no. 2:111–126.

21. M. H. Bazerman, K. A. Wade-Benzoni, and F. Benzoni (1996), "A Behavioral Decision Theory Perspective to Environmental Decision Making," in D. M. Messick and A. Tenbrunsel, eds., *Ethical Issues in Managerial Decision Making* (New-York: Russell Sage), 256–274.

22. Wade-Benzoni, "Thinking About the Future."

23. E. A. Mannix and G. L. Loewenstein (1992), "The Effects of Interfirm Mobility and Individual Versus Group Decision Making on Managerial Time Horizons," *Organizational Behavior and Human Decision Processes* 59, no. 3:371–390.

24. N. Weinstein (1980), "Unrealistic Optimism About Future Life Events," *Journal of Personality and Social Psychology* 39, no. 5:806–820.

25. E. Babad and Y. Katz (1991), "Wishful Thinking–Against All Odds," *Journal of Applied Social Psychology* 21:1921–1938.

26. R. M. Kramer (1994), "Self-Enhancing Cognitions and Organizational Conflict," working paper; T. Tyler and R. Hastie (1991), "The Social Consequences of Cognitive Illusions," in M. H. Bazerman, R. J. Lewicki, and B. H. Sheppard, eds., *Research in Negotiation in Organizations*, vol. 3 (Greenwich, Conn.: JAI Press), 69–98.

27. Interview on *Frontline* (1991, May 21), Public Broadcasting System.

28. Zimmermann, "If World War III Comes, Blame Fish," 59–60.

29. McGinn, "Promoting Sustainable Fisheries," 74.

30. B. Runolfsson (1997), "Fencing the Ocean," *Regulation* 3:7.

31. J. Marsh (1997, April), "North Pacific Fisheries Environment," *Contemporary Economic Policy* 15:44–51.

32. E. Ostrom (1990), *Governing the Commons* (New York: Cambridge University Press).

33. U.S. Department of Transportation, Research and Special Programs Administration (1993, November), *Journey-To-Work Trends in the United States and Its Major Metropolitan Areas, 1960–1990*, http://www.bts.gov/ntl/DOCS/473.html.

34. M. Replogle (1993, April 30), *Transportation Conformity and Demand Management: Vital Strategies for Clean Air Attainment*, Environmental Defense Fund, http://www.bts.gov/tmip/papers/airqual/vsca/toc.htm.

35. A. Ehrenhalt (1999, May), "The Czar of Gridlock," *Governing Magazine*, 20.

36. G. Easterbrook (1999, March 15), "Suburban Myth," *New Republic*, 22.

37. M. Gordon (1963), *Sick Cities* (New York: MacMillan), 41–42.

38. J. Calfee and C. Winston (1998), "The Value of Automobile Travel Time: Implications for Congestion Policy," *Journal of Public Economics* 69, no. 1:83–102.

39. P. Pae (1997, March 29), "Higher Tolls in the Works for Drivers on Struggling Dulles Greenway," *Washington Post*, B3.

40. J. Blum and D. Hedgpeth (1999, August 3), "Dulles Greenway Raises Weekday Toll," *Washington Post*, B03.

41. L. V. Mapes (1999, April 28), "Chinook Listing Faces Court Challenge," *Seattle Times*, B3.

42. L. V. Mapes (1999, March 14), "Salmon on the Brink," *Seattle Times*, A1.

43. T. Kenworthy (1999, June 4), "U.S., Canada Reach Landmark Pact on Pacific Salmon Fishing," *Washington Post*, A17.

44. Ibid.

Chapter 6

1. R. Lacayo (1999, December 13),"Rage Against theMachine," *Time*, 16.

2. J. Stiglitz (1998), "The Private Uses of Public Interests: Incentives and Institutions," *Journal of Economic Perspectives* 12, no. 2:3–22.

3. Anonymous (2000, July 8), "Happy Birthday, Señor Fox," *The Economist*.

4. M. Mendoza (1998, November 24), "U.S. Brussels Sprout Trade at Risk," Associated Press Dispatch.

5. Anonymous (2000, January 15), "The Standard Question," *The Economist*.

6. H. Hagre (2000), "Development and the Liberal Peace: What Does It Take to Be a Trading State?" *Journal of Peace Research* 37, no. 26:5; J. R. O'Neal and B. Russett (1999), "Assessing the Liberal Peace with Alternative Specifications: Trade Still Reduces Conflict," *Journal of Peace Research* 36, no. 2:423.

7. Anonymous (1999, November 24), "The Engine of Economic Growth," BBC News Online, http://news.bbc.co.uk.

8. J. D. Sachs and A. Warner (1995), "Economic Reform and Process of Global Integration," *Brooking Papers on Economic Activity*:1–117.

9. J. Morris (1999, November 23), "Free Trade Benefits All," BBC News Online, http://news.bbc.co.uk.

10. J. Baron (1996), "Do No Harm," in D. Messick and A. Tenbrunsel, eds., *Codes of Conduct: Behavioral Research Into Business Ethics* (New York: Russell Sage), 197–213.

11. Ibid.

12. Ibid.

13. Anonymous (2000, January 29), "The Biosafety Protocol—A Conventional Argument," *The Economist*.

14. Anonymous (1999, October 9), "Embracing Greenery," *The Economist.*

15. E. Olson (2000, October 23), "Malaysia Says U.S. Failed to Obey Ruling on Shrimp," *New York Times,* W1.

16. K. Moran (1999, December 6), "Bush Urged to Do More in Turtle Preservation," *Houston Chronicle,* A19.

17. P. Singer (1993), *Practical Ethics,* 2d ed., (Cambridge: Cambridge University Press), 219. Originally from the World Bank's *World Development Report,* 1978.

18. In 1993 dollars, adjusted to account for differences in purchasing power across countries.

19. S. R. Berger (2001, January 20), Editorial: "A Global Gap That Open Markets Can't Close," *New York Times,* A23.

20. Ibid.

21. The World Bank Group (2000, September 28), *Trends in Poverty Over Time,* http://www.worldbank.org/poverty/mission/up3.htm.

22. The World Bank Group (2000, December 21), *Health: The Problem of AIDS and Malaria,* http://www.worldbank.org/poverty/data/trends/aids.htm.

23. The World Bank Group (1993), *Trends in Poverty Over Time,* http://worldbank.org.

24. P. Unger (1996), *Living High and Letting Die: Our Illusion of Innocence* (Oxford: Oxford University Press).

25. S. Milgram (1974), *Obedience to Authority* (New York: Harper and Row).

26. D. Fetherstonhaugh, P. Slovic, S. Johnson, and J. Friedrich (1997), "Insensitivity to the Value of Human Life: A Study of Psychophysical Numbing," *Journal of Risk and Uncertainty* 14, no. 3:283–300; see also J. Baron (1997), "Confusion of Relative and Absolute Risk in Valuation," *Journal of Risk and Uncertainty* 14, no. 3:301–309.

27. B. Goldwater (1961), *Conscience of a Conservative* (New York: McFadden Books), 98.

28. L. Rohter (1996, July 19), "To U.S. Critics, a Sweatshop; to Hondurans, a Better Life," *New York Times,* A1.

29. Following its adoption by the U.N., the Convention on the Rights of the Child was ratified by all but two member countries, Somalia (which does not currently have a recognized government) and the United States, where ratification has been bogged down in Congress. Nations that ratify the convention are required to bring their legislation in line with its provisions. Although some U.S. senators have opposed the treaty, arguing that it will strip away parental rights and foster immoral behavior among children, passage is expected to occur eventually.

30. The World Bank Group (2001), "The World Bank and Vietnam," http://www.worldbank.org.

31. The World Bank Group (2001), "Country Data Profile: Bolivia," http://www.worldbank.org.

32. T. Hawkins and M. Holman (2000, May 15), "Long Snakes, Short Ladders," *Financial Times,* 20.

33. J. Kahn (2000, June 1), "World Bank Cites Itself in Study of Africa's Bleak Performance," *New York Times,* A9.

34. Ibid.

35. UNICEF (1997), *UNICEF Report on Child Labor: The State of the World's Children* (New York: UNICEF), http://www. unicef.org/sowc97.

36. UNICEF (1995), *The Progress of Nations* (New York: UNICEF), http://www. unicef.org/pog95.

37. Associated Press dispatch (1993, December 26), "U.S. Denies Request for $3 Million to Fight TB," *New York Times,* 19.

38. Encyclopedia Britannica Online (2000, July 21), "Borlaug, Norman Ernest," http://www.britannica.com.

39. Easterbrook, G. (1997, January), "Forgotten Benefactor of Humanity," *The Atlantic Monthly,* 75–82.

40. The World Bank Group (2001, April 10), "Assessing Aid Overview," http://worldbank.orf/research/aid/overview.htm.

41. W. Underhill (1999, March 1), "Is It Payback Time?" *Newsweek,* 46.

42. Ibid.

43. Ibid.

44. T. Karon (1999, June 23), "Why IMF's Charity Has a Sting in Its Tail," *Time* Daily, http://www.time.com/time/daily.

45. Transparency International (1996, September 20), *The TI Source Book: Executive Summary,* http://www.transparency.org/documents/source-book/summary.html.

46. The Organization for Economic Cooperation and Development (2001, January 19) "Welcome to the OECD Anti-Corruption Unit," http://www.oecd.org/daf/nocorruption/index.htm.

47. Transparency International (2001, January 5), "National Chapters and Contacts," http://www.transparency.org/organisation/chapters/index.html.

48. This paragraph draws on S. Rose-Ackerman (1999), "'Grand' Corruption and the Ethics of Global Business," Working Paper Series, Social Science Research Network; also Program for Studies in Law, Economics and Public Policy, Yale Law School, Working Paper No. 221.

49. Encyclopedia Britannica (1999), Year in Review 1998: "Military Affairs," *Encyclopedia Britannica Online,* www.britannica.com.

50. SIPRI (1998), *SIPRI Yearbook 1998: Military Expenditures,* http://editors.sipri.se/pubs/yb98/ch6.html. This is a chapter summary from E. Sköns, A.

Courades Allebeck, E. Loose-Weintraub, and R. Weidacher (1998), *SIPRI Yearbook 1998: Armaments, Disarmament and International Security* (Oxford: Oxford University Press).

51. H. Morris (1999, October 4), "Zimbabwe Misled IMF on Congo War: Fund Probes Big Discrepancy in Figures for Cost of Intervention," *Financial Times*, 1.

52. News Digest (1999, June 12), "IMF Praises Defense Cuts," *Financial Times*, 6.

53. B. Crosette (2000, June 9), "Death Toll in Congo's 2-Year War Is at Least 1.7 Million, Study Says," *New York Times*, A1.

54. The World Bank Group (1998), *The Leadership Challenges of Demilitarization in Africa, Arusha, Tanzania, July 22–24, 1998: Summary of the Conference Report*, http://www.worldbank.org.

55. Ibid.

56. M. Wines (2000, December 28), "For All of Russia, Biological Clock Is Running Out," *New York Times*, A1.

57. United Nations Development Programme (1998), *World Fertility Patterns 1997*, http://www.undp.org.

58. Ibid.

59. P. H. Gleick (1995, September), "Human Population and Water: To the Limits in the 21st Century," American Association for the Advancement of Science, http://www.aaas.org/international/psd/fisheries/gleick.htm.

60. J. Bongaarts (1994a), "Population Policy Options in the Developing World," *Science* 263:771–776; J. Bongaarts (1994b), "The Impact of Population Policies: Comment," *Population and Development Review* 20:616–620.

61. J. C. Caldwell, et al. (1999), "The Bangladesh Fertility Decline: An Interpretation," *Population and Development Review* 25:67–84.

62. United Nations Development Programme (1999), *World Contraceptive Use, 1998*, http://www.undp.org.

63. United Nations Development Programme (1999), "Levels and Trends of Contraceptive Use As Assessed in 1998: Key Findings," http://www.undp.org/popin/wdtrends.

64. P. H. Kostmayer (2001, January 25), "Bush 'Gags' the World on Family Planning," *Chicago Tribune*, 23.

65. "EU Chief Attacks Bush on Abortion Cash" (2001, January 23), CNN.com and Reuters combined report: http://www.cnn.com.

66. M. Olson (1998), "The Key to Economic Development," *Population and Development Review* 24, 369–379.

67. Worldwatch Database Disk (2000), *Internet Host Density, by Region, 1991-1998*, compiled by Worldwatch Institute using data from Network Wizards, ITU, U.S. Census Bureau.

68. K. Arrow, et al. (1995, April), "Economic Growth, Carrying Capacity, and the Environment," *Science* 268, no. 5210:520–521.

69. South Asia Environment Unit, The World Bank (1999), "South Asia Region," *Environment Matters: Annual Review* (Washington, D.C.: The World Bank), 32–35.

70. S. R. Bull and L. L. Billman (2000), "Renewable Energy: Ready to Meet Its Promise?" *The Washington Quarterly: Global Trends, A Glimpse Ahead* 23, no. 1:229.

71. P. Aldhous (1993, July 9), "World Bank Report Calls for Network to Bolster Research," *Science* 261, no. 5121:155.

72. W. Dowell (2000, January 24), "Addressing Africa's Agony," *Time*, 36.

73. J. Sachs (1999, August 14), "By Invitation: Helping the World's Poorest," *The Economist*, 11, 16.

74. Ibid.

75. J. Bongaarts (1996), "Population Pressure and the Food Supply System in the Developing World," *Population and Development Review* 22, no. 3:483–503.

76. Easterbrook, "Forgotten Benefactor."

77. International Center for Tropical Agriculture: http://www.ciat.cgiar.org.

78. Anonymous (1999, September 19), "Research from the Ground Up," *The Economist*, 90.

79. Consultative Group on International Agriculture Research: http://www.cgiar.org.

80. From an award search of the National Science Foundation Web site: http://www.nsf.gov.

Chapter 7

1. The information in this paragraph comes from S. H. Schneider, ed. (1996), *Encyclopedia of Climate and Weather* (Oxford: Oxford University Press).

2. J. M. Wallace and P. V. Hobbs (1977), *Atmospheric Science: An Introductory Survey* (San Diego: Academic Press).

3. J. D. Mahlman (1997, November 21), "Uncertainties in Projections of Human-Caused Climate Warming," *Science* 278, no. 5342:1416–1417.

4. G. Easterbrook (1995), *A Moment on the Earth: The Coming Age of Environmental Optimism* (New York: Viking).

5. P. Shabecoff (1985, November 3), "Scientists Warn of Earlier Rise in Sea Levels," *New York Times*, 23.

6. E. W. Coldglazier (1990), "Scientific Uncertainties, Public Policy, and Global Warming: How Sure Is Sure Enough?" Energy, Environment, and Resources Center Manuscript, University of Tennessee, Knoxville, Tenn.

7. S. H. Schneider (1989, February 10), "The Greenhouse Effect: Science and Policy," *Science* 243, no. 4892:771–781.

8. R. A. Kerr (1998, September 25), "Among Global Thermometers, Warming Still Wins Out," *Science* 281, no. 5385:1948–1949.

9. Assuming that population doubles and that world economic growth continues at 2 to 3 percent per year.

10. W. D. Nordhaus (1999), "Discounting and Public Policies That Affect the Distant Future," in P. R. Portney and J. P. Weyant, eds., *Discounting and Intergenerational Equity* (Washington, D.C.: Resources for the Future), 145–162.

11. R. Monastersky (1995, September 30), "Iron Versus the Greenhouse: Oceanographers Cautiously Explore a Global Warming Therapy," *Science News* 148:220.

12. R. H. Limbaugh (1992), *The Way Things Ought to Be* (New York: Pocket Books); R. H. Limbaugh (1993), *See, I Told You So* (New York: Pocket Books).

13. T. C. Schelling (1992), "Some Economics of Global Warming," *American Economic Review* 82:1–14.

14. K. A. Wade-Benzoni, A. E. Tenbrunsel, and M. H. Bazerman (1996), "Egocentric Interpretations of Fairness in Asymmetric, Environmental Social Dilemmas: Explaining Harvesting Behavior and the Role of Communication," *Organizational Behavior and Human Decision Processes* 67:111–126.

15. H. Dunphy (1999, July 8), "Market for Pollution Credits Viable," Associated Press dispatch.

16. Anonymous (1999, June 18), "Climate Change: Emissions Trading Could Save Money," *Green News.*

17. J. Kaiser (1998, November 6), "Pollution Permits for Greenhouse Gases?" *Science* 282, no. 5391:1025.

18. Ibid.

19. M. J. Sandel (1997, December 16), "Emissions Trading Defeats Purpose of Global Pact," *Minneapolis Star Tribune,* 21A.

20. Schelling, "Some Economics of Global Warming."

21. K. Lewin (1947), "Group Decision and Social Change," in T. M. Newcomb and E. L. Hartley, eds., *Readings in Social Psychology* (New York: Holt, Rinehart, and Winston).

22. M. Gerzon (1997), *A House Divided* (New York: Tarcher/Putnam).

23. J. Baron (1997), "Political Action Vs. Voluntarism in Social Dilemmas and Aid for the Needy," *Rationality and Society* 9:307–326.

Index

fishing, 133, 139
foreign indigenous, 123–124
gas, 188
mining, 108–109, 108*t4.1*
natural death of, 107
the poor and, 102
reduction of, 139
timber, 111–113, 119
travel, 148
Suffering
closeness and action against, 173
lack of concern for, 157
Superfund, 46, 110

Taiwan, 181
Tamoxifen, 14
Tariffs, 162
Tax credits, 94
Tax Reform Act of 1986, 73
Taxation
corporate incentives and reduction in,
80, 82, 102–104, 133
as prevention to fish depletion, 140, 141
school, 62–63
sports teams and government, 68–74,
90–91, 93
tax credit prudence in, 94
Technology
developing nations and, 194
new *vs.* old, 9–10
Telemarketing
not-for-profits and, 83–87, 85*t3.1*, 89, 98
Terrorists, 4
Texas, 80, 93
Thailand, 181
Thalidomide, 31, 37
3M, 55–56
Timber industry
clean cut, 45
environment and, 45–47, 50–54, 168
governmental subsidies for, 103
lobbying of, 119
lost of jobs in, 107
species protection *vs.* jobs in, 47
subsidies for, 111–113
Tissue plasminogen activator (TPA), 33
Tobacco industry
assistance to, 99–100, 103, 117
health issues for, 99–100
lobbying by, 117–119

regulation rebuked by, 116–117
Tolls, 148–149
Tort laws, 3
Tots for Tots, 85
Trade agreements
benefits of, 162–163
resistance to, 164–165
Trade barriers
loosening of, 183–184
Tradeoffs
compromise with, 59–61, 64
global warming and, 214–219
sacrifices with, 156, 215–218
unwise, 6
Transparency International, 186–187
Turkey, 143
Turtle excluder devices (TED), 167–168
Twins, Minnesota, 71

Uganda, 188
Ulysses, 76–77
Union Carbide, 58
Unions, 184
United Nations, 189–190
United Nations Children's Fund
(UNICEF), 171–172, 176–178
United Nations Environment Program,
203–204
United Nations Food and Agriculture
Organization, 134
United States, 151–152
global warming and, 206, 212, 216
Universities
political lobbying of, 122–123
Unocal Corporation, 51
USDA. *See* Department of Agriculture

Vaccines, 12–14, 41, 196–197, 198
Venezuela, 186
Vermont, 62–63, 226
Vietnam, 178
Visatacion Associates, 53
Volkswagen, 80–81
Voting, 96

War, 188–189
prevention of, 161
Warner Lambert, 36
Warnings, 14
Watergate, 113